Adobe® InDesign® CS5

ILLUSTRATED

Adobe® InDesign® CS5

ILLUSTRATED

Ann Fisher

COURSE TECHNOLOGY
CENGAGE Learning

Australia • Brazil • Japan • Korea • Mexico • Singapore • Spain • United Kingdom • United States

COURSE TECHNOLOGY
CENGAGE Learning

Adobe® InDesign® CS5—Illustrated
Ann Fisher

Executive Editor: Marjorie Hunt

Product Manager: Katherine C. Russillo

Associate Acquisitions Editor: Brandi Shailer

Associate Product Manager: Michelle Camisa

Editorial Assistant: Kim Klasner

Director of Marketing: Cheryl Costantini

Senior Marketing Manager: Ryan DeGrote

Marketing Coordinator: Kristen Panciocco

Developmental Editor: Barbara Waxer

Senior Content Project Manager: Jennifer Goguen McGrail

Art Director: GEX Publishing Services

Print Buyer: Fola Orekoya

Text Designer: GEX Publishing Services

Copyeditor: Andrew Therriault

Proofreader: Brandy Lilly

Indexer: Elizabeth Cunningham

QA Reviewers: Jeff Schwartz, Danielle Shaw, Marianne Snow, Susan Whalen

Cover Designer: GEX Publishing Services

Cover Artist: Mark Hunt

Composition: GEX Publishing Services

For product information and technology assistance, contact us at
Cengage Learning Customer & Sales Support, 1-800-354-9706
For permission to use material from this text or product, submit all requests online at **www.cengage.com/permissions**
Further permissions questions can be emailed to
permissionrequest@cengage.com

Library of Congress Control Number: 2010932362

ISBN-13: 978-0-538-47787-1

ISBN-10: 0-538-47787-3

Cengage Learning
20 Channel Center Street
Boston, MA 02210
USA

Cengage Learning is a leading provider of customized learning solutions with office locations around the globe, including Singapore, the United Kingdom, Australia, Mexico, Brazil, and Japan. Locate your local office at:
international.cengage.com/region

Cengage Learning products are represented in Canada by Nelson Education, Ltd.

To learn more about Course Technology, visit **www.cengage.com/coursetechnology**

To learn more about Cengage Learning, visit **www.cengage.com**

Purchase any of our products at your local college store or at our preferred online store **www.cengagebrain.com**

Adobe product screen shot(s) reprinted with permission from Adobe Systems Incorporated

Adobe®, Dreamweaver®, Flash®, InDesign®, Illustrator®, and Photoshop® are either registered trademarks or trademarks of Adobe Systems Incorporated in the United States and/or other countries. THIS PRODUCT IS NOT ENDORSED OR SPONSORED BY ADOBE SYSTEMS INCORPORATED, PUBLISHER OF ADOBE® DREAMWEAVER®, FLASH®, INDESIGN®, ILLUSTRATOR®, AND PHOTOSHOP®.

CREDITS: Fig D-1 Scott Bauer USDA/ARS; Fig H-5 Buddy Dog Humane Society, Inc., www.buddydoghs.org

Printed in the United States
1 2 3 4 5 6 7 16 15 14 13 12 11 10

Brief Contents

Preface x

InDesign CS5

Unit A: Getting Started with InDesign CS5.. InDesign 1

Unit B: Working with Text .... InDesign 25

Unit C: Working with Objects .... InDesign 53

Unit D: Working with Graphics .... InDesign 77

Unit E: Using Master Pages... InDesign 99

Unit F: Working with Layers .... InDesign 121

Unit G: Working with Color and Tables.. InDesign 143

Unit H: Adding Interactivity and Exporting Documents........................... InDesign 169

Glossary.. Glossary 193

Index.. Index 197

Contents

Preface x

InDesign CS5

Unit A: Getting Started with InDesign CS5 ....**InDesign 1**

Understanding Page Layout Software...InDesign 2

Starting InDesign ....InDesign 4
Understanding more about links

Exploring the InDesign Workspace...InDesign 6
Using custom workspaces

Creating a New Document...InDesign 8

Naming and Saving a Document...InDesign 10
Understanding Adobe InDesign CS5 Preferences

Working with Panels..InDesign 12
Working in Normal and Preview modes
Working with panels

Working with Guides..InDesign 14
Using the grid feature in InDesign

Using Adobe Help ....InDesign 16

Practice ....InDesign 18

Unit B: Working with Text ....**InDesign 25**

Creating Text Boxes..InDesign 26

Placing and Flowing Text..InDesign 28

Formatting Text..InDesign 30
Using the Story Editor
Kerning and Tracking

Formatting Paragraphs..InDesign 32
Formatting controls on the Control panel

Creating and Applying Paragraph Styles ....InDesign 34
Understanding parent/child relationships with styles

Modifying a Paragraph Style...InDesign 36
Using the Fill with Placeholder Text feature

Creating and Applying Character Styles..InDesign 38

Applying Bullets to Text..InDesign 40

Finding and Changing Text ....InDesign 42
Find/Change dialog box options

Practice ....InDesign 44

Unit C: Working with Objects ....**InDesign 53**

    Working with Smart Guides...InDesign 54

    Creating an Object ....InDesign 56

        Converting shapes

    Transforming an Object ....InDesign 58

        The Transform Again command

        Editing corners

    Arranging and Locking an Object...InDesign 60

        Selecting objects

    Stepping and Repeating an Object..InDesign 62

        Using the Move command

    Using Live Distribute...InDesign 64

        Rotating an object

    Using the Align Panel...InDesign 66

    Modifying Corners and Strokes ....InDesign 68

    Practice ....InDesign 70

Unit D: Working with Graphics ....**InDesign 77**

    Understanding Bitmap and Vector Graphics....................................InDesign 78

        Understanding resolution issues

    Placing a Graphic into a Frame..InDesign 80

        Placing multiple images

    Working with the Content Indicator...InDesign 82

        Other uses of the Direct Selection tool

    Transforming Frame Contents ....InDesign 84

    Using the Links Panel..InDesign 86

        Printing an InDesign document with linked files

    Replacing a Linked Image and Embedding a File ....InDesign 88

        Changing Links panel options

        Editing a link

    Adding Graphics to a Library...InDesign 90

        Viewing and sorting library items

    Practice ....InDesign 70

Unit E: Using Master Pages...**InDesign 99**

    Creating a Multipage Document ....InDesign 100

        Inserting pages

    Creating Master Items..InDesign 102

        Numbering options

    Overriding Master Items ....InDesign 104

        Removing local overrides

    Modifying a Master Page..InDesign 106

        Moving document pages

Creating a New Master Page..InDesign 108

    Master text frames

Applying Master Pages ....InDesign 110

    Using options on the Pages Panel menu

    Detaching master items

Working with Master Pages..InDesign 112

    Loading master pages

    Preventing shuffling

Practice ....InDesign 114

Unit F: Working with Layers ....**InDesign 121**

Placing an Object on a Layer ....InDesign 122

Changing Layer Options ....InDesign 124

    Selecting page items

Creating a New Layer ....InDesign 126

    Using the Arrange commands with multiple layers

Duplicating a Layer..InDesign 128

Locking and Hiding a Layer ....InDesign 130

Moving an Object to Another Layer ....InDesign 132

    Merging layers

Changing Layer Order...InDesign 134

    Pasting layers into a document

Practice ....InDesign 136

Unit G: Working with Color and Tables ....**InDesign 143**

Creating a Process Color ....InDesign 144

Selecting a Spot Color ....InDesign 146

    Creating a new tint swatch

Creating a Gradient..InDesign 148

    Filling text with a gradient fill

    Changing the view of the Swatches panel

Using the Gradient Swatch Tool ....InDesign 150

    Using the Gradient panel

Creating a Table...InDesign 152

    Using the Table panel

Formatting Table Cells ....InDesign 154

    Converting text to tables and tables to text

Inserting, Merging, and Splitting Table Cells..InDesign 156

    Creating a table style

Setting Tabs in a Table..InDesign 158

    Creating a new tint swatch

Practice ....InDesign 160

Unit H: Adding Interactivity and Exporting Documents ....**InDesign 169**

    Creating a Document for the Web..InDesign 170

    Creating a Hyperlink...InDesign 172

        Using the Web swatch library

    Creating an Animation ....InDesign 174

    Exporting a Document as a Flash Player File...InDesign 176

        Understanding Global Security

    Creating a Button..InDesign 178

        Adding sample buttons

    Creating a Rollover..InDesign 180

        Working with effects

        Using the Preflight panel

    Exporting a Document as an Interactive Adobe PDF File ....InDesign 182

        Creating an Export preset

    Understanding Export Options for the Web ....InDesign 184

        Packaging a document

    Practice ....InDesign 186

Glossary...**Glossary 193**

Index ....**Index 197**

Preface

Welcome to *Adobe® InDesign® CS5—Illustrated*. The unique page design of the book makes it a great learning tool for both new and experienced users. Each skill is presented on two facing pages so that you don't have to turn the page to find a screen shot or finish a paragraph. See the illustration on the right to learn more about the pedagogical and design elements of a typical lesson.

This book is an ideal learning tool for a wide range of learners—the "rookies" will find the clean design easy to follow and focused with only essential information presented, and the "hot shots" will appreciate being able to move quickly through the lessons to find the information they need without reading a lot of text. The design also makes this a great reference after the course is over!

Coverage

This text is organized into eight units. In these units, students learn how to work with the InDesign interface, along with objects, text, vector and bitmap graphics. They will also use the Links, Pages, and Layers panels to organize their publications. In addition, students will learn about color options in InDesign, and create tables and interactive documents.

Each two-page spread focuses on a single skill.

Introduction briefly explains why the lesson skill is important.

A case scenario motivates the the steps and puts learning in context.

UNIT D
InDesign CS5

Understanding Bitmap and Vector Graphics

Graphic files come in many formats. Two formats that are commonly placed into InDesign documents are bitmap and vector. A **bitmap graphic** is a graphic that is made up of **pixels**: tiny color squares arranged in a grid that are used to display graphics shown on a monitor or television screen. Scanned photographs and photographs taken from a digital camera are bitmap graphics. Files created in an image-editing software program, such as Adobe Photoshop, are another example of bitmap graphics. If you zoom in on a bitmap graphic or greatly increase its size, you can see its pixels. A **vector graphic** is a graphic that is made up of **vectors**, which are straight or curved line segments connected by **anchor points** (small dots), much like a completed connect-the-dots drawing. Vector graphics are created in drawing programs such as Adobe Illustrator. They are an ideal format for illustrations and logos because they can be resized in page layouts without losing image quality. Vector graphics can be manipulated in InDesign using the Pen tool and the Direct Selection tool. You can add, move, and delete anchor points and line segments to change the shape of the vector. Before working with the images you'll use in the advertisement, you review the properties of bitmap and vector graphics.

STEPS

1. **Start InDesign, open ID D-1.indd from the drive and folder where you store your Data Files, then save it as Graphics**
   The file includes one bitmap image of papayas and one vector image of an apple.

2. **Click the workspace switcher on the Application bar, then click Essentials**

3. **Click the Zoom tool 🔍 on the Tools panel**
   You will use the Zoom tool to enlarge your view of the bitmap image to view the pixels.

4. **Drag a small rectangle with the Zoom tool pointer 🔍 over the papayas image in the approximate location shown in Figure D-1, then release the mouse button**
   The dotted rectangle that appears as you drag the Zoom tool pointer is called a **marquee**. Everything inside the marquee will be enlarged on the screen when you release the mouse pointer. At a high zoom percentage, you can easily see the pixels that make up the image.

5. **Click View on the Application bar, then click Fit Page in Window**

6. **Click the Direct Selection tool ▶ on the Tools panel, then position the Direct Selection tool pointer ▶ near the upper-right edge of the red apple until it appears with a small line segment next to it ▶**
   When the Direct Selection tool pointer is positioned over the edge of an unselected vector graphic, the anchor points and line segments become visible. As shown in Figure D-2, the pointer is over a line segment, indicated by the tiny line segment icon next to the arrow pointer.

QUICK TIP
In order to manipulate a vector graphic's anchor points and line segments in InDesign, you must copy and paste it from Illustrator to InDesign. If you use the Place command, the vector graphic will not be editable.

7. **Click any one of the anchor points on either side of the line segment, then drag slowly in any direction to change the location of the anchor point and the shape of the apple, as shown in Figure D-3**
   Most vector graphics are created in Adobe Illustrator but they can be manipulated in Adobe InDesign using the same tools.

8. **Save your work, then close the Graphics file**

InDesign 78

Working with Graphics

Tips and troubleshooting advice, right where you need it–next to the step itself.

x

Large screen shots keep students on track as they complete steps

Brightly colored tabs indicate which section of the book you are in.

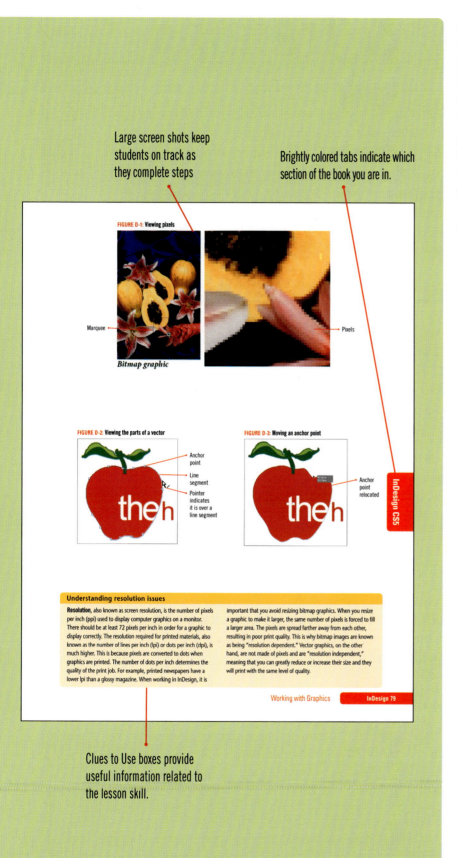

FIGURE D-1: Viewing pixels

Marquee

Pixels

Bitmap graphic

FIGURE D-2: Viewing the parts of a vector

Anchor point

Line segment

Pointer indicates it is over a line segment

FIGURE D-3: Moving an anchor point

Anchor point relocated

InDesign CS5

Understanding resolution issues

Resolution, also known as screen resolution, is the number of pixels per inch (ppi) used to display computer graphics on a monitor. There should be at least 72 pixels per inch in order for a graphic to display correctly. The resolution required for printed materials, also known as the number of lines per inch (lpi) or dots per inch (dpi), is much higher. This is because pixels are converted to dots when graphics are printed. The number of dots per inch determines the quality of the print job. For example, printed newspapers have a lower lpi than a glossy magazine. When working in InDesign, it is important that you avoid resizing bitmap graphics. When you resize a graphic to make it larger, the same number of pixels is forced to fill a larger area. The pixels are spread farther away from each other, resulting in poor print quality. This is why bitmap images are known as being "resolution dependent." Vector graphics, on the other hand, are not made of pixels and are "resolution independent," meaning that you can greatly reduce or increase their size and they will print with the same level of quality.

Working with Graphics   InDesign 79

Clues to Use boxes provide useful information related to the lesson skill.

Assignments

The lessons use MegaPixel, a design agency, as the case study. MegaPixel has many clients including The Happy Apple, an organic supermarket, and BreakTime, a student-travel company. The assignments on the light yellow pages at the end of each unit increase in difficulty. Additional case studies provide a variety of interesting and relevant exercises for students to practice skills.

Assignments include:

- **Concepts Reviews** consist of multiple choice, matching, and screen identification questions.

- **Skills Reviews** provide additional hands-on, step-by-step reinforcement.

- **Independent Challenges** are case projects requiring critical thinking and application of the unit skills. The Independent Challenges increase in difficulty, with the first one in each unit being the easiest. Independent Challenges 2 and 3 become increasingly open-ended, requiring more independent problem solving.

- **Real Life Independent Challenges** are practical exercises to help students with their everyday lives by focusing on important and useful essential skills, including creating business cards, greeting cards, schedules, and booklets.

- **Advanced Challenge Exercises** set within the Independent Challenges provide optional steps for more advanced students.

- **Visual Workshops** are practical, self-graded capstone projects that require independent problem solving.

Assessment & Training

SAM 2010: SKILLS ASSESSMENT MANAGER *SAM*

SAM 2010 is designed to help bring students from the classroom to the real world. It allows students to train and test on important computer skills in an active, hands-on environment.

SAM's easy-to-use system includes powerful interactive exams, training, and projects on the most commonly used Microsoft® Office applications. SAM simulates the Office 2010 application environment, allowing students to demonstrate their knowledge and think through the skills by performing real-world tasks such as bolding word text or setting up slide transitions. Add in live-in-the-application projects and students are on their way to truly learning and applying skills to business-centric document.

Designed to be used with the Illustrated Series, SAM includes handy page references, so students can print helpful study guides that match the Illustrated Series textbooks used in class. For instructors, SAM also includes robust scheduling and reporting features.

STUDENT EDITION LABS

Our Web-based interactive labs help students master hundreds of computer concepts, including input and output devices, file management and desktop applications, computer ethics, virus protection, and much more. Featuring up-to-the-minute content, eye-popping graphics, and rich animation, the highly interactive Student Edition Labs offer students an alternative way to learn through dynamic observation, step-by-step practice, and challenging review questions.

COURSENOTES

Course Technology's CourseNotes are six-panel quick reference cards that reinforce the most important and widely used features of a software application in a visual and user-friendly format. CourseNotes serve as a great reference tool during and after the student completes the course. CourseNotes for Microsoft Office 2010, Word 2010, Excel 2010, Access 2010, PowerPoint 2010, Windows 7, and more are available now!

COURSECASTS Learning on the Go. Always Available…Always Relevant.

Our fast-paced world is driven by technology. You know because you are an active participant—always on the go, always keeping up with technological trends, and always learning new ways to embrace technology to power your life. Let CourseCasts, hosted by Ken Baldauf of Florida State University, be your guide into weekly updates in this ever-changing space. These timely, relevant podcasts are produced weekly and are available for download at http://coursecasts.course.com or directly from iTunes (search by CourseCasts). CourseCasts are a perfect solution to getting students (and even instructors) to learn on the go!

Instructor Resources

The Instructor Resources CD is Course Technology's way of putting the resources and information needed to teach and learn effectively into your hands. With an integrated array of teaching and learning tools that offer you and your students a broad range of technology-based instructional options, we believe this CD represents the highest quality and most cutting edge resources available to instructors today. Many of these resources are available at www.cengage.com/coursetechnology. The resources available with this book are:

• **Instructor's Manual**—Available as an electronic file, the Instructor's Manual includes detailed lecture topics with teaching tips for each unit.

• **Sample Syllabus**—Prepare and customize your course easily using this sample course outline.

• **PowerPoint Presentations**—Each unit has a corresponding PowerPoint presentation that you can use in lecture, distribute to your students, or customize to suit your course.

• **Figure Files**—The figures in the text are provided on the Instructor Resources CD to help you illustrate key topics or concepts. You can create traditional overhead transparencies by printing the figure files. Or you can create electronic slide shows by using the figures in a presentation program such as PowerPoint.

• **Solutions to Exercises**—Solutions to Exercises contains files students are asked to create or modify in the lessons and end-of-unit material. Also provided in this section is a document outlining the solutions for the end-of-unit Concepts Review, Skills Review, and Independent Challenges.

• **Data Files for Students**—To complete the units in this book, your students will need Data Files. You can post the Data Files on a file server for students to copy. The Data Files available on the Instructor Resources CD are also included on a CD located at the front of the textbook.

Instruct students to use the Data Files List included on the CD found at the front of the book and the Instructor Resources CD. This list gives instructions on copying and organizing files.

• **ExamView**—ExamView is a powerful testing software package that allows you to create and administer printed, computer (LAN-based), and Internet exams. ExamView includes hundreds of questions that correspond to the topics covered in this text, enabling students to generate detailed study guides that include page references for further review. The computer-based and Internet testing components allow students to take exams at their computers, and also saves you time by grading each exam automatically.

Read This Before You Begin

This book assumes the following:

1. The software has been registered properly. If the product is not registered, students must respond to Registration and dialog boxes each time they start the software.
2. Default tools in the Tools panel might differ, but tool options and other settings do not carry over to the EOU or between units.
3. Students know how to create a folder using a file management utility.
4. After introduction and reinforcement in initial units, the student will be able to respond to the dialog boxes that open when saving a file. Later units do not provide step-by-step guidance.
5. Panels, windows, and dialog boxes have default settings when opened. Exceptions may occur when students open these elements repeatedly in a lesson or in the unit.
6. Students will be instructed in the early units on how to update missing links. Later units do not provide step-by-step guidance.
7. The few exercises that do contain live type were created using commonly available fonts. Nevertheless, it is possible, that students may run into a missing font issue when opening a data file. In that case, students should use an available font that is similar to the size and weight of the type shown in the lesson.

Frequently Asked Questions

What are the Minimum System Requirements (Windows)?

- Intel® Pentium® 4 or AMD Athlon® 64 or faster processor with 1GB RAM (2GB recommended)

- Microsoft® Windows Vista or Windows 7

- 1.6GB of available hard disk space (2 GB recommended)

- Color monitor with 16-bit color video card

- DVD-ROM

- Adobe Flash Player 10 (for exporting SWF files)

What are Data Files and where are they located?

The Data Files for this text are mostly InDesign files that you will use to complete the steps in the lessons and end-of-unit material. The Data Files for this text are located on a CD included at the front of this book. Insert the CD into a CD-ROM drive to access the files. Your instructor may have you copy them to a network or removable drive.

What software was used to write and test this book?

This book was written and tested with Adobe InDesign CS5 using a typical installation of Microsoft Windows 7 with Aero turned on.

Do I need to be connected to the Internet to complete the steps and exercises in this book?

Some of the exercises in this book assume that your computer is connected to the Internet. If you are not connected to the Internet, see your instructor for information on how to complete the exercises.

What do I do if my screen is different from the figures shown in this book?

This book was written and tested on computers with monitors set at a resolution of 1280 × 1024. If your screen shows more or less information than the figures in the book, your monitor is probably set at a higher or lower resolution. If you don't see something on your screen, you might have to scroll down or up to see the object identified in the figures.

Other Adobe® CS5 Titles

Adobe® Dreamweaver® CS5—Illustrated
Sherry Bishop (0538478691)

Ten units provide essential training on using Dreamweaver CS5 to create Web sites. Coverage includes creating a Web site, developing Web pages, formatting text, using and managing images, creating links and navigation bars, using CSS to layout pages, and collecting data with forms.

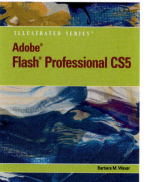

Adobe® Flash® Professional CS5—Illustrated
Barbara Waxer (053847789X)

Eight units provide essential training on using Adobe Flash Professional CS5, including creating graphics, text, and symbols, using the Timeline, creating animation, creating buttons and using media, adding interactivity, and integrating Flash projects with other CS5 programs.

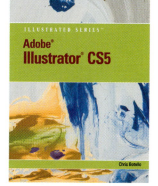

Adobe® Illustrator® CS5—Illustrated
Chris Botello (1111221960)

Eight units cover essential skills for working with Adobe Illustrator CS5 including drawing basic and complex shapes, using the Pen tool, working with blends, compound paths and clipping masks, creating pattern fills and gradient fills for objects, and designing stunning 3D effects.

Adobe® Photoshop® CS5—Illustrated
Chris Botello (0538477814)

Eight units offer thorough coverage of essential skills for working with Adobe Photoshop from both the design and production perspective, including creating and managing layer masks, creating color effects and improving images with adjustment layers, working with text and combining text and imagery, and using filters and layer styles to create eye-popping special effects.

I ♥ ILLUSTRATED SERIES™

For more information on the Illustrated Series, please visit:
www.cengage.com/ct/illustrated

Acknowledgements

Author Acknowledgements

I very much enjoyed writing this book, mostly because of the great team that I had to work with. I would like to thank Nicole Pinard, Vice President, Publisher at Course Technology, Marjorie Hunt, Executive Editor and Brandi Shailer, Associate Acquisitions Editor for giving me this opportunity. I would also like to thank our Product Manager, Jennifer Goguen McGrail and Kate Russillo, Project Manager. Jennifer and Kate were always available to me when I had a question and were wonderful to work with. Barbara Waxer, both my friend and developmental editor, brought ideas and energy into this project. Her wonderful karma was transmitted from New Mexico to Boston and into the pages of this book. Barbara also provided me with beautiful images to use in the book. Thank you too, to Anita Quintana of Media Mantis Designs and Santa Fe Community College. Anita designed the Happy Apple logo and the Newsletter document found in Unit A.

And of course, thank you to our wonderful QA reviewers, Jeff Schwartz, Susan Whalen, Danielle Shaw, and Marianne Snow, whose sharp eyes and sharp minds found room for correction and improvement.

Finally, I would like to thank my family and friends who supported me and made me laugh during this past year.

– **Ann Fisher**

Getting Started with InDesign CS5

Files You Will Need:

Newsletter.indd
Boutique Flyer.indd
ID A-1.indd

Adobe InDesign CS5 is part of the Adobe Creative Suite 5 (CS5) family of software programs. InDesign is a page layout software program used to design and produce documents that can be printed or used on the Web. You can create anything from a simple business card to a large book. You can also export InDesign documents for use in Adobe Dreamweaver and Flash. If you are working toward a career as a print or Web designer, knowledge of InDesign is a must. MegaPixel is a graphic arts service bureau and design agency. You work as a designer at MegaPixel and use Adobe InDesign to create print and Web documents for a number of clients.

OBJECTIVES
Understand page layout software
Start InDesign
Explore the InDesign workspace
Create a new document
Name and save a document
Work with panels
Work with guides
Use Adobe Help

Understanding Page Layout Software

Adobe InDesign is a page layout software program. **Page layout software** includes tools that allow you to easily position text and graphics on document pages. For example, using InDesign, you could create a newsletter that includes articles and pictures on each page. You can place pictures and text next to each other, on top of each other, or beside each other—wherever you want them to go. If you can imagine what you want or need on paper, you can create it in InDesign as long as you are familiar with its tools and features. MegaPixel has hired an assistant, Chris, to help you out. You demonstrate InDesign's features to Chris using a newsletter you created for The Happy Apple, an organic supermarket, as shown in Figure A-1.

DETAILS

Using InDesign, you can accomplish the following:

- ### Create and place text
  You can create text in InDesign and then format it. In addition to choosing fonts and font sizes, you can change the color of text and control the spacing between each character. You can also place text from another source, such as Microsoft Word, in an InDesign document.

QUICK TIP
If you are familiar with the Pen tool in Illustrator or Photoshop, you will be ready to use the Pen tool in InDesign.

- ### Create and place graphics
  You can create simple graphics in InDesign with the shape tools and the Pen tool. You can also place illustrations and photographs from other programs, such as Illustrator and Photoshop, in InDesign documents.

- ### Choose from many colors
  InDesign contains many color samples, called **swatches**, to choose from. The Swatches panel includes the basic colors used for printed materials. There are also other color libraries to choose from for special purposes. For example, there is a library of Web colors for documents created for the Web.

- ### Position objects easily
  InDesign offers many features that help you position text and graphics with accuracy. You can snap objects to ruler guides or a grid. You can also use the Transform panel and the Control panel to define an object's width, height, rotation angle, and vertical and horizontal location. The Align panel allows you to align and distribute objects by their tops, bottoms, centers, or sides.

- ### Store items
  Libraries are storage containers for items that you use repeatedly and want easy access to when working in InDesign. Company logos, legal jargon, and contact information are good examples of items to store in a library. Libraries look just like panels, but they are actually InDesign documents that are saved with the .indl extension. Libraries are not linked to one InDesign document; they can be opened and used with any InDesign documents.

- ### Create interactive buttons and hyperlinks
  In InDesign, you can use buttons and hyperlinks to design clickable areas in a document that link to a Web page, another file, or another page in your document. Hyperlinks and buttons that are created in InDesign become usable (clickable) when you export an InDesign document as an Adobe PDF (Portable Document Format) document or as a Web format.

- ### Export documents
  You can export an InDesign document as another file type so that it can be used in another program. For example, you can export an InDesign document as a Flash Player file (SWF) or as a Flash Professional CS5 file (FLA).

Text created and formatted in InDesign

The Happy Apple News

Logo created in Adobe Illustrator

Volume 24 October 22, 2013

New Employees

Text created in Microsoft Word and placed in InDesign

The Happy Apple has recently hired four new employees. Please welcome Kim de Peyster, our new Nutrition Consultant, Natalie Williams, head of Accounting, and Julia Goodman, Administrative Assistant to the Human Resources department. All three employees will work at the Corporate Offices in Lexington, Massachusetts.

New job listings will be posted on December 1, 2013 in the employee cafeteria. For more information, contact Helen in Human Resources.

Three adorable youngsters claim their pumpkins at last week's Pumpkin Fair in Jamaica Plain, MA. The Happy Apple supplied all of the cider and baked goods for the event. Fun was had by all.

Photographs placed in frames

Styles applied to similar text elements

Kim de Peyster, Nutrition Consultant

Natalie Williams, Head of Accounting

Julia Goodman, Administrative Assistant, Human Resources

Training Seminars

The Happy Apple is offering two training seminars for all part-time and full-time employees. Training seminars are free of charge and are encouraged for those of you who would like to hear more about careers at The Happy Apple or learn about other departments.

Childcare will be available and refreshments will be served. Hope to see you there.

SEMINAR 1
Flower Arranging
November 7, 2013, 7:00 pm - 8:30 pm.

SEMINAR 2
Keeping a Happy Customer
November 14, 2013, 7:00 pm - 8:30 pm.
Seminars will be held in the employee lounge in our Concord store.

Employee of the Month
Zachary Bairos:
Customer Service

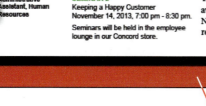

Nomination forms for the Employee of the Month award are in the Employee cafeteria.

The next employee of the month award will be announced on November 1, 2013. Winners receive an extra vacation day!

Drop shadow effect added to photograph

www.thehappyapple.com

Simple graphics created with shape tools

InDesign CS5

Starting InDesign

When you start InDesign for the first time, you will see the InDesign Welcome Screen. The Welcome Screen offers options for opening a recent document, creating a new document, or visiting one of Adobe's community Web sites. If you do not wish to view the Welcome Screen upon starting InDesign, you can click the Don't show again check box in the lower-left corner of the window. When you start InDesign without the Welcome Screen, the program opens without any documents open. You start InDesign and open a document so that you can familiarize Chris with the program.

STEPS

TROUBLE

Macintosh users: To open InDesign, double-click the hard drive icon on the desktop, double-click the Applications folder, double-click the Adobe InDesign CS5 folder, then double-click Adobe InDesign CS5. While performing the steps in this book, if you see the Missing Fonts dialog box, you can choose to use the substitute font supplied by InDesign or click Find Font, choose another font in the Find Font dialog box, then click OK.

1. **Click the Start button 🪟 on the taskbar, point to All Programs, click Adobe (or the name of the Adobe folder in the Start menu) if necessary, then click Adobe InDesign CS5**

   The InDesign window opens, showing the default workspace, as shown in Figure A-2. You may see the Welcome Screen in the center of the window when InDesign opens. The Welcome Screen will not be used in this unit. To close the Welcome Screen, click the Don't show again check box in the lower-left corner, then click the Close button. At a lower monitor resolution, your Application bar may be two rows instead of one.

2. **Click File on the Application bar, then click Open**

   The Open a File dialog box opens.

3. **Navigate to the location where you store your Data Files, click Newsletter.indd, then click Open**

   Newsletter.indd opens in InDesign, and a warning box appears stating that the document contains links to missing or modified files. You'll learn more about links in a later lesson, and you can explore now by reading the *Understanding more about links* Clues to Use below.

4. **Click Update Links in the warning box**

   The warning box closes, and the Newsletter document opens with the Links panel open on the right side of the workspace, as shown in Figure A-3.

5. **Close the Links panel**

Understanding more about links

When you place a photo or a picture in InDesign, you are only placing a preview of it for viewing. Each preview is linked to the original artwork and its location on the hard drive. This helps to keep each InDesign document's size small and manageable. If you move the photos or pictures that you placed in InDesign to a new location or modify them after you placed them in InDesign, InDesign asks you to find them by showing you the warning box stating that some files may be missing or modified. In many cases, the linked files are not missing; they have just been copied to a CD or copied onto a network. InDesign needs to know their new location in order to open the document correctly.

FIGURE A-2: InDesign window

FIGURE A-3: Newsletter document

Links panel

Exploring the InDesign Workspace

A workspace is where your work is created. Workspaces typically include an area designated for creating a finished product, much like a painter would use a canvas to create a painting. The InDesign workspace allows you to focus on your work without getting distracted by tools and panels. When you start InDesign for the first time, you see the default workspace, called "Essentials," with the Control panel and Tools panel along the top and left side of the InDesign window. You examine the workspace elements with Chris.

The InDesign workspace includes the following features, as shown in Figure A-4:

- The **document tab** appears just above the horizontal ruler and includes the document's name, its current magnification level, and a Close button. When more than one document is open, a tab appears for each document and the document tabs appear in a horizontal row. Click a document tab to view that document in the window. You can drag a document tab out of the group to open it in a stand-alone window.

- The **Application bar** sits at the top of the workspace and includes several menus. To open a menu, click the menu name on the Application bar. Each menu lists commands that relate to the menu category. To the right of the menu names are workspace and view options.

- The **Control panel** is located directly beneath the Application bar and above the horizontal ruler. On a Macintosh, the Control panel appears above the document window. When you select an object, the Control panel displays information about that object, such as its size and location on the page.

- The **Tools panel** contains the tools available in InDesign. There are tools for creating objects, such as the Rectangle tool, tools for transforming objects, such as the Rotate tool, and tools for changing the page view and navigating the workspace, such as the Zoom tool and the Hand tool. Some tools have a small black triangle in the lower-right corner. This indicates that additional tools are available beneath that tool. Click and hold the tool to see the hidden tools.

- **Panels** are small windows that contain options for working with selected objects. You make choices in panels by clicking buttons, choosing items from lists, or using a command on the panel menu. Panels are positioned on the right side of the workspace and are identified by a name and an icon.

- The **document window** is the central area that represents the open InDesign document. It resembles a piece of paper and is surrounded by a black border. The black border represents the page border. The default document window size is 8.5" × 11". Notice the two red rectangles at the top and bottom of the publication. These elements extend to the page borders on one or more sides, a printing issue known as **bleeding**. To print this document correctly, making sure that red bleed elements are not trimmed too close, a special bleed guide is added to the document. Bleed elements are enlarged by .25" on each side that they touch the page border. This allows for any margin of error that may occur when the document is trimmed.

- The **pasteboard** is the gray or white area surrounding the document window. You can place items on the pasteboard before actually inserting them on the page. The pasteboard color is white when you view your document window with guides and gray when you view the window without guides.

- The horizontal and vertical **rulers** run along the top and left sides of the document window and pasteboard area. They are helpful for measuring and positioning objects.

- The **status bar** is at the bottom of the workspace. The status bar gives you the status of what is going on at the moment. For example, the status bar shows which page is active in a multipage document.

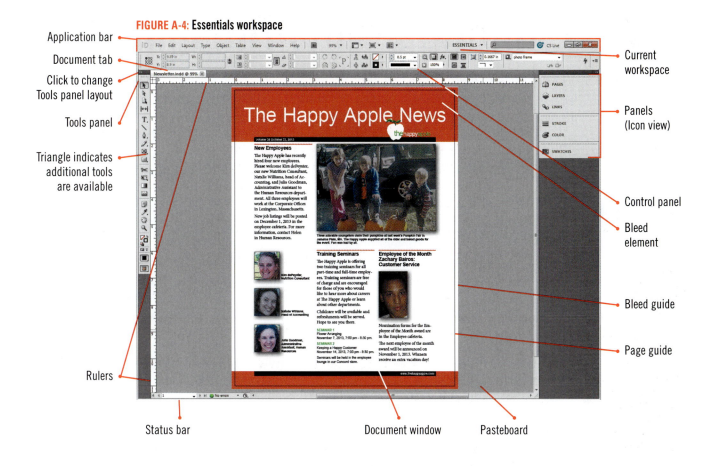

Application bar

Document tab

Click to change
Tools panel layout

Tools panel

Triangle indicates
additional tools
are available

Rulers

Status bar

Document window

Pasteboard

Current
workspace

Panels
(Icon view)

Control panel

Bleed
element

Bleed guide

Page guide

Using custom workspaces

InDesign offers custom workspaces for specific types of InDesign projects. For example, the Interactive workspace displays the Animation, Timing, Preview, Media, Object States, and Buttons panels, all of which would be useful when creating an interactive document. To choose a custom workspace, click Window on the Application bar, point to Workspace, and then click one of the eight workspace names. You can also create your own custom workspace with a unique name. For example, you may prefer to hide all of the panels in order to maximize your document window, or you may want the Tools panel to be a lot closer to your layout. InDesign makes it very easy to create the workspace you want and then save

it. Once the workspace is set up as you like it, click Window on the Application bar, point to Workspace, then click New Workspace. In the New Workspace dialog box, name the workspace, choose whether you want the new workspace to capture panel locations and/or menu customization, and then click OK. Your custom workspace will be added to the list of custom workspaces. The name of the current workspace appears in the workspace switcher on the right side of the Application bar. "Essentials" is the default workspace name. To switch to a different workspace, click the workspace switcher on the Application bar, and then click the name of the workspace you want to use.

Creating a New Document

Before you create a new InDesign document, you should know what it is that you'd like to create. Planning helps you make the right choices in the New Document dialog box. To create a new document, click File on the Application bar, point to New, then click Document to open the New Document dialog box. You can save your document settings in the New Document dialog box for future use. MegaPixel's client, The Happy Apple organic supermarket, is offering a new service for its customers: a low-interest Happy Apple credit card. You need to create an in-store flyer advertising the credit card. You show Chris how to create a new document.

STEPS

TROUBLE

If you do not see Reset Essentials as an option, click Window on the Application bar, point to Workspace, then click [Essentials].

1. **With the Newsletter document open, click File on the Application bar, click Close, click No (Win) or Don't Save (Mac) to reject the changes to the Newsletter document made when the links were fixed, click Window on the Application bar, point to Workspace, then click Reset Essentials**

   The workspace returns to the Essentials workspace, which displays the Pages, Layers, Links, Stroke, Color, and Swatches panels.

2. **Click Edit (Win) or InDesign (Mac) on the Application bar, point to Preferences, then click General**

   The Preferences dialog box opens with the options for the General category showing.

3. **Click Units & Increments on the left side of the dialog box, click the Horizontal list arrow under Ruler Units, click Inches if necessary, click the Vertical list arrow, click Inches if necessary, then click OK to close the dialog box**

   Inches will be used as the unit of measurement on the horizontal and vertical rulers.

TROUBLE

If the current Document Preset shown in the New Document dialog box is not [Default], click the Document Preset list arrow, then click [Default] before proceeding to Step 5.

4. **Click File on the Application bar, point to New, then click Document**

   The New Document dialog box opens, as shown in Figure A-5, showing [Default] as the Document Preset. A **preset** is a collection of all of the settings in the New Document dialog box, saved and stored with a descriptive name and available for future use.

5. **Click the Intent list arrow, notice that you can choose between Print and Web, then click Print, the default setting**

   The flyer you are creating will be printed. When you choose Web from the Intent list arrow, InDesign changes the unit of measurements to **pixels** (px), the unit of measure for on-screen resolution.

6. **Click the Page Size list arrow to view the standard sizes that are available**

   The default page size is Letter, which is 8.5" × 11". Other options include Legal, which is 8.5" × 14" and used for legal documents; Tabloid, which is 11" × 17" and used for small newspaper formats; and A4, which is the international standard paper size. Note that you can also create a custom size.

7. **Press [Esc] to close the list, then click the Facing Pages check box to remove the check mark**

   The New Document dialog box changes to display settings for a document that does not contain facing pages. Facing pages are used in multiple-page documents, such as magazines, that require left and right pages. **Facing pages** are also known as **spreads**. When you deselect the Facing Pages check box, the Document Preset changes from [Default] to [Custom] and the Inside and Outside margin setting labels change to Left and Right.

QUICK TIP

Vertical margin guides are called column guides.

8. **Double-click the Top text box of the Margins section, type 1, then press [Tab]**

   The three other margin settings also change to 1 because the Make all settings the same button in the Margins area is currently selected.

9. **Click OK to close the New Document dialog box**

   A letter-sized document with 1-inch margins appears in the workspace, as shown in Figure A-6. The name of the document, "Untitled-1," appears on the document tab. The margins are indicated in the document by colored lines called **margin guides**.

FIGURE A-5: New Document dialog box

Document Preset list arrow

Intent list arrow

Page Size list arrow

Landscape button

Portrait button

Make all settings the same button (selected)

FIGURE A-6: New document

Default name of document

Horizontal and vertical rulers in inches

Margin guides

Naming and Saving a Document

Saving your work is very important so that you don't lose anything that you've created. To save a document, click File on the Application bar, and then click Save. The first time that you save a new document, the Save As dialog box opens, asking you to name the document and to choose a location in which to store it. Once saved, the new filename, followed by the InDesign filename extension **.indd**, appears on the document tab. Once a document is named and saved, you should continue to save your work on a regular basis, such as every 10 minutes. You save the new document with a unique name.

STEPS

1. **Click File on the Application bar, then click Save As**

   The Save As dialog box opens, as shown in Figure A-7. The default name of the file appears highlighted in the File name text box (Win) or the Save As text box (Mac). Below this text box is the Save as type list arrow (Win), or the Where up and down arrows and the Format up and down arrows (Mac). The default file type is InDesign CS5 document.

2. **Click the Save in list arrow (Win) or the Save As down arrow (Mac), then navigate to the location where you store your Data Files**

3. **Type Credit Card Flyer in the File name text box (Win) or the Save As text box (Mac), then click Save**

   The file's new name, Credit Card Flyer.indd, appears on the document tab.

> **TROUBLE**
> If your document is already a floating window, move on to Step 5.

4. **Drag the document tab down to the document window, then release the mouse button when the blue outline around the document window disappears**

   The document becomes a floating window without the document tab and the document name is incorporated into a title bar.

5. **Drag the floating window in the workspace so that you can see more of the pasteboard, as shown in Figure A-8**

   Working with floating windows is useful if you need to see artwork in another document while you work in the current one.

6. **Click the title bar, then slowly drag it in an upward direction until you see the blue border reappear (Win) or until it is just below the Option bar (Mac), then release the mouse button**

   The document tab reappears.

FIGURE A-7: Save As dialog box

Your location might differ → Save in: Data Files

File name text box → File name: Untitled-1.indd

Save as type list arrow → Save as type: InDesign CS5 document

Your files might differ →

Name	Date modified	Type
Boutique Flyer	12/13/2013 8:48 AM	InDesign
ID A-1	12/13/2013 8:48 AM	InDesign
Newsletter	12/13/2013 8:41 AM	InDesign

Recent Places
Desktop
Libraries
Computer
Network

☑ Always Save Preview Images with Documents

Save
Cancel

FIGURE A-8: Creating a floating document window

*Credit Card Flyer.indd @ 98%

Understanding Adobe InDesign CS5 Preferences

You can make changes to InDesign based on your personal preferences. For example, you can choose to use an Italian dictionary instead of the default English dictionary to check the spelling in your document; you can have InDesign underline misspelled words in olive green instead of the default red; or you can change the default color of guides and margin guides. These settings and many more are available in the InDesign Preferences dialog box. To open the Preferences dialog box, click Edit (Win) or InDesign (Mac) on the Application bar, point to Preferences, then click a preference category, such as Guides & Pasteboard, to open the dialog box. Click a different category on the left side of the dialog box to change categories. Keep in mind that in order for the settings you change to stick to all future documents, no documents can be open while you make changes in the Preferences dialog box. If a document is open when you change preference settings, the changes will only affect the current open document.

InDesign CS5

Working with Panels

Panels are moveable objects in the workspace. Sometimes known as "floating panels," they can be dragged anywhere, even into the document window. Panels contain buttons, check boxes, and menus you can use to work with and format InDesign objects. For example, the Swatches panel includes color swatches for applying colors to objects. To open a panel in the workspace, click the panel's name or icon. If you don't see the panel you need in the workspace, click Window on the Application bar, then click the panel name. You demonstrate to Chris how panels work.

STEPS

1. **Click Window on the Application bar, point to Workspace, then click Reset Essentials**

   If necessary, all default panel locations are restored. The most commonly used panels in InDesign appear on the right side of the default workspace: Pages, Layers, Links, Stroke, Color, and Swatches.

QUICK TIP

Click the Expand Panels button ▶▶ in the upper-right corner above the panel groups to show all of the panel groups in full view. When all panels are expanded to full view, click the Collapse to Icons button ◀◀ in the upper-right corner to close all of the panel groups.

2. **Click Swatches on the right side of the workspace**

   As shown in Figure A-9, the Swatches panel opens and is displayed in full view.

3. **Click and hold the Swatches panel tab, then drag it to the document window**

   The Swatches panel becomes a stand-alone panel. When you create a stand-alone panel, you can drag it wherever you need it in the workspace.

4. **Click the Panel options button ▾≣, then click Large Swatch**

   The color swatches in the Swatches panel are displayed in a larger size, making it easier to see them. Each panel has a panel options button that opens a menu of commands that you can use to change the contents and display of the panel.

5. **Click ▾≣, then click Name**

   The color swatches in the Swatches panel return to their default size, listed by name.

6. **Drag the Swatches panel tab to just below the Color panel on the right side of the workspace until a light blue line appears under the Color panel, then release the mouse button**

   The Swatches panel is collapsed and returned back to its original icon state and location.

Working in Normal and Preview modes

Normal mode is the default view when InDesign opens; it displays all of the non-printing elements, such as frame borders, guides, grids, margin guides, and column guides. **Preview mode** hides all of the non-printing elements so that you can focus on your layout without distraction. You can quickly switch from one mode to the other by pressing [W].

FIGURE A-10: New guide

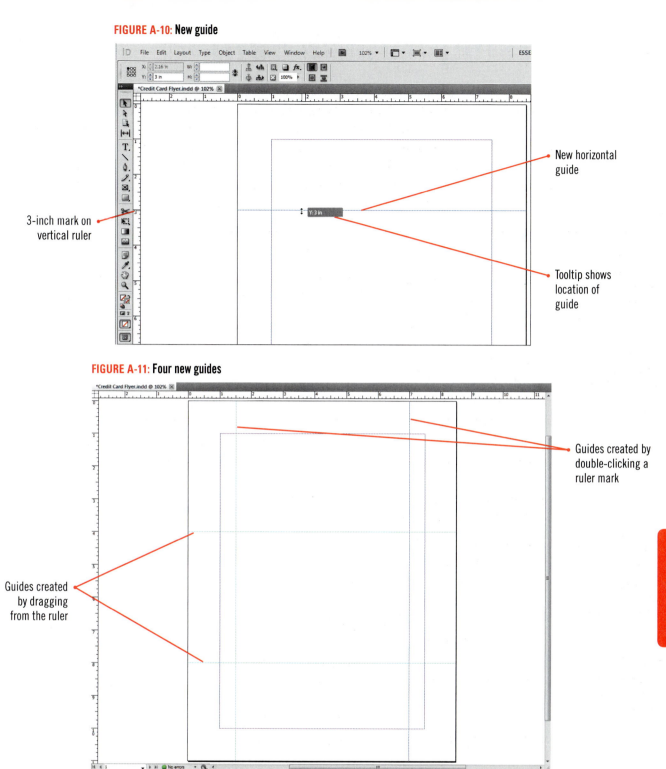

3-inch mark on vertical ruler

New horizontal guide

Tooltip shows location of guide

FIGURE A-11: Four new guides

Guides created by double-clicking a ruler mark

Guides created by dragging from the ruler

Using the grid feature in InDesign

The **grid** is a preset group of vertical and horizontal lines equidistant from each other in the document window, much like traditional grid paper. There are only two grids: the **baseline grid**, useful for working with columns of text, and the **document grid**, useful for aligning objects. Grids are most useful when your design requires you to place multiple items the same distance from each other, such as a dozen check boxes that are part of a checklist. You can change the grid settings, such as its color and spacing, in the Grids section of the Preferences dialog box. To turn the grid on or off, click View on the Application bar, point to Grids & Guides, then click either Show Baseline Grid or Show Document Grid. You can also choose to snap objects to the grid. To do so, click View on the Application bar, point to Grids & Guides, then click Snap to Document Grid. As you drag an object toward a grid line, the snap feature pulls it, much like a magnetic pull, and aligns it with the gridline.

Using Adobe Help

The Adobe Community Help window opens with help topics and resources for Adobe Illustrator CS5 in the right pane. The help topics are categorized by subject, such as Text and Graphics. You can expand a subject by clicking the plus sign to the left of a subject name to view subtopics in that category. Clicking a topic name displays information about that topic. You can also search for a specific keyword or phrase by typing it in the Search text box on the left side of the window. Results found from the search are listed below the Search text box. Each result is a link to a web page from where the information was found. After getting the flyer started and creating a rectangle frame, you take some time to look for more information about working with graphics using InDesign Help.

STEPS

QUICK TIP
If you see the Local Content Update dialog box, click Cancel.

1. **Click Help on the Application bar, then click InDesign Help**

   As shown in Figure A-12, the Adobe Community Help window opens. You may also see the Local Content Update dialog box. This dialog box allows you to update local content in the Help window.

2. **Click Graphics in the Help window**

   As shown in Figure A-13, a list of topics about graphics appears.

3. **Click Placing graphics, then click Place multiple graphics**

   As shown in Figure A-14, an article about placing multiple graphics opens in the window.

4. **Read the article, then close the Help window**

5. **Close Credit Card Flyer.indd, click File on the Application bar, then click Exit (Win), or click InDesign on the Application bar, then click Quit InDesign (Mac) to exit InDesign**

FIGURE A-12: Adobe InDesign CS5 Help

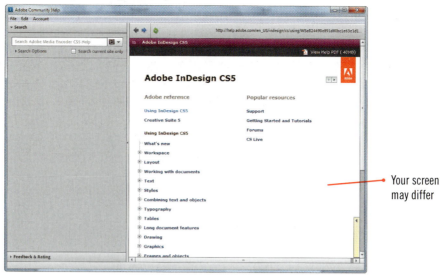

Your screen may differ

FIGURE A-13: Graphics Help topic

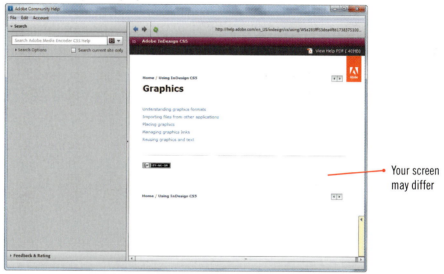

Your screen may differ

FIGURE A-14: Help topic about placing multiple graphics

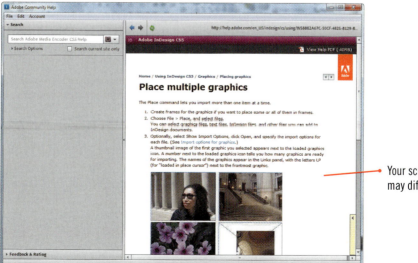

Your screen may differ

Practice

SAM

For current SAM information, including versions and content details, visit SAM Central (http://www.cengage.com/samcentral). If you have a SAM user profile, you may have access to hands-on instruction, practice, and assessment of the skills covered in this unit. Since various versions of SAM are supported throughout the life of this text, check with your instructor for the correct instructions and URL/Web site for accessing assignments.

Concepts Review

Label the elements of the InDesign screen shown in Figure A-15.

FIGURE A-15

1. _____   4. _____
2. _____   5. _____
3. _____

Match each term with the statement that best describes it.

6. Pixel
7. Preset
8. [W]
9. Panel
10. Pasteboard

a. Small floating windows that contain options for working with selected objects
b. Unit of measure used for onscreen resolution
c. Switches from Normal to Preview mode
d. Area where you can place objects before putting them on the page
e. Collection of all of the settings in the New Document dialog box

Select the best answer from the list of choices.

11. **Which of the following is found in the New Document dialog box?**
    - **a.** Intent list arrow
    - **b.** Preferences
    - **c.** Workspace switcher
    - **d.** Panel list arrow

12. **How can you create a guide without dragging the mouse pointer?**
    - **a.** Use the Guide dialog box
    - **b.** Double-click a ruler mark on the ruler
    - **c.** Click View on the Application bar, then click Create Guide
    - **d.** Double-click the Y Location value

13. **What is the name of the default workspace?**
    - **a.** Print
    - **b.** Preset
    - **c.** Exploring
    - **d.** Essentials

14. **Which panel displays the vertical or horizontal location of a selected guide?**
    - **a.** Guides
    - **b.** Control
    - **c.** Essentials
    - **d.** Location

Skills Review

1. **Understand page layout software.**
   - **a.** List three types of documents you can create using Adobe InDesign.
   - **b.** List four things you can do when working in InDesign.

2. **Start InDesign.**
   - **a.** Start InDesign using the process appropriate for your operating system and computer.
   - **b.** Open the document Boutique Flyer.indd from the location where you store your Data Files.
   - **c.** Click Update Links in the warning box, if necessary.

3. **Explore the InDesign workspace.**
   - **a.** Locate the following items in the InDesign workspace.
     - Title tab (Win) or Title bar (Mac)
     - Application bar
     - Control panel
     - Horizontal and vertical rulers
     - Tools panel
     - Status bar
     - Panels
     - Document window
     - Pasteboard
   - **b.** Click File on the Application bar, click Close, then click No (Win) or Don't Save (Mac).

4. **Create a new document.**
   - **a.** Open the New Document dialog box using a command on the File menu.
   - **b.** Click the Document Preset list arrow, then click [Default], if necessary.
   - **c.** Verify that the Intent list arrow is set to Print.
   - **d.** Click the Page Size list arrow to view the standard sizes that are available, then click Compact Disc.
   - **e.** Remove the check mark in the Facing Pages check box.
   - **f.** Double-click 0.5 in the Top text box of the Margins section, type **1**, then press [Tab].
   - **g.** Click OK to close the New Document dialog box.

5. **Name and save a document.**
   - **a.** Click File on the Application bar, then click Save As.
   - **b.** Click the Save in list arrow (Win) or the Save As down arrow (Mac), then navigate to the location where you store your Data Files.

c. Type **CD Cover** in the File name text box (Win) or the Save As text box (Mac), then click Save.

d. Drag the document tab down to the document window, then release the mouse button when the blue outline around the document window disappears. (*Hint*: If your document is already a floating window, move on to Step 5e.)

e. Click the title bar, then slowly drag it in an upward direction until you see the blue border reappear (Win) or until it is just below the Option bar (Mac), then release the mouse button.

6. **Work with panels.**

a. Click Window on the Application bar, point to Workspace, then click Reset Essentials.

b. Click the Stroke icon to open the Stroke panel group and display the Stroke panel in full view.

c. Drag the Stroke Panel tab to the document window.

d. Click the Panel options button, click Stroke Styles, then click Cancel.

e. Drag the Stroke panel tab on top of its original group so that the Stroke panel tab overlaps the Color panel tab.

f. Click the double-arrow icon in the upper-right corner of the Stroke panel group to collapse the group.

7. **Work with guides.**

a. Click the horizontal ruler, drag to approximately the 1.5-inch mark on the vertical ruler to create a horizontal guide, then release the mouse button.

b. Create another horizontal guide at the 2.5-inch mark on the vertical ruler.

c. Create a vertical guide by double-clicking the .5-inch mark on the horizontal ruler.

d. Save your work, then compare your screen to Figure A-16.

8. **Use Adobe Help.**

a. Click Help on the Application bar, then click InDesign Help.

b. Click Frames and objects in the list of categories.

c. Click the Selecting objects topic, then click Select objects.

d. Read the article, then close the Help window.

e. Click File on the Application bar, then click Exit (Win), or click InDesign on the Application bar, then click Quit InDesign (Mac) to exit InDesign.

FIGURE A-16

Independent Challenge 1

Your cousin wants to start creating her own greeting cards rather than buying them. She is looking for someone to create a greeting card template for her so that she can easily place her graphics when creating the cards in InDesign. You offer to help her by creating an InDesign document with the appropriate settings. She has requested a simple postcard style card that is 5 inches wide and 4 inches high.

a. Start InDesign.

b. Open the New Document dialog box to create a new document.

c. Change the Document Preset to [Custom], then verify that the Intent setting is set to Print.

d. Change the width of the new document to **5** inches and the height to **4** inches.

e. Change all four margin settings to **0.5** inches, if necessary.

f. Click the Landscape orientation button.

g. Remove the check mark in the Facing Pages check box, if necessary.

h. Click OK to close the New Document dialog box, then save the document as **Postcard**.

i. Compare your screen to Figure A-17, then close the Postcard document and exit InDesign.

FIGURE A-17

Independent Challenge 2

You have recently been promoted from stock room manager to customer service associate at The Software Depot. You need to get up to speed on new software programs so that you can answer customer questions. Your first assignment is to prepare yourself for answering customer inquiries about customizing InDesign.

a. Start InDesign.

b. Create a new document using the Default settings in the New Document dialog box, then save the new document as **Sample**.

c. Display the rulers, if necessary.

d. Click the Pages panel tab, then drag it to the document window, then drag the Links panel to the document window.

e. Click the Links panel tab, drag it to the bottom of the Pages panel, then release the mouse button when a blue line appears. (*Hint*: If the Links panel is too tall, click the Show/Hide Link Information button on the panel to collapse the lower half of the panel.)

Independent Challenge 2 (continued)

f. Click Window on the Application bar, then click Text Wrap.

g. Add the Text Wrap panel to the Pages and Links panel group.

h. Drag the new arrangement of docked panels from the top, dark gray bar to the left side of the document window so that it is near the Tools panel, then compare your screen to Figure A-18.

Advanced Challenge Exercises

- Click Window on the Application bar, point to Workspace, then click New Workspace.
- Save the workspace as **Custom Workspace**.
- Click Window on the Application bar, point to Workspace, then click [Typography].
- Click Window on the Application bar, point to Workspace, then click Custom Workspace.

i. Save your work, close the Sample document, then exit InDesign.

FIGURE A-18

Independent Challenge 3

Your family decides to have a last-minute yard sale this weekend. You've made a flyer advertising the sale and decide to adjust some of the document settings so that you can use it again in the future.

a. Start InDesign, open ID A-1.indd, update the links in the document if necessary, then save it as **Yard Sale**.

b. Select the top guide, which is at the 3.25-inch mark on the vertical ruler, then press [Delete].

c. Select the bottom guide, then drag it down until it snaps to the top of the text box at the bottom of the document.

d. Create a new horizontal guide anywhere on the page, and then change its Y Location value to 3 on the Control panel.

e. Deselect the new horizontal guide, press [W] to view your document without guides.

Independent Challenge 3 (continued)

f. Compare your document to Figure A-19.

g. Press [W] to make the guides visible again.

h. Click View on the Application bar, point to Grids & Guides, then click Lock Guides.

Advanced Challenge Exercises

- Open the Guides & Pasteboard category in the Preferences dialog box.
- Click the Margins list arrow, then click Dark Green.
- Click the Columns list arrow, then click Red.
- Click the Preview Background list arrow, then click Teal.
- Click OK to close the Preferences dialog box.

i. Save the Yard Sale document, close it, then exit InDesign.

Yard Sale
Saturday, August 30, 2013
34 Elm Road
9:00 am - 2:00 pm

Books, Clothing, Toys, Kitchen appliances
and more!

Real Life Independent Challenge

Your professor has provided a bonus question during the first week of your graphic arts class. If you get the answer right, you'll receive 10 points, so you're determined to find the answer. The question is:

"What is a character style?"

a. Start InDesign.

b. Access InDesign Help to find the answer to the above question.

c. Record your answer in a word-processing program or on paper.

d. Exit InDesign.

Visual Workshop

Create a new [Default] size document with 1-inch margins. Save the document as **Guides**, then create the guides shown in Figure A-20. Save the document and then exit InDesign.

Working with Text

Files You Will Need:

ID B-1.indd
Letter.doc
ID B-2.indd
Boy reading.jpg
Book News.doc
Invitation Text.doc
ID B-3.indd
Ski jump.jpg
ID B-4.indd
ID B-5.indd
Uhaul.jpg
ID B-6.indd
Gingerbread
  house.tif

Text is one of the most important features in InDesign. Even in a small amount such as a title, text can greatly influence the overall design of a publication. The job of text is to grab its viewers' attention and deliver a message to them successfully. In InDesign there are many text features that you can use to control how text appears in a document and to give text a personality all its own. Each month, the president of The Happy Apple writes a customer newsletter and MegaPixel helps her format it attractively in InDesign.

OBJECTIVES

Create text boxes

Place and flow text

Format text

Format paragraphs

Create and apply paragraph styles

Modify a paragraph style

Create and apply character styles

Apply bullets to text

Find and change text

Creating Text Boxes

Text boxes, also referred to as text frames, are containers for text. When you create a text box, a flashing cursor appears in the upper-left corner of the box, ready for you to start typing. The amount of text you can fit horizontally in a text box depends on the size of the text box because text automatically wraps to the next line once it hits the right side of the text box. You can copy and paste text from another source into InDesign or place a text file in an InDesign document using the Place command. You create a text box in the first column of the newsletter, then copy it to the second and third columns.

STEPS

QUICK TIP
Update links if necessary.

1. **Start InDesign, open ID B-1.indd from the location where you store your Data Files, then save the document as November News**

   The document opens with the standard newsletter elements already in place, such as the margin guides, the newsletter heading, and the Happy Apple logo.

2. **Click the workspace switcher on the Application bar, then click Reset**

   The workspace is returned to Essentials. Any floating panels are restored to their default locations.

3. **Click the Type tool T. on the Tools panel, then position the Type tool on the left margin guide**

   The Type tool pointer changes color when it is directly over a guide.

4. **Click and drag the Type tool pointer to create a text box of any height that snaps to the left margin guide, the bottom margin guide and the guide that defines the right side of the first column, as shown in Figure B-1, then release the mouse pointer**

   A text box is added to the page and the cursor is flashing in the upper-left corner of the text box. InDesign pages can have one or more columns. The space between two columns is called the **gutter**.

5. **Click the Selection tool ▶ on the Tools panel, then click the lower-left reference point on the Control panel**

   When you click the Selection tool, a bounding box appears around the text box to indicate it is selected. You can change the size and location of the selected text box using the Control panel. Clicking the lower-left reference point on the Control panel selects the reference point as the fixed point for the object. When you resize the object, changes emanate from the fixed reference point.

6. **Double-click the Height (H) value on the Control panel, type 6, then press [Enter] (Win) or [return] (Mac)**

   The height of the text box is added to the top of it. The bottom of the text box remains affixed to the bottom margin guide.

7. **Press and hold [Alt] (Win) or [option] (Mac), then slowly drag the text box to the right, as shown in Figure B-2**

   The double-white arrow icon indicates that you are duplicating the selected object.

8. **Drag the copy of the text box so that it snaps to the second column margin guides and the bottom margin guide, then release the mouse pointer**

   The document contains two text boxes.

QUICK TIP
To find out the width of the gutter, click Layout on the Application bar, then click Margins and Columns to view the Gutter value in the Margins and Columns dialog box.

9. **Repeat Steps 7 and 8 using the middle text box to add a third text box to the third column, then save your work**

   You created three text boxes into which you can place text for the newsletter.

New text box

Guide that defines the right
side of the first column

Bottom margin guide

Double-arrow pointer

Placing and Flowing Text

In multipage documents, such as magazines or books, text usually comes from other sources like Microsoft Word. You can place all of the text contained in a file created in another source in InDesign using the Place command on the File menu. Once placed, you can flow text into many text boxes throughout the pages in an InDesign document. Flowing text (also known as **threading** text) into text boxes can be compared to pouring a pitcher of water into a series of water glasses until there is no more water to pour. Table B-1 details all of the methods that you can use to flow text. The Happy Apple's newsletter is in Microsoft Word format. You plan to place the text into the first text box and then flow it into the second and third.

STEPS

1. **Click View on the Application bar, then click Zoom In**

   The magnification level increases and can be seen in the document name tab. Continue to zoom in for a better view, if necessary.

2. **Click the Hand tool 👋 on the Tools panel, then drag the page into better view, if necessary**

   You can return to a view of the entire page or spread by double-clicking the Hand tool on the Tools panel. You can also access this view, called "Fit Page in Window," on the View menu or by pressing [Ctrl][0] (Win) or ⌘[0] (Mac).

3. **Click the Type tool T on the Tools panel, then click inside the first text box**

   The flashing cursor appears in the text box. The text you place will flow into this text box.

   QUICK TIP
   You can flow text into text boxes on pages that are not near each other. For example, you can place a text file in a text box on page 1 of a document and then flow some of it or the rest of it into another text box on page 7.

4. **Click File on the Application bar, click Place, navigate to the location where you store your Data Files, click Letter.doc, then click Open**

   All of the text contained in the Letter file is flowed into the text box. The entire text box is filled and, as shown in Figure B-3, a red overset text icon appears at the bottom of the text box, indicating that there is more text available than this text box can display. The text is displayed with the formatting that was applied to it in Microsoft Word.

5. **Click the Selection tool ▶ on the Tools panel, then click the overset text icon ⊞**

   When you click the overset text icon, the pointer becomes a loaded text pointer with a link icon, indicating that the text that is about to be placed is part of the same text file that filled the previous text box.

6. **Click anywhere in the second text box**

   The remaining text fills the second text box. A link is established between the two text boxes. If you were to delete all of the text from these two text boxes and then place a new text file into the first text box, the overset text would automatically flow into the second text box because of the established link. Deleting flowed text from the text boxes does not delete the link.

7. **Click ⊞ in the second column, then click the third text box so that the text fills the three columns**

   Your columns should resemble the columns in Figure B-4.

   QUICK TIP
   To see text threads, the Selection tool must be selected.

8. **Click View on the Application bar, point to Extras, then click Show Text Threads**

   The blue text thread shows the flow of text from the first text box to the second and from the second to the third. Viewing text threads is helpful if you are not sure how text boxes are linked and how text is flowing in a document.

9. **Click View on the Application bar, point to Extras, click Hide Text Threads, then save your work**

FIGURE B-3: Text placed in the text box

November 2013

Dear Customers,
While driving to work the other day, I noticed how hungry I was. I tried to remember what I had for breakfast. And, then I realized that I had rushed out of the house with a travel mug of coffee. Some breakfast! I was trying to get a few errands done before work—pick up the antique linen tablecloth at the dry cleaners and silver polish at the department store. Many of you can probably relate to this type of running around as you get ready for Thanksgiving and of course, the December holidays.
I'd like to give you some tips and advice for staying healthy during this time of year. If we do not fuel our bodies, we run the risk of becoming worn down and more susceptible to germs and viruses. Some great on-the-go breakfast foods include oatmeal bars, granola bars, bananas, cheese, and almonds. You may be surprised that almonds would be a good start to your day. Almonds are

→ Overset text icon

FIGURE B-4: Linked text

November 2013

Dear Customers,
While driving to work the other day, I noticed how hungry I was. I tried to remember what I had for breakfast. And, then I realized that I had rushed out of the house with a travel mug of coffee. Some breakfast! I was trying to get a few errands done before work—pick up the antique linen tablecloth at the dry cleaners and silver polish at the department store. Many of you can probably relate to this type of running around as you get ready for Thanksgiving and of course, the December holidays.
I'd like to give you some tips and advice for staying healthy during this time of year. If we do not fuel our bodies, we run the risk of becoming worn down and more susceptible to germs and viruses. Some great on-the-go breakfast foods include oatmeal bars, granola bars, bananas, cheese, and almonds. You may be surprised that almonds would be a good start to your day. Almonds are

full of nutrition. About a quarter cup of almonds packs 6 grams of protein! Almonds contain no cholesterol, trans-fat, or sodium. They contain Vitamin E, magnesium and calcium. For the entire month of November and December, the following almonds will be on sale at all Happy Apple stores:
Eat Smart Shelled almonds
Eat Smart Sliced almonds
Eat Smart Oil-roasted almonds
Sunset Dry-roasted almonds
Sunset Blanched almonds
Below you will find a simple recipe that include almonds. It is easy to make and great for kids and adults on the go!
Hit the Trails Mix
Ingredients
1 cup of sliced or whole shelled almonds
1 cup of raisins
1 cup of banana chips
1 cup of carob chips
1 cup of salted peanuts
Directions
Mix all of the ingredients together in a large bowl.
Serve in small bowls or plastic sandwich bags.
Serves 4

Cheers,

Jonathan Brim

TABLE B-1: Methods for flowing text

method	steps	result
Manual text flow	Click the overset text icon, then click a page or a text box on a page to flow more text into it. Repeat steps as needed.	Text is added to one page or one text box at a time.
Semi-autoflow	Click the overset text icon, then press and hold [Alt] (Win) or [option] ⌘ (Mac) each time you click the text boxes into which to flow the remaining text.	Each time a text box is filled, the pointer remains a loaded text icon and is ready to fill the next text frame. Unlike manual text flowing, you do not need to click the overset text icon again in order to keep flowing text from one text box to another.
Autoflow	Click the overset text icon, then press and hold [Shift] when you click another text box or another page.	Additional text boxes and pages are automatically created until all text is visible in the document.
Fixed-page autoflow	Click the overset text icon, then press and hold [Shift][Alt] (Win) or [shift][option] ⌘ (Mac) when you click a text box or page.	All text is flowed into the document without any new pages or text boxes created. Overset text must be set manually.

Formatting Text

Formatting text means changing the way that it looks without changing its meaning. In InDesign, there are many ways to change the look of your text. You can choose a typeface for your text. A **typeface** is a design created for a set of characters including the alphabet, numbers, and some symbols. A **font** is a set of characters based on a typeface using a specific size and style. For example, the Arial Narrow font is based on the typeface Arial. You can change the size, color, and style of text using the Control panel, the Character panel, and the Swatches panel. You magnify the "A letter from the President" text and then format it using the Control panel.

STEPS

1. **Click the** Zoom tool 🔍 **on the Tools pane, then drag the** Zoom tool pointer ⊕ **around "A letter from the President" at the top of the first column**

    A letter from the President is in a text box that spans the first two columns.

2. **Click the** Type tool T. **on the Tools panel, then double-click the word** letter

    Double-clicking selects a word. To select a line of text, triple-click a word in the line. To select a paragraph, click the text four times. Click the text five times to select all of the text in a text box.

3. **Triple-click the word** letter **to select the entire line**

    Text must be selected in order to change its appearance. When text is selected, the Control panel displays text formatting controls, as shown in Figure B-5. The Control panel identifies the current font and size, among other attributes, applied to the selected text.

QUICK TIP

To copy the format from one text box to another, select the text that you want to change, click the Eyedropper tool on the Tools panel, then click the text that has the format you want to apply.

4. **Click the** Font list arrow **on the Control panel, then click** Times New Roman **(Win) or point to** Times New Roman, **then click** Regular **(Mac)**

    The text font changes to Times New Roman.

5. **Click the** Font Size list arrow **on the Control panel, then click** 24 pt

    The text font size increases to 24 pt.

6. **Double-click the** Hand tool 🖐 **on the Tools panel to fit the page in the window**

7. **Click the** Type tool T. **on the Tools panel, click anywhere in the word** President, **then compare your text to Figure B-6**

    The Control panel identifies the new font and font size applied to the text. If you click the cursor within a line or a paragraph, the character attributes of that text are displayed on the Control panel.

8. **Click the** Selection tool ▶ **on the Tools panel, click** Object **on the Application bar, then click** Text Frame Options

    The Text Frame Options dialog box opens, where you can format the location of the text within the text box.

9. **Click the** Align list arrow, **click** Center, **click** OK, **then save your work**

    The text is vertically centered in the text box.

Using the Story Editor

InDesign provides a special window, called the Story Editor, for you to use to edit text that is already placed. It is much easier to see text in the Story Editor than on the InDesign page because it fills the entire screen, much like working in a word-processing program. To work in the Story Editor, click the Type tool on the Tools panel, click in the section of text that you wish to edit, click Edit on the Application bar, then click Edit in Story Editor. The Story Editor opens and you'll see the cursor in the same place that you clicked in the text. The Control panel is available at the top of the Story Editor, enabling you to make formatting changes in addition to editing the text. Once you make changes to the text, simply click the Close button in the Story Editor window and you'll be back in the original text box in InDesign.

FIGURE B-5: Selected text

Font and
font size
applied to
selected text

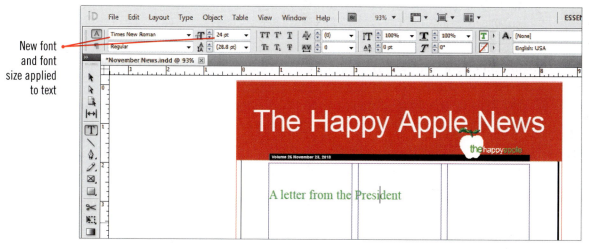

FIGURE B-6: Formatted text

New font
and font
size applied
to text

Kerning and Tracking

On the Character panel, you can control the space between two or more characters using the Kerning and Tracking settings. **Kerning** means to change the space between just two characters. **Tracking** means to change the space between all characters in a selection of text, such as a headline or an entire paragraph. To kern a pair of characters, click the Type tool cursor between the two characters, then click the Kerning list arrow and choose a preset value or use the Kerning up and down arrows to change the value in increments of 1/1000 of an em space. An **em space** is a printing measurement and is represented by the size of a the letter *m* in the current font and font size. A negative kerning value decreases the space between two characters and a positive kerning value increases the space. To track text, highlight the text and then choose a preset value using the Tracking list arrow or use the up and down arrows provided.

Formatting Paragraphs

Paragraphs are lines of text that are separated by the space created when you press [Enter] (Win) or [return] (Mac). For example, if you type *Monday*, press [Enter] (Win) or [return] (Mac), then type *Tuesday*, you have created two paragraphs—one on each line. Like text, you can format paragraphs by changing paragraph properties such as leading and alignment. **Leading** (pronounced "LED-ing") is the amount of space between the baselines of two lines of type. **Alignment** refers to the way a paragraph is horizontally spread out between the left and right sides of a text box. Table B-2 describes the available paragraph alignment buttons on the Control panel and the Paragraph panel. You format the title paragraph that introduces the letter by aligning it in the center of the first column.

STEPS

1. Click the Zoom tool 🔍 on the Tools panel, then drag the Zoom tool pointer ⊕ around "A letter from the President"

2. Click Type on the Application bar, then click Show Hidden Characters, if necessary
   A **hidden character** is a symbol that represents something else, such as a space between words. It does not print. Notice the pound sign (#) that follows "President." This pound sign is a hidden character that represents the end of a story. The term "story" refers to all of the text in one text box or all of the text in linked text boxes.

> **QUICK TIP**
> To force text onto a new line without creating a new paragraph, press [Shift] [Enter] (Win) or [shift][return] (Mac). This is known as creating a **soft return**.

3. Click the Type tool T. on the Tools panel, click after "President," press [Enter] (Win) or [return] (Mac), then compare your screen to Figure B-7
   A paragraph end symbol (another hidden character) appears after "President," indicating that "A letter from the President" is one paragraph. If you were to type a new line, you would be creating a second paragraph. The pound sign indicates that the end of the story now appears on the second line. The blue dots indicate spaces between words and are hidden characters.

4. Click Edit on the Application bar, then click Undo Paragraph Return to remove the new paragraph

> **QUICK TIP**
> If necessary, drag the Paragraph panel out of the way so that you have a good view of the paragraph you are formatting.

5. Click Type on the Application bar, then click Paragraph to open the Paragraph panel
   The Paragraph panel appears in the workspace. The Paragraph panel has many settings for changing the structure of a paragraph. To change values in the Paragraph panel text boxes, you can double-click the existing value and then type a new value, or click the up and down arrows to the left of each text box to choose a preset value.

> **QUICK TIP**
> If you select a text box with the Selection tool and then make changes in the Paragraph panel, the changes will apply to all paragraphs in the text box.

6. Triple-click the "A letter from the President" paragraph
   The entire paragraph is selected.

7. Click the Align center button ☰ on the Paragraph panel
   The text is horizontally centered between the left and right edges of the text box.

8. Click View on the Application bar, then click Fit Page in Window

9. Click Edit on the Application bar, click Deselect All, then save your work
   Your centered "A letter from the President" paragraph should look similar to the paragraph in Figure B-8.

Formatting controls on the Control panel

The Control panel has two buttons that allow you to switch between formatting characters and formatting paragraphs. The two buttons are at the far left side of the panel. The Letter "A" button is the Character Formatting Controls button. Click this button to display options for formatting characters, such as Font Size, Superscript, and All Caps, on the left side of the Control panel. The ¶ button is the Paragraph Formatting Controls button. Click this button to display options for formatting paragraphs, such as alignment and indentation, on the left side of the Control panel.

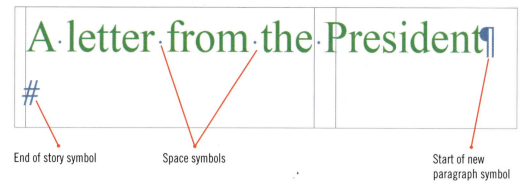

A·letter·from·the·President¶

\#

End of story symbol   Space symbols   Start of new
paragraph symbol

FIGURE B-8: Center-aligned text

The·Happy·Apple·News#

Volume 25 November 23, 2013#

A·letter·from·the·President#

TABLE B-2: Paragraph alignment options

button	type of alignment	description
	Align left	Lines are aligned on the left border of a text box.
	Align center	Lines are centered between the left and right borders of a text box.
	Align right	Lines are aligned on the right border of a text box.
	Justify with last line aligned left	Lines are evenly distributed so that they align on both the right and left borders of a text frame. The last line in the paragraph is aligned on the left border.
	Justify with last line aligned right	Lines are evenly distributed so that they align on both the right and left borders of a text frame. The last line in the paragraph is aligned on the right border.
	Justify with last line aligned centered	Lines are evenly distributed so that they align on both the right and left borders of a text frame. The last line in the paragraph is centered.
	Justify all lines	Lines are evenly distributed so that they align on both the right and left borders of the text box.
	Align towards spine	Used with left and right pages; text in a text box on a left page is right-aligned and any text that flows onto a right page is left-aligned.
	Align away from spine	Used with left and right pages; text in a text box on a left page is left-aligned and any text that flows onto a right page is right-aligned.

Creating and Applying Paragraph Styles

You have seen how to use the Paragraph panel to format an individual paragraph. **Paragraph styles** are useful when you want to format *several* paragraphs in a document. Paragraph styles work by lumping paragraph formatting options, such as indents, spacing before and after paragraphs, and alignment, into one named style. You simply apply the style to the paragraph and all of the formatting saved with the style is applied. Paragraph styles also enable you to control character formatting for paragraph text, such as font, size, style, and color. An **indent** is a blank space between text and its margin or frame border. You create a paragraph style in the New Paragraph Style dialog box named "Body," and then apply it to paragraphs in the newsletter using the Paragraph Styles panel.

1. **Verify that none of the text boxes are selected, click Type on the Application bar, then click Paragraph Styles**

   The Paragraph Styles panel opens, showing two available styles, [Basic Paragraph] and Normal. The [Basic Paragraph] style uses the Minion Pro font and 12 pt font size, which are the default text settings in InDesign. The Normal style was applied to the Letter document in Microsoft Word and was brought over to InDesign when the document was placed.

2. **Click the Panel options button 🔽, then click New Paragraph Style**

   The New Paragraph Style dialog box opens. It includes paragraph and character formatting categories.

3. **Type Body in the Style Name text box, then click Basic Character Formats on the left side of the dialog box**

4. **Click the Font Family list arrow, click Arial, click the Font Style list arrow, click Regular, then change the Font Size to 12 pt, if necessary**

5. **Click Indents and Spacing on the left side of the dialog box**

6. **Click the Alignment list arrow, click Left, double-click the Space Before text box, type .25, press [Tab], type .25 in the Space After text box, compare your New Paragraph Style dialog box to Figure B-9, then click OK**

   When the Body style is applied to text, each paragraph will be left-aligned, the lines in each paragraph will not be indented, and there will be .25 inches of blank space before and after every paragraph. The text in the paragraphs will be Arial, 12-point, Regular.

   QUICK TIP

   If you see a plus sign (+) following a paragraph style name in the Paragraph Styles panel, this means that additional formatting was applied to the currently selected text after the paragraph style was applied to it. You can remove the additional (or local) formatting and reapply a style by pressing [Alt] (Win) or [option] (Mac) when you click the style name in the panel.

7. **Click the Type tool T on the Tools panel, if necessary, click the paragraph While driving to work four times, then click Body on the Paragraph Styles panel**

   The Body style is applied to the paragraph.

8. **Apply the Body paragraph style to the two paragraphs in the letter that begin with "I'd like to give you some tips" and "Below you will find"**

9. **Deselect all, compare your screen to Figure B-10, then save your work**

FIGURE B-10: Applied paragraph style

Understanding parent/child relationships with styles

You can create a new paragraph or character style from an existing paragraph or character style by basing one on the other. When you base one style on another, you pick up all of the formatting choices of one style and modify them to quickly make a new style. Doing so creates a parent/child relationship between the new style and the existing style. The original style becomes the parent and the new style based on the parent becomes the child. A link is formed between the two styles. The parent and child styles are identical at first, but you can further modify the child style to differentiate it from the parent. However, if you make a change to the parent style, that change will automatically be reflected in the child style. For example, if you change the font from Times New Roman to Calibri in

the parent style, the font also changes to Calibri in the child style. Every paragraph that is formatted with both parent and child styles in the document will automatically change to the Calibri font. To create a child style based on a parent style, click the Based On list arrow in the General category of the New Paragraph Style or New Character Style dialog box, then choose the parent style that you want to base the new (child style) on. To base a style on an existing style without creating the parent/child relationship, select the style, click the Panel options button, and then click Duplicate Style. The new style will be an unlinked duplicate that you can then modify to your needs.

Modifying a Paragraph Style

Once you've applied paragraph styles to the text in a document, you may need to make a change to one or more of the paragraph style settings. For example, you may not like the way the text is aligned or you may need to change the font size. You can make any necessary changes to a paragraph style by double-clicking the paragraph style in the Paragraph Styles panel. Doing so will open the Paragraph Style Options dialog box, which contains all of your original formatting choices. Once you make the necessary changes, close the dialog box. The text to which the style is applied in the document is automatically updated with the changes to the style. You decide to change the paragraph alignment to Left Justify to improve the look of the text in the columns and to decrease the space before and after each paragraph.

STEPS

1. **Double-click Body in the Paragraph Styles panel**

   The Paragraph Style Options dialog box opens. It includes all of the formatting choices made for the Body paragraph style.

2. **Click Indents and Spacing on the left side of the dialog box**

3. **Click the Alignment list arrow, then click Left Justify**

4. **Click the down arrow next to Space Before one time to change the value in the Space Before text box to 0.1875**

5. **Change the Space After value to 0.1875, then compare your Paragraph Style Options dialog box to Figure B-11**

6. **Click OK to close the dialog box, then compare your screen to Figure B-12**

   All of the paragraphs with the Body paragraph style applied are updated with the new settings.

Using the Fill with Placeholder Text feature

InDesign documents can contain lots of text. When you are using InDesign to create a book or a magazine, you may want to experiment with how text will look in your publication and how it will flow before the text is ready to be placed. For example, you may want to determine which font and size to use for text in order to make it spread over a certain number of pages. To fill text boxes with "fake text" while you await the "real text," click Type on the Application bar, then click Fill with Placeholder Text. **Placeholder text** is made up of text that is divided into words of different lengths, often in Latin, to represent how real text will flow in your document. An example of placeholder text is: *Em ilit lummod tat. Ut ad ercil ecte magna adignibh et at.* When you are ready to replace the placeholder text with the real text, simply select all of the placeholder text and delete it. Any links between text boxes will be preserved so that the new text will automatically flow from one text box to another. You can also replace the provided placeholder text with your own placeholder text by saving a text document as Placeholder.txt in the InDesign application folder.

FIGURE B-11: Paragraph Style Options dialog box

FIGURE B-12: Updated paragraph styles

A letter from the President#

November 2013¶

¶

Dear Customers,¶

While driving to work the other day, I noticed how hungry I was. I tried to remember what I had for breakfast. And, then I realized that I had rushed out of the house with a travel mug of coffee. Some breakfast! I was trying to get a few errands done before work—pick up the antique linen tablecloth at the dry cleaners and silver polish at the department store. Many of you can probably relate to this type of running around as you get ready for Thanksgiving and of course, the December holidays. ¶

I'd like to give you some tips and advice for staying healthy during this time of year. If we do not fuel our bodies, we run the risk of becoming worn down and more susceptible to germs and viruses. Some great on-the-go breakfast foods include oatmeal bars, granola bars, bananas, cheese, and almonds. You may be surprised that almonds would be a good start to your day. Almonds are full of nutrition. About a quarter cup of almonds packs 6 grams of protein! Almonds contain no cholesterol, trans-fat, or sodium. They contain Vitamin E, magnesium and calcium. For the entire month of November and December, the following almonds will be on sale at all Happy Apple stores.¶

Eat Smart Shelled almonds¶
Eat Smart Sliced almonds¶
Eat Smart Oil-roasted almonds¶
Sunset Dry-roasted almonds¶
Sunset Blanched almonds¶

Below you will find a simple recipe that include almonds. It is easy to make and great for kids and adults on the go!¶

Hit the Trails Mix¶
Ingredients¶
1 cup of sliced or whole shelled almonds¶
1 cup of raisins¶
1 cup of banana chips¶
1 cup of carob chips¶
1 cup of salted peanuts¶
Directions¶
Mix all of the ingredients together in a large bowl. Serve in small bowls or plastic sandwich bags.¬
Serves 4¶
¶
¶
¶
Cheers,¶
¶
Jonathan Brim⤸

InDesign CS5

Creating and Applying Character Styles

Character styles work very much like paragraph styles, except that they are created just for characters. Character styles are perfect for short pieces of text, such as headings, labels, or titles. Imagine you have an InDesign document outlining your top five vacation choices, and you want to apply the same font, font size, and color to each vacation destination. You can choose the font, font size, and color; group them together as a character style; and save the style with a special name on the Character Styles panel. Then you could apply the character style to the vacation text in the document. You decide to create a character style for the Eat Smart brand name because it is The Happy Apple's in-house brand, and you want it to stand out from the rest of the text in the President's letter. You create a character style named "Eat Smart" and then apply it to each instance of "Eat Smart" in the letter.

STEPS

QUICK TIP

If necessary, drag the Character Styles panel out of the way so that you can easily see the text you are formatting.

1. **Click Type on the Application bar, then click Character Styles**

   The Character Styles panel opens, showing one available style called "[None]." The pencil icon with a slash through it next to [None] indicates that this style cannot be changed or deleted.

2. **Click the Character Styles Panel options button ▾≡, then click New Character Style**

   The New Character Style dialog box opens. On the left side of the dialog box are seven categories of possible formatting options for characters. The General category is where you name the character style. The Basic Character Formats and Character Color categories offer the most common formatting choices, such as font, style, font size, and color.

3. **Make sure the default style name in the Style Name text box is highlighted, then type Eat Smart**

   The default style name is replaced by "Eat Smart." This is the name of the style that will appear in the Character Styles panel.

4. **Click Basic Character Formats on the left side of the dialog box, click the Font Family list arrow, scroll down and then click Arial, click the Font Style list arrow, click Italic, click the Size list arrow, click 11 pt, then compare your New Character Style dialog box to Figure B-13**

5. **Click Character Color on the left side of the dialog box, scroll down and click the C=15 M=100 Y=100 K=0 (red) swatch, then click OK**

   The new style, called "Eat Smart," appears on the Character Styles panel.

6. **Use the Zoom tool 🔍 to zoom in on the five almond products listed in the second column**

7. **Click the Type tool T. on the Tools panel, select the first instance of "Eat Smart" in the list, then click Eat Smart on the Character Styles panel**

   The Eat Smart style is applied to the Eat Smart text.

QUICK TIP

To modify an existing character style, double-click its name in the Character Styles panel, change settings as desired in the Character Style Options dialog box, then close the dialog box. The text to which the style is applied in the document is automatically updated with the changes to the style.

8. **Apply the Eat Smart character style to the other two instances of Eat Smart, deselect the text, compare your screen to Figure B-14, then save your work**

   The Eat Smart character style places emphasis on the Eat Smart brand.

9. **Reset the Essentials workspace, click View on the Application bar, then click Fit Page in Window**

FIGURE B-13: New Character Style dialog box

New Character Style

General	**Style Name:** Eat Smart
Basic Character Formats	Location:
Advanced Character Formats	Basic Character Formats
Character Color	
OpenType Features	**Font Family:** Arial
Underline Options	**Font Style:** Italic
Strikethrough Options	**Size:** 11 pt **Leading:**
	Kerning: **Tracking:**
	Case: **Position:**

☑ Underline   ☑ Ligatures   ☑ No Break
☑ Strikethrough

☐ Preview   OK   Cancel

FIGURE B-14: Character style applied to text

Text with character style applied

New character style

Happy Apple stores:¶

Eat Smart Shelled almonds¶
Eat Smart Slic...onds¶
Eat Smart Oil-r... almonds¶
Sunset Dry-roasted almonds¶
Sunset Blanched almonds¶

Below you will find a simple

CHARACTER STYLES
[None]
[None]
Eat Smart

Applying Bullets to Text

Bullets are small symbols, such as circles or squares, that you can insert before the beginning of a paragraph. Bullets are typically used for an unsorted list of items, such as what to bring on a weekend trip. Use numbers instead of bullets for items that need to be in a specific order, such as driving directions or instructions for assembling a bookshelf. To apply bullets or numbers, first select the paragraphs to which you want to apply bullets, click Type on the Application bar, point to Bulleted & Numbered Lists, then choose either Apply Bullets or Apply Numbers. You can also use the Bullets and Numbering dialog box to apply bullets. This dialog box offers more options for bullets than using the menu commands. You apply a shaded-circle bullet to the five almond products mentioned in the letter to set them apart from the rest of the text.

1. Click the Zoom tool 🔍 on the Tools panel, then drag the Zoom tool pointer ⊕ around the five almond products in the second column

2. Click the Type tool T. on the Tools panel, then triple-click Eat Smart Shelled almonds
   The first paragraph is selected.

3. Press and hold [Shift], then press ↓ four times to select the next four lines
   To select lines above or below a selected line, press [Shift] ↑ or [Shift] ↓.

> **QUICK TIP**
> You can also apply bullets or numbers to selected text by clicking the Bulleted List button or the Numbered List button on the Control panel.

4. Show the Paragraph panel, click the Paragraph Panel options button ☰, then click **Bullets and Numbering**
   The Bullets and Numbering dialog box opens.

5. Click the List Type list arrow, click Bullets, then click Add
   The Add Bullets dialog box opens. The Add Bullets dialog box lets you choose new bullets from the available fonts installed on your computer. You want to choose a shaded circular bullet.

6. Click the Font Family list arrow, then click Wingdings
   Wingdings is a font family made up of many symbols.

7. Click the down scroll arrow twice, click the eleventh solid square bullet in the ninth row (GID:131), as shown in Figure B-15, then click OK
   The bullet is added to the Bullet Character list in the Bullets and Numbering dialog box.

> **QUICK TIP**
> To preview the bullet in the selected tab position in the document, click the Preview check box in the Bullets and Numbering dialog box.

8. Click the new bullet (GID:131) in the Bullet Character list, change the First Line Indent value to 0, change the Left Indent value to 0, change the Tab Position value to 0.125 in, and then click OK
   The Tab Position setting determines how far the beginning of the paragraph will be from the bullet. The Bullets and Numbering dialog box closes and the new bullet is added to each of the five selected paragraphs. Notice that the beginning of each paragraph is 0.25 inches away from each bullet.

9. Double-click the Hand tool 🖐 on the Tools panel, click Edit on the Application bar, click **Deselect All**, then save your work
   Compare your screen to Figure B-16.

FIGURE B-15: Add Bullets dialog box

FIGURE B-16: Bullets applied to paragraphs

Finding and Changing Text

You may need to make changes to text in InDesign after you have typed it or placed it. In long documents, finding specific words or phrases can be time-consuming. The Find/Change dialog box offers a great way to find text quickly and change it, if necessary. For example, you could use the Find/Change dialog box to find and replace each instance of "Pacific" with the word "Atlantic." Using the Find/Change dialog box guarantees that you won't miss any instances of the word you want to change in the document. In the letter he submitted, the President mistakenly referred to the Sunrise brand as the Sunset brand. You need to find all instances of "Sunset" and change them to "Sunrise," and you also must add the registered trademark symbol after "Sunrise" each time it appears.

STEPS

1. Click Edit on the Application bar, then click Find/Change

The Find/Change dialog box opens. You do not have to select text in order to use the Find/Change dialog box.

2. Type Sunset in the Find what text box, then type Sunrise in the Change to text box

> **QUICK TIP**
> To find and change fonts, click Type on the Application bar, then click Find Font. The Find Font dialog box lets you replace one font with another.

3. Click the Special characters for replace button 🔍 to the right of the Change to text box, point to Symbols, then click Registered Trademark Symbol

In the Change to text box, "^r" appears next to "Sunrise," as shown in Figure B-17. "^r" represents the registered trademark symbol (®) that will appear after "Sunrise" when it replaces "Sunset" in the document. A registered trademark symbol is a special symbol associated with the legal protections given a product whose name distinguishes it from other products.

4. Click Find

The first occurrence of the word "Sunset" is highlighted. You may need to drag the Find/Change dialog box out of the way to see the highlighted text.

5. Click Change

Sunrise® replaces Sunset in the text box in the document.

6. Click Change All

Clicking Change All replaces all instances of "Sunset" in the document with "Sunrise®." A dialog box appears telling you that one replacement was made when you clicked the Change All button.

7. Click OK, then click Done to close the Find/Change dialog box

8. Click the Type tool 🅣 if necessary, click before the B in "Below you will find" at the bottom of the second column, press [Enter] (Win) or [return] (Mac) three times to push the paragraph to the top of the third column, then save your work

9. Deselect all, press [W] to view your document without any frame borders, guides, or hidden characters showing, then compare your newsletter to Figure B-18

10. Click Window on the Application bar, point to Workspace, click Reset Essentials, then close November News and exit InDesign

Find/Change dialog box options

There are many options that you can choose for your search in the Find/Change dialog box. You can search for text as whole words; for example, you can define a word like "pen" as a whole word so that the Find/Change feature will not alert you each time it finds "pen" in words such as "pencil" and "happen." To search for whole words, click the Whole Word button ▤ in the Find/Change dialog box. You can have the Find/Change feature look for only upper- or lowercase versions of words by clicking the Case Sensitive button [Aa] in the dialog box. You can also choose to search the current document or all open documents for an instance of text. Click the Search list arrow in the dialog box and then choose either Document or All Documents. In addition to replacing text with special characters such as trademark symbols, hyphens, and dashes, you can find special characters by clicking the Special characters for replace button 🔍 next to the Find what text box and choosing the character that you want to replace.

FIGURE B-17: Find/Change dialog box

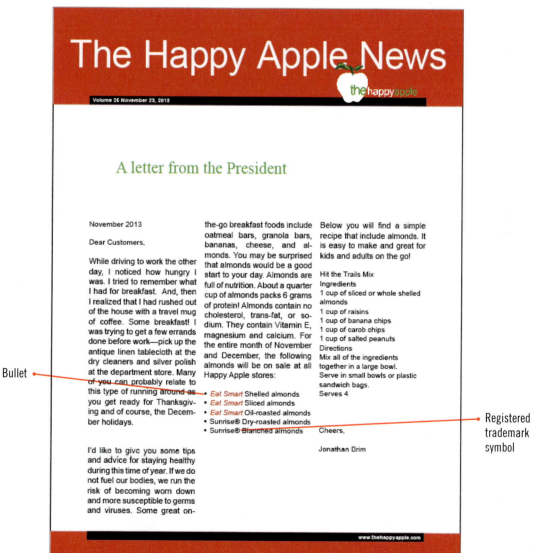

FIGURE B-18: Finished newsletter

Bullet

Registered trademark symbol

Practice

For current SAM information, including versions and content details, visit SAM Central (http://www.cengage.com/samcentral). If you have a SAM user profile, you may have access to hands-on instruction, practice, and assessment of the skills covered in this unit. Since various versions of SAM are supported throughout the life of this text, check with your instructor for the correct instructions and URL/Web site for accessing assignments.

Concepts Review

Label the elements of the InDesign screen shown in Figure B-19.

FIGURE B-19

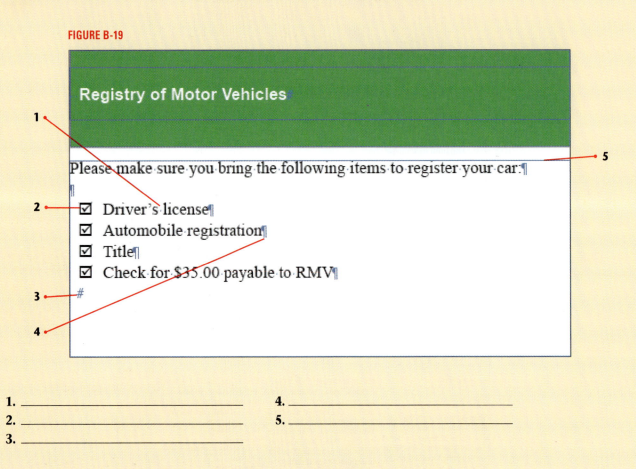

1. _____
2. _____
3. _____
4. _____
5. _____

Match each term with the statement that best describes it.

6. Threading
7. Gutter
8. Bullets
9. Paragraphs
10. Leading

a. Space between two columns
b. Lines of text that are separated by the space created when you press [Enter] (Win) or [return] (Mac)
c. Vertical space from one baseline to the next
d. To flow text from one text box to another
e. Small symbols

Select the best answer from the list of choices.

11. **What is all of the text in a text box, or all of the text in linked text boxes, called?**
  a. Type
  b. Story
  c. Book
  d. Document

12. **Which type of alignment evenly distributes all lines of text between the left and right edges of a text box?**
  a. Align center
  b. Justify all lines
  c. Align towards spine
  d. Align left

13. **What is the blank space between text and its margin or frame border called?**
  a. Indent
  b. Bullet
  c. Gutter
  d. Return

14. **How do you modify an existing paragraph style?**
  a. Click the Find/Change dialog box
  b. Select the text with the paragraph style applied, then make changes in the Control panel
  c. Double-click the paragraph style name in the Paragraph Styles panel
  d. Double-click the paragraph style name in the New Paragraph Style dialog box

Skills Review

1. **Create text boxes.**
  a. Start InDesign, open ID B-2.indd from the location where you store your Data Files, update the links if necessary, then save the document as **School News**.
  b. Click the workspace switcher, click Reset Essentials, click Edit (Win) or InDesign (Mac) on the Application bar, point to Preferences, then click Guides & Pasteboard.
  c. Click the Guides in Back check box to add a check mark if necessary, then click OK.
  d. Click the Type tool on the Tools panel if necessary, then position the Type tool on the left margin guide.
  e. Click and drag the Type tool to create a text box of any height that snaps to the bottom margin guide and the guide that defines the right side of the first column.
  f. Click the Selection tool, then click the lower-left reference point in the Control panel, if necessary.
  g. Double-click the Height (H) value on the Control panel, type **6.5**, then press [Enter] (Win) or [return] (Mac). (*Hint*: If the X Location value of the lower-left reference point is not 1 and/or the Y Location value is not 10, double-click the X Location value, type **1** if necessary, press [Tab], type **10** if necessary as the Y Location value, then press Enter (Win) or [return] (Mac).)
  h. Click the Type tool, position it on the right margin guide in the second column, then drag the Type tool pointer to create a text box above "READ" that snaps to the right margin guide and to the guide that defines the left side of the second column.
  i. Click the Selection tool, then verify that the bottom-left reference point is still selected on the Control panel.
  j. Change the Y Location value on the Control panel to **4.8 in**, then change the Height (H) value to **2.5 in**.

2. **Place and flow text.**
  a. Click the Type tool, then click inside the text box in the first column.
  b. Click File on the Application bar, click Place, navigate to the location where you store your Data Files, click Book News.doc, then click Open.
  c. Click the Selection tool, click the overset text icon, then click anywhere in the second text box.
  d. Click View on the Application bar, point to Extras, then click Show Text Threads.
  e. Click View on the Application bar, point to Extras, then click Hide Text Threads.
  f. Save the document.

Skills Review (continued)

3. Format text.

   a. Click the Zoom tool, then drag the Zoom tool pointer around "A letter from the Principal", the date, and "Dear Parents" at the top of the first column.

   b. Click the Type tool, then double-click the word "Principal."

   c. Triple-click the word "Principal" to select the entire line.

   d. Click the Font list arrow on the Control panel, scroll up in the list if necessary, then click **Segoe Script** or another font if you do not have Segoe Script installed on your computer. (*Hint*: If the Paragraph Formatting Controls button is selected on the Control panel, the character formatting options appear on the right side of the Control panel.)

   e. Click the Font Size list arrow, then click **14 pt**.

   f. Change the font of the date and "Dear Parents" to Times New Roman.

   g. Double-click the Hand tool to fit the page in the window.

   h. Click the Selection tool, then click the pasteboard to deselect the text box.

   i. Save your work.

4. Format paragraphs.

   a. Click the Zoom tool, then drag the Zoom tool pointer around "A letter from the Principal."

   b. Click Type on the Application bar, then click Show Hidden Characters.

   c. Identify the end of the story by finding the pound sign hidden character.

   d. Click the Type tool, then triple-click the text.

   e. Click Type on the Application bar, then click Paragraph.

   f. Click the Align center button on the Paragraph panel.

   g. Double-click the Hand tool to fit the page in the window.

   h. Click the Selection tool, then click the pasteboard to deselect the text box.

   i. Save your work.

5. Create and apply paragraph styles.

   a. Click Type on the Application bar, then click Paragraph Styles.

   b. Click the Paragraph Styles Panel options button, then click New Paragraph Style.

   c. Type **Paragraphs** in the Style Name text box.

   d. Click Basic Character Formats on the left, change the font to Times New Roman and the font size to **11 pt**.

   e. Click Indents and Spacing on the left side of the dialog box.

   f. Click the Alignment list arrow, then click Left.

   g. If necessary, change the First Line Indent value to **0**, then change the Left Indent value to **0**.

   h. Click the Space Before up arrow four times until you see **0.25** in the text box, change the Space After value to **0.25**, then click OK.

   i. Click the Type tool if necessary, click the first paragraph after "Dear Parents," which starts with "While I was at the supermarket" four times, then click Paragraphs on the Paragraph Styles panel.

   j. Apply the Paragraphs paragraph style to the next paragraph starting with "Speaking of books."

   k. Save your work.

6. Modify a paragraph style.

   a. Double-click Paragraphs in the Paragraph Styles panel.

   b. Click Indents and Spacing on the left side of the dialog box.

   c. Click the Alignment list arrow, then click Left Justify.

   d. Change the Space After value to **0.125 in**, and then change the Space Before value to **0.125 in**.

   e. Click the Type tool, if necessary, click before the "O" in "Owen" at the bottom of the first column, then press [Enter] (Win) or [return] (Mac) to push the line of text to the beginning of the next column.

   f. Click OK to close the dialog box, then save your work.

7. Create and apply character styles.

  a. Click Type on the Application bar, then click Character Styles.

  b. Click the Character Styles Panel options button, then click New Character Style.

  c. Make sure the default style name in the Style Name text box is highlighted, then type **Popular Books**.

  d. Click Basic Character Formats on the left side of the dialog box, click the Font Family list arrow, scroll down if necessary and then click Calibri, click the Font Style list arrow, click Italic, click the Size list arrow, then click 11 pt.

  e. Click Character Color on the left side of the dialog box, scroll down and click the C=100 M=90 Y=10 K=0 (blue) swatch, then click OK.

  f. Use the Zoom tool to zoom in on the eight books listed at the top of the second column.

  g. Click the Type tool, select the name of the first book ("Owen Foote, Super Spy"), then click Popular Books on the Character Styles panel. (*Hint*: Do not select the author name.)

  h. Apply the Popular Books character style to the remaining seven books.

  i. Fit the document page in the window again, deselect all, then save your work.

8. Apply bullets to text.

  a. Click the Zoom tool, then drag the Zoom tool pointer around the eight book titles in the second column.

  b. Click the Type tool, then triple-click "Owen Foote, Super Spy, by Stephanie Greene."

  c. Press and hold [Shift], then press the down arrow seven times to select the next seven lines.

  d. Click Type on the Application bar, then click Paragraph to open the Paragraph panel, if necessary.

  e. Click the Paragraph Panel options button, then click Bullets and Numbering.

  f. Click the List Type list arrow, click Bullets, then click Add.

  g. Click the Font Family list arrow, then click Wingdings.

  h. Click the second bullet in the ninth row (GID:122), then click OK.

  i. Click the new bullet (GID:122) in the Bullet Character list.

  j. Change the Tab Position value to 0.125 in, then click OK to close the dialog box. (*Hint*: If the tab position is too big, change the Tab Position value to 0 in.)

  k. Double-click the Hand tool, click Edit on the Application bar, click Deselect All, then save your work.

9. Find and change text.

  a. Click Edit on the Application bar, then click Find/Change.

  b. Type **our school librarian** in the Find what text box, type **Mrs. DiVito** in the Change to text box, then click Find.

  c. Click Change All, click OK, then click Done to close the Find/Change dialog box.

  d. Deselect all, press [W] to hide the frame borders, then compare your newsletter to Figure B-20.

  e. Click Window on the Application bar, point to Workspace, then click Reset Essentials.

  f. Save your work, then close the School News document and exit InDesign.

FIGURE B-20

InDesign CS5

Independent Challenge 1

You work for an international foreign exchange student program. The company is celebrating 10 years in business. The owners are planning a special presentation and dinner in honor of this milestone and you are in charge of designing a postcard-style invitation. The details of the party are given to you as a text file. You use InDesign to format the text.

a. Start InDesign, then create a new document.

b. In the New Document dialog box, change the Width to **4** inches and the Height to **5** inches, change each of the four margin values to **0.5** inches if necessary, then close the New Document dialog box.

c. Save the new document as **Party Invitation**.

d. Create a text box that snaps to the inside of all four margin guides. (*Hint*: The X Location of the bottom-left reference point should be .5, the Y Location should be 4.5, the Width of the text box should be 3, and the Height of the text box should be 4.)

e. Click File on the Application bar, then click Place.

FIGURE B-21

f. Place the Data File called "Invitation Text.doc" into the text box.

g. Show hidden characters.

h. Open the Paragraph panel.

i. Select all of the paragraphs in the text box, double-click the value in the Space After text box in the Paragraph panel, type **.25**, then press [Enter].

j. Center-align all paragraphs.

k. Click in the first paragraph before the "t" in "ten," then press [Shift][Enter] (Win) or [shift][return] (Mac).

l. Change the font for all paragraphs to Edwardian Script ITC or to a similar font if you do not have Edwardian Script ITC installed on your computer.

m. Change the font size of the first three paragraphs to **18** pt, then change the font of the last three paragraphs to **15** pt. (*Hint*: Type **15** in the Font Size text box to change the font size to 15, because 15 pt is not an option on the Font Size list.)

n. Hide the hidden characters, deselect all, press [W], then compare your screen to Figure B-21.

o. Save the document, then exit InDesign.

Please join us as we celebrate
ten years in business.

Saturday, February 5, 2013

The Ritz Carlton Hotel, Boston

Slide Show – 6:00 pm

Dinner and Dancing - 7:00 pm until midnight

Black tie optional

Independent Challenge 2

You work for a magazine called *The Greater Outdoors*. Each month, one of your responsibilities is to design the type on the magazine cover. You try to use just the right fonts, sizes, colors, and styles so that the text on the cover helps deliver the message that is represented by the cover photo.

a. Start InDesign.

b. Open ID B-3.indd, then save it as **Magazine**.

Independent Challenge 2 (continued)

c. Using the character and paragraph formatting features in InDesign and any fonts installed on your computer, format the text in the five text boxes on the magazine cover. (*Hint*: You may need to resize text boxes if you change font sizes. Use the Selection tool to resize the text boxes.)

d. Create a paragraph style called **Date**, use Right as its Alignment value, then apply it to the February 2013 text.

e. Apply bullets to the three items listed underneath "In this issue:".

f. Deselect all, press [W] to preview the page, then compare your screen to Figure B-22.

FIGURE B-22

Advanced Challenge Exercise

- Display the Character panel if it is not already displayed.
- Zoom in on the magazine title, "The Greater Outdoors."
- Click the Type tool, then click between the "t" and the "d" in the word "Outdoors."
- In the Character panel, click the Kerning up arrow once to change the Kerning value to 10, then notice the new space between the two characters.
- Kern the space between the "a" and the "t" in the word "Greater" so that the new Kerning value is also 10.
- Triple-click "The Greater Outdoors," then change the Baseline Shift value to 8 pt in the Character panel.
- Deselect all, then fit the page in the window.

g. Save the document, then exit InDesign.

Independent Challenge 3

You are known in your family as the creative one. Your uncle is opening a new café and wants to create a unique menu template for the daily specials that will be offered. He is interested in seeing different samples of text options for the menu. You create four samples using placeholder text and the text formatting features in InDesign.

a. Start InDesign.

b. Open ID B-4.indd, then save it as **Daily Specials**.

c. Click the Type tool in the first text box in the top-left corner.

d. Fill the text box with placeholder text using the Type menu.

e. Fill the remaining three text boxes with placeholder text.

f. Create four paragraph styles for each text box and name them **Sample 1**, **Sample 2**, **Sample 3**, and **Sample 4**. Use any font, style, size, color, and indents and spacing options that you like. (*Hint*: Each time you create a new paragraph style, be sure that Based On is set to [No Paragraph Style].)

g. Modify any paragraph styles, as necessary. Do not worry if the overset text icon appears on one or more of the text boxes.

Independent Challenge 3 (continued)

h. Save your work, deselect all, then compare your screen to Figure B-23.

Advanced Challenge Exercise

- Open the Paragraph Style Options dialog box for the Sample 1 paragraph style.
- Click the Preview check box to see changes that you make applied to the Sample 1 style.
- Click Basic Character Formats in the Paragraph Style Options dialog box.
- Change the Leading value, then change the Tracking value. Notice how the paragraph is affected.
- Click OK to close the Paragraph Style Options dialog box.

i. Save the document, then exit InDesign.

FIGURE B-23

Fuga. Officidelent qui quunt untotatur?

Laborem quunt. Ebitibus ad quam, cone nissi dolorepresed eum dolorem aspel inient et ulpa serum harum vere sequiscias am vellabor sequam, nestiis dus dolorup tatecatur, sit acero tem liquoss ediate liatur? Quid moluptaepro con repe nestiam nist illorio temporissit aut omnis quatemquasin eiciet im faccus doluptistis mil ipiet laborum, ea conseque volest lamust, quiaero officia cor aut magnam enecti nosanis nobitasperia que cupiendunti tectae solore, volor modipsam expelit rescillab incit quas quisquia sunt et pore eatur, odicit exerfero od quatur alibus, que la nit, comnim lisitatem faccum quae

Natiis nonsendendae cus conseditat.

Ut repro blabo. Itatiis aditatq uunturem consenihil in prero consequi dolorem volo et officiate omnis et as siti dusda accupid ma nobitate nonseque sit as sedi rati sed ut arum et repta nobit, officimet prat et laceribus, voluptatio bea dernatem ipide omnim aut aut molor aut ut vernat que volumqu asitatist, te occaboreic totati voluptas dollant ipiendisquae natust, omni quis int, optas etur? Quiature di bea solorest quidic tet, qui alitio quas sum re parchil iquidissin nonem sunt autatem porehent volestrum, ut experi con expedisi sitia doluptio eaque voluptas est maiore est ma quia int aliae volendit, sit,

Today's Specials

Catem qui commodipsam, nonsequosame mint labore dem dellaborios dolent facepel icienianis everum labor asi vitiossit essed eum lacius doluptat fugiand aesciam, et voluptas si nobit aut eati que resedit, cus am voloratem quiasi omnis il is endunti orectem utentur arit arum quia digendandit, quunt explibust quia quibus.

Onet aut odipsam nobit ditae rectem quide et, cus remped mincit estorro magnam, con cum rera volupta tquaestin necto volorepra noneste mporere ra dolesserrunt earum corectur, solectium si ullam fuga. Ut iunt voluptam nati tendus, omnimus apiendam fugit, sectus dolenis etur minvernam faccus

Ibus, voluptati to dis aboreprest volorepudis estem dolut vendundebis sed estiuntiis ma quid quo etur simos ad molupta epelis aut quate ratate peri idicturibus doluptatquis aliquias nempore ictem. Is eius morescius et hicitibus, is paribus il moloribus.

Tenducit, aliquiatem re dipsante eos dellupi deniatur, volendi orepelia pa dolore vene dolorerro ex estius sunt, quia nissi con re es evelloriae veliciis sed mod esed moloreped qui alia ius et et restior sandusa nduciis enducid ut ut aut aliciant iliquiatium et aliqui culpa venectate nam faciis rese venis idestio imporero cor modi in parciaecea voluptio eos voluptatus essunt iur?

Real Life Independent Challenge

You are moving out of state and need to sell some household items that you do not plan to take with you. Create a flyer in InDesign advertising three items that you would like to sell. (*Hint*: If you can't think of anything, use a dishwasher, computer table, and treadmill as the items in the flyer.) Include the item name, description, and price.

a. Start InDesign.

b. Open ID B-5.indd, then save it as **Moving Sale**.

c. Click the Type tool after "Moving Sale," then press [Enter] (Win) or [return] (Mac) twice.

d. Type the first item you would like to sell, then press [Enter] (Win) or [return] (Mac) to start a new paragraph.

e. Type a short description of the item, press [Enter] (Win) or [return] (Mac) to start a new paragraph, type the price, then press [Enter] (Win) or [return] (Mac).

f. Repeat Steps d and e to enter at least two more items for sale. (*Hint*: Do not insert extra paragraph returns between each price and the next item. You will use paragraph styles to insert space.)

g. Create a paragraph style named **Item**, using any formatting choices you like.

h. Create a paragraph style named **Description**, using any formatting choices you like, then do the same to create a paragraph style named **Price**. Include a Space After value for the Price style to create a space between the three items.

i. Apply the three styles to the three items, descriptions, and prices. You may want to modify one or more of the styles after you have applied them to the text to improve the appearance of the text.

j. Create a small text box at the bottom of the page listing your contact information, then format the Moving Sale text using any formatting you like.

k. Deselect all, press [W], save your work, then compare your screen to Figure B-24.

Advanced Challenge Exercise

- Create a new paragraph style named **Title**.
- In the New Paragraph Style dialog box, click the Based On list arrow, then click Item.
- Make formatting changes to the Title style, then close the dialog box.
- Apply the Title style to the Moving Sale text.

l. Save your work, then exit InDesign.

FIGURE B-24

Moving Sale

Dishwasher
Less than one year old, great condition
$200.00

Computer Table
Good for small living space
$150.00

Treadmill
Folds up easily for storing
$400.00

Call Ann: 555-111-5555

Visual Workshop

Open ID B-6.indd, then save it as **Gingerbread House**. Format the text so that it resembles the text shown in Figure B-25. (*Hint*: The font used in the sample is Cambria, 22 point. The bullets used in the sample are Wingdings 2 GID:146.) Also, apply a .25-inch Space After value for the first paragraph to visually separate it from the list. Save the document and then exit InDesign.

FIGURE B-25

Everything you need to make a gingerbread house:

◇ Small milk cartons
◇ Graham crackers
◇ Royal frosting
◇ Peppermint candies
◇ Gum drops
◇ Licorice sticks
◇ M&M's®
◇ Necco Wafers®
◇ Small candy canes
◇ Hershey's Kisses®
◇ Lemonheads®
◇ Red Hots®
◇ Mint leaves
◇ Plastic knives
◇ Paper plates
◇ Paper towels

Working with Objects

Files You Will Need:

ID C-1.indd
Skiing.jpg
ID C-2.indd
Holiday.psd
ID C-3.indd
ID C-4.indd
Flowers 2.jpg

When working with InDesign, there are many types of objects that you can add to your document pages. Graphics such as photos and illustrations are one type; other types include shapes, lines, text boxes, Microsoft Excel charts, and Microsoft Word tables. You can modify objects in InDesign using many tools, panels, and menu commands. For example, you can scale an object, rotate an object, or add color to it. You can group it with other objects, or change its transparency or location on the page. At MegaPixel, your boss has assigned you a new client, BreakTime, a company that organizes trips for high school students. The owner, Jennifer, asks you to help her with a "Save the Date" mailer to build some excitement about an upcoming ski trip to Utah. She has supplied you with an InDesign file containing basic details and a photo, and asks you to show her how to improve it by adding some simple graphics.

OBJECTIVES

Work with smart guides

Create an object

Transform an object

Arrange and lock an object

Step and repeat an object

Use Live Distribute

Use the Align panel

Modify corners and strokes

Working with Smart Guides

Smart guides are guides that appear automatically as you position objects on a page. Smart guides are visual clues that let you know when the object you are positioning is touching a side or the center of another object, a margin guide, or the center of the page. To use smart guides, you need to select the Smart Guides command. You can change the color of smart guides in the Guides & Pasteboard section of the Preferences dialog box. You open the InDesign file from Jennifer and decide to reposition the photo using smart guides.

STEPS

QUICK TIP
Update links if
necessary.

1. **Start InDesign, navigate to the drive and folder where you store your Data Files, then open ID C-1.indd**

   The document opens with some basic information and a photo. The document size is 8.5" wide by 5.5" tall; a typical postcard size for an advertisement that you may receive in the mail.

2. **Save the document as Ski Trip, then change the workspace to Essentials, if necessary**

3. **Click the workspace switcher on the Application bar, then click Reset Essentials, if necessary, to close any open panels**

4. **Click View on the Application bar, point to Grids & Guides, then, if there is not a check mark next to Smart Guides, click Smart Guides to select it**

   If there is a check mark next to Smart Guides, the feature is on.

5. **Click the Selection tool on the Tools panel, if necessary**

6. **Click the photo, slowly drag it to the right until you see a vertical green guide, as shown in Figure C-1, then release the mouse button**

   The vertical green guide is a smart guide that appears when the center of the photo touches the left edge of the text box. Smart guides turn green when one object touches another.

7. **Drag the photo slightly to the left until you see a vertical pink guide, as shown in Figure C-2, then release the mouse button**

   The pink guide is also a smart guide, indicating that the center of the photo is touching the horizontal center of the page. Smart guides are pink, like margin guides, when one object is aligning with the page and not another object.

8. **Slowly drag the photo upward until you see a pink smart guide appear showing the vertical center of the page, keep adjusting the position of the photo until you see both the horizontal and vertical center smart guides, as shown in Figure C-3, then release the mouse button**

   The photo is perfectly centered horizontally and vertically with the page.

9. **Save your work**

FIGURE C-1: Viewing the smart guide

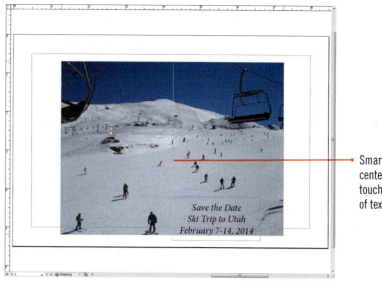

Smart guide represents center of photo touching left edge of text box

FIGURE C-2: Pink smart guide

Smart guide represents horizontal center of page

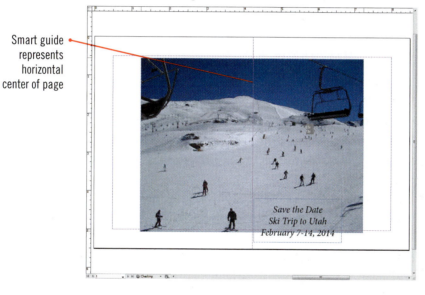

FIGURE C-3: Viewing horizontal and vertical smart guides

Intersection of smart guides

InDesign CS5

Creating an Object

Sometimes the only type of object you need for your publication is a simple shape. Shapes can add visual interest to a document and serve as a background for text. The tools for creating shapes include the Rectangle, Ellipse, and Polygon tools. To select a shape tool, click and hold down the mouse button on the Rectangle tool (or currently selected shape tool) on the Tools panel, and then select the shape tool you want to use. With a shape tool selected, you can create a shape manually by dragging in the document, or you can click in the document to open the shape's dialog box and define its settings. You use the Swatches panel to add color to the fill and stroke (border) of your shape, and the Stroke panel to change the weight (thickness) and style of the stroke. You want to show Jennifer how you create a rectangle shape to serve as a background object in the flyer, and then format the rectangle's fill and stroke.

STEPS

> **QUICK TIP**
>
> You can also create a rectangle by clicking the Rectangle tool, clicking the page, and then entering width and height values in the Rectangle dialog box.

1. **Click the Rectangle tool ▣ on the Tools panel**

2. **Position the Rectangle tool pointer -¦- on the left side of the page**

3. **Drag to create a rectangle that is approximately the size of the one shown in Figure C-4, then release the mouse button**

   The rectangle is selected, indicated by the **bounding box**. A bounding box is a rectangle whose size matches the width and height of the selected object. The bounding box includes eight selection handles that can be used to resize the object. The bounding box appears when an object is selected and then disappears when the object is deselected.

> **TROUBLE**
>
> If the Rectangle is not selected, click the Selection tool ▸ on the Tools panel, then click the edge of the rectangle to select it.

4. **Verify that the rectangle is still selected, then click the Swatches panel icon ▦ on the right to open the Swatches panel**

   The rectangle has a black stroke that is 1-point wide applied to it by default.

> **QUICK TIP**
>
> You can change the tint (amount) of a color by dragging the Tint slider on the Swatches panel, then choosing a new value. For example, you can fill or stroke an object with 50% of a color for a lighter shade.

5. **Click the Fill button ▨ on the Tools panel, if necessary, then scroll to and click Orange on the Swatches panel**

   To apply a fill color to an object, the Fill button must be in front of the Stroke icon on the Tools panel. The rectangle is filled with orange, as shown in Figure C-5. To apply a new stroke color to an object, click the Stroke button to bring it in front of the Fill button. You can create new colors on the Color panel by dragging the C, M, Y, and K sliders. When you create a color, right-click the Swatch button on the Color panel and then click Add to Swatches.

6. **Click the Stroke button ▢ on the Tools panel, then scroll to and click [None] on the Swatches panel**

   The stroke is removed from the rectangle.

7. **Close the Swatches panel, then save your work**

Converting shapes

You can convert an existing shape into a different shape using the Convert Shape command on the Object menu. Click a shape in the document window, click Object on the Application bar, point to Convert Shape, then click one of the available shapes in the list. You can choose from Rectangle, Rounded Rectangle, Beveled Rectangle, Inverse Rounded Rectangle, Ellipse, Triangle, Polygon, Line, and Orthogonal Line.

FIGURE C-4: Creating a rectangle

Rectangle

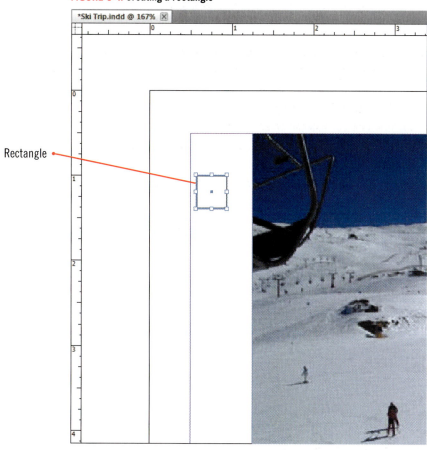

FIGURE C-5: Rectangle with orange fill color

Rectangle filled
with orange

Fill button

Stroke button

Transforming an Object

When you transform something, you change its appearance. For example, you can rotate an object 45° or scale an object 50% to make it half its original size. The Transform commands in InDesign include Move, Scale, Rotate, Shear, and Flip. You can also transform objects using buttons on the Transform panel or the Control panel. You can change the width and height of an object and its location on the page. Before you transform an object, you choose a reference point from which to transform it. This point is called the **point of origin**, and it is the point of the selected object that remains fixed during the transformation. You show Jennifer how to use the Control panel to change the location of the rectangle and to change its width and height.

STEPS

1. Click the Selection tool on the Tools panel, if necessary, then click the orange rectangle to select it

2. Locate the current value in the X Location text box on the Control panel, as shown in Figure C-6

   The X Location value is the horizontal location of one of nine possible reference points on the selected rectangle. The nine reference points match the locations of the nine selection handles on the bounding box. In Figure C-6, the X Location value is 0.58 and the upper-left reference point is selected. This means that the horizontal location of the upper-left point of the rectangle is 0.58. (Your selected reference point and your X Location value might be different.)

3. Make sure the upper-left reference point is selected on the Control panel, double-click the X Location value, type 0, then press [Tab]

   The upper-left corner of the rectangle frame jumps to the new X location, aligned with the 0" mark on the horizontal ruler. On the Control panel, the value in the Y Location box is now selected.

4. Type 0 in the Y Location box, then press [Enter] (Win) or [return] (Mac)

   The upper-left corner of the rectangle frame moves to the upper-left corner of the page, aligned with the 0" mark on both the horizontal and vertical rulers, as shown in Figure C-7.

5. Double-click the value in the W (Width) text box in the Control panel, type 8.5, then press [Tab]

   The width of the rectangle frame increases to 8.5" On the Control panel, the value in the H (Height) text box is selected.

6. Type 5.5 in the H (Height) text box, then press [Enter] (Win) or [return] (Mac)

   The height of the rectangle increases to 5.5", the same height as the page. The rectangle fills the page and covers the text and photo. We will send it behind the text and photo to be a background image in the next lesson.

7. Save your work

The Transform Again command

Once you transform an object, you can apply the same transformation again if you choose the Transform Again command on the Object menu. For example, if you want to rotate an object incrementally, you can rotate it once—say 5°—and then click Object on the Application bar and click Transform Again to rotate it another 5°.

FIGURE C-6: Identifying the reference point

X Location
text box

Upper-left
reference point

Upper-left point
on rectangle

FIGURE C-7: Aligning the rectangle with the upper-left corner of the page

Your W and H
values might
differ

Upper-left corner
of rectangle is
aligned with
upper-left corner
of page

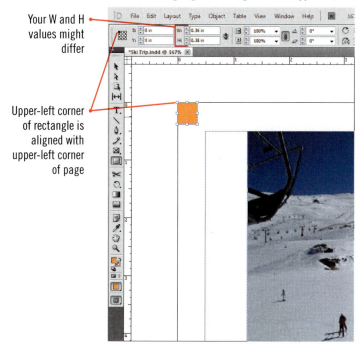

Editing corners

When you select an object with the Selection tool, a small yellow square appears on the right side of the bounding box. You can click this square to edit all corners of the object. When you click the square, it disappears and is replaced by four yellow diamonds on each corner of the bounding box. Clicking and dragging a diamond allows you to set the corner size. As you drag, you will see the value of the roundness of each corner. When you drag one corner, all of the corners change in the same amount. Press and hold [Shift] to manipulate only one corner. This can give way to some very interesting shapes. Press and hold [Alt] (Win) or [option] (Mac) while clicking a yellow diamond to change the shape into a new one.

Arranging and Locking an Object

InDesign objects are vertically stacked in a document, like a pile of papers, from bottom to top in the order that they are created or placed. For example, if you create a red circle and then a blue circle, the blue circle is "above" the red circle because it was the most recently created object. If the circles are side by side, they look like they are on the same level; but if you drag the blue circle over the red circle, the blue circle overlaps the red circle and hides part of it. You can easily change the vertical order of InDesign objects using the Arrange commands on the Object menu. Once an object is on the correct level in the stack and you no longer need to modify it, you may want to lock it. Locking an object ensures its location on the page will not be disrupted. It is also easier to select an item on top of a locked item because you won't select the locked item by mistake. You show Jennifer how to send the orange rectangle behind the photo and the text, and then lock it.

STEPS

1. **Verify that the orange rectangle is still selected**

2. **Click Object on the Application bar, point to Arrange, then click Send Backward**

   The Send Backward command sends the selected object or objects back one level only in the document. The Send to Back command sends the selected object or objects to the back-most level of the document. The rectangle moves back one level behind the text box. The text box was the last object created before the rectangle was created.

3. **Click Object on the Application bar, point to Arrange, then click Send Backward**

   The rectangle moves back one more level behind the photo, as shown in Figure C-8. The orange rectangle is now underneath all other objects in the document. The orange rectangle serves as a background image. Since it no longer needs to be modified, it is a good idea to lock it.

4. **Verify that the orange rectangle is still selected, click Object on the Application bar, then click Lock**

   The orange rectangle is locked, indicated by the padlock icon shown in Figure C-9. Locked items cannot be selected or modified. To unlock an item, click Object on the Application bar, then click Unlock All on Spread.

5. **Click the photo to select it, then repeat Step 4 to lock it**

   Having the orange rectangle and the photo locked will make it easier to work with new objects on top of them.

6. **Click the pasteboard to deselect all, press [W] to view your work without guides, then save your work**

7. **Press [W] to return to Normal view**

FIGURE C-8: Moving the rectangle to the back

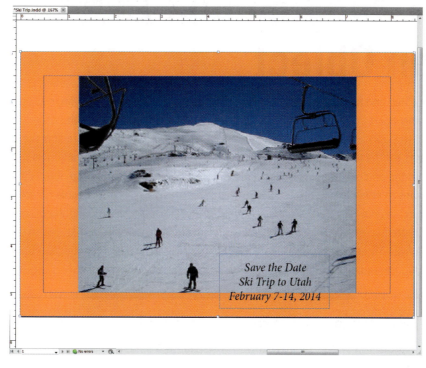

FIGURE C-9: Locking the orange rectangle

Padlock icon

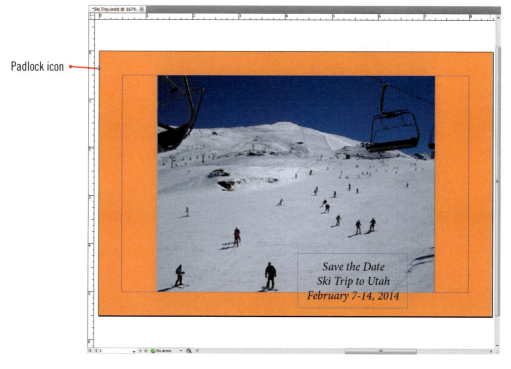

Selecting objects

The Select commands on the Object menu allow you to select an object in a document regardless of which level it is on. For example, if a text box is hidden by a large frame and you cannot click it with-out moving the large frame out of the way, you can click the large frame, click Object on the Application bar, point to Select, then click Next Object Below to select the text box. Once the text box is selected, you could click Object on the Application bar, point to Arrange, and then click Bring to Front to bring the text box on top of the large frame. The placement of the large frame would not be affected. Another way to find and select a hidden object is to press [Ctrl] (Win) or [⌘] (Mac) and click continuously where you believe the object is hidden until you see the bounding box for the hidden object appear.

InDesign CS5

Stepping and Repeating an Object

The Step and Repeat feature in InDesign offers a quick solution for creating multiple identical objects spaced evenly apart from each other. Using Step and Repeat, you first select the object or objects that you would like to duplicate. Next, enter the number of objects you wish to create and the vertical and/or horizontal offset for the new objects. Vertical and horizontal offset values determine how far the copies will be offset from the original. After using Step and Repeat, it is a good idea to group objects together. To **group** objects means to select two or more objects, then make them into one selectable object by clicking Group on the Object menu. When objects are grouped, it is impossible for their alignment and distribution to become disrupted unless you ungroup the objects first. Jennifer would like you to create a design element for the flyer. You create a small square and then use the Step and Repeat dialog box to create a pattern. You group the squares that make up the pattern, and then step and repeat two copies of the pattern.

STEPS

1. Click the Rectangle tool on the Tools panel, click in the approximate location shown in Figure C-10, then release the mouse button

   The Rectangle dialog box opens.

2. Type .25 in the Width text box, press [Tab], type .25 in the Height text box, then click OK

   A small square appears on the page.

3. Open the Swatches panel, change the fill color of the square to [None], then change the stroke color to C=100 M=90 Y=10 K=0 (blue)

4. Verify that the square is still selected, click Edit on the Application bar, then click Step and Repeat

   The Step and Repeat dialog box opens.

5. Click the Preview check box to select it in the Step and Repeat dialog box

   The Preview feature lets you see the results of what you enter in the Step and Repeat dialog box before you close the dialog box.

TROUBLE

If you get a warning dialog box after entering 11 in the Count text box, change the Vertical and/or Horizontal text boxes to 0 first, then go back and enter the Count value.

6. Type 11 in the Count text box, press [Tab] until the Vertical Offset text box is highlighted, type 0.3125, press [Tab], then type 0 in the Horizontal Offset text box, as shown in Figure C-11

   Eleven new squares appear below the original square; each one 0.3125 inches away from the other.

7. Click OK to close the Step and Repeat dialog box, click Object on the Application bar, then click Group

   A dashed line appears around the squares, indicating they are one group. The 12 squares are now treated as one selectable object.

8. Verify that the group is still selected, click Edit on the Application bar, then click Step and Repeat

9. Type 2 in the Count text box, press [Tab] twice, type 0.1875 in the Vertical text box, press [Tab], type 0.3125 in the Horizontal text box, then click OK

   Three columns of squares appear.

10. Deselect the grouped squares, then compare your screen to Figure C-12

    You quickly created a simple pattern starting out with just one square.

FIGURE C-10: Location for creating rectangle

Click Rectangle
tool pointer here

FIGURE C-11: Step and Repeat dialog box

Preview check box

FIGURE C-12: A simple pattern created using Step and Repeat

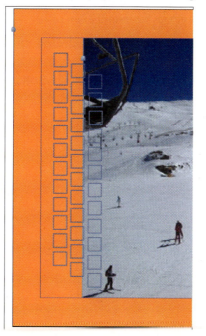

Using the Move command

In InDesign, you can move an object using a specific vertical and/or horizontal offset. You can also move and copy the selected object. The Move command in InDesign is similar to the Step and Repeat command, but is more practical when you are moving one item and do not need to create multiple copies or a pattern. You move objects using the Move dialog box. Entering a positive value in the Horizontal text box in the Move dialog box moves an item to the right of its original location. Entering a negative number moves an object to the left of its original location. Entering a positive value in the Vertical text box moves an item below its original location. Entering a negative value in the Vertical text box moves an item above its original location.

Using Live Distribute

To **distribute** objects is to place equal space between three or more objects. You can distribute objects using options on the Align panel or using the Live Distribute feature. The distribute options on the Align panel are useful when you want to distribute objects using a specific value. The Live Distribute feature is a better choice when you want to manually distribute objects until you achieve the exact result you are looking for. To use the Live Distribute feature, you select three or more objects, then press and hold the Spacebar while you drag a bounding box handle. As you drag, the space between the objects continually changes proportionally to reflect the amount and direction that you drag the mouse pointer. You show Jennifer how easy it is to modify the square pattern using the Live Distribute feature.

STEPS

1. Make sure the Selection tool ▶ is selected on the Tools panel

2. Click the **first group of squares** by clicking the edge of one of the squares, press and hold **[Shift]**, then click the **second and third groups of squares** so that all three groups are selected, as shown in Figure C-13

   One bounding box surrounds the three selected objects.

3. Position the mouse pointer over the lower-right selection handle of the bounding box

   As shown in Figure C-14, the mouse pointer becomes a resize pointer.

   > **TROUBLE**
   > If you start to drag the selection handle before pressing [Spacebar], you will resize the objects instead of distributing them. Undo your last step and then try again.

4. Click the **selection handle**, press **[Spacebar]**, drag the **pointer** slowly to the right, then drag to the left until the distribution of the three groups resembles the configuration shown in Figure C-15

5. Release the mouse button and then release **[Spacebar]**

   Overlapping the three groups has created a new pattern.

6. Verify that the three groups are still selected, click **Object** on the Application bar, then click **Group**

   Grouping the three objects will ensure that the distribution among them will not be altered.

7. Save your work

Rotating an object

To **rotate** an object means to turn it around an axis or center point. In InDesign, there are multiple ways to rotate an object. You can manually rotate an object by placing the pointer outside of the bounding box. The pointer becomes a rounded arrow that you can drag to rotate the selected object. You can also use the Rotate commands on the Object menu. For example, you can choose to rotate an object 90° Clockwise. Finally, you can choose to use the Rotate dialog box by clicking the Rotate tool, and then clicking the page.

Enter a value in the Rotate dialog box and then click OK or Copy to rotate and copy the object. Double-clicking the Rotate tool rotates the selected object around the selected reference point on the Control panel. Or, you can select an object, click the Rotate tool, and press and hold [Alt] (Win) or [option] (Mac) while you click a specific point on the object. The Rotate dialog box opens and the rotation angle that you enter will take effect from the point that you clicked.

FIGURE C-13: Selecting the three groups

Bounding box

FIGURE C-14: Locating the resize pointer

Resize pointer

FIGURE C-15: Creating a new pattern

Using the Align Panel

To **align** objects means to position one or more selected objects in relation to each other, in relation to the margins of a document, or in relation to the boundaries of the page or spread. When you align multiple objects with each other, you can align them by their edges or by their center points. You use the Align panel to align objects. You duplicate the pattern and align the two patterns and the text box by their top edges.

STEPS

1. Drag the group of squares so that they are inside the left margin guide, as shown in Figure C-16

2. Verify that the group of squares is still selected, press and hold [Alt] (Win) or [option] (Mac), drag the group of squares to the right side of the page to create a duplicate of the pattern, then release the mouse button when the duplicate is positioned inside the right margin guide, as shown in Figure C-17

   You will now align the two patterns and the text box by their top edges.

3. Click Window on the Application bar, point to Object & Layout, then click Align

   The Align panel opens. The Align panel has three rows of buttons: the top row includes align buttons, the second row includes distribute buttons, and the bottom row includes distribute spacing buttons.

4. Make sure the Selection tool ▶ is selected on the Tools panel, click the pattern on the left, press and hold [Shift], click the edge of the text box, then click the pattern on the right

   All three objects are selected. You need at least three objects selected in order to align them.

5. On the Align panel, click the Align to list arrow, then click Align to Selection if necessary

   When Align to Selection is chosen, items are aligned with each other according to the location of the outer-most of the aligned edges in the selection. The Align to Page command aligns selected items using the boundaries of the page. The Align to Spread command aligns selected items using the boundaries of the left and right pages in the spread. The Align to Margins command aligns selected items within the margins.

6. On the Align panel, click the Align top edges button 🔲

   The text box and the two grouped patterns are aligned by their top edges, as shown in Figure C-18.

7. Deselect all, click the Type tool 🔲 In the Tools panel, then highlight the text in the text box

8. Show the Swatches panel, then click [Paper] to change the text color to white

9. Deselect the text box, close the Align panel, then save your work

FIGURE C-16: Positioning the pattern

Pattern is inside
left margin guide

FIGURE C-17: Duplicating the pattern

Save the Date
Ski Trip to Utah
February 7-14, 2014

Drag duplicate pattern
to the Inside of the
right margin guide

FIGURE C-18: Aligning three objects by their top edges

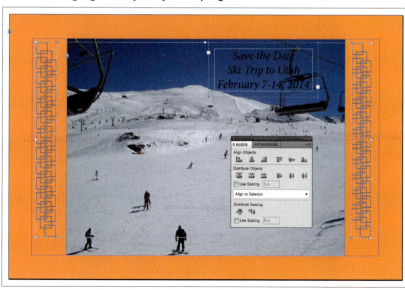

Save the Date
Ski Trip to Utah
February 7-14, 2014

Modifying Corners and Strokes

In InDesign, you can modify the corners of a rectangular shape using the Corner Options dialog box, which offers five types of corners, such as Rounded and Beveled. Like most dialog boxes, you can preview the settings applied to the selected object before closing the dialog box. To better see the changes made to corners, a thick stroke is recommended. You change the weight of a stroke on the Stroke panel. Jennifer asks if you can place an interesting border around the photo. You place a 4-point black stroke on the photo and then change its corners to Inverse Rounded.

STEPS

1. Click Window on the Application bar, point to Workspace, then click Reset Essentials

2. Click the Stroke panel icon ☰ to open the Stroke panel

3. Click Object on the Application bar, then click Unlock All on Spread

   The orange rectangle and the photo are unlocked. The photo needs to be unlocked so that you can add a border to it.

4. Click the Selection tool ▶ on the Tools panel, click the pasteboard to deselect all, then click the photo

5. Click the Stroke button ☐ on the Tools panel, then click Black on the Swatches panel

6. On the Stroke panel, click the Weight list arrow, then click 4 pt

   As shown in Figure C-19, a 4-point stroke is added to the frame of the photo. The stroke is aligned to the center of the frame by default. On the Stroke panel, you can choose to align a stroke to the inside, outside, or center of the selected object's frame.

7. Click Object on the Application bar, then click Corner Options

   The Corner Options dialog box opens. The dialog box consists of four settings, one for each corner of the selected frame. Each setting includes the option to choose a corner style and size.

8. Click the top-left down arrow, then click Inverse Rounded, as shown in Figure C-20

   All four boxes change to Inverse Rounded because the Make all settings the same button ⬚ is selected. You can apply different styles to each corner by deactivating the Make all settings the same button.

9. Click OK, deselect all, press [W] to view the document without guides, then compare your screen to Figure C-21

10. Save your work, then exit InDesign

FIGURE C-19: Applying a 4-point stroke

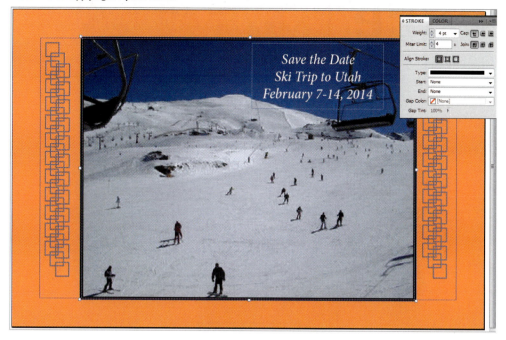

FIGURE C-20: Corner Options dialog box

Top-left corner setting

Blue dot indicates the selected corner

Top-left down arrow

Inverse Rounded style

Make all settings the same button

FIGURE C-21: Completed project

Practice

Concepts Review

For current SAM information, including versions and content details, visit SAM Central (http://www.cengage.com/samcentral). If you have a SAM user profile, you may have access to hands-on instruction, practice, and assessment of the skills covered in this unit. Since various versions of SAM are supported throughout the life of this text, check with your instructor for the correct instructions and URL/Web site for accessing assignments.

Label the elements of the InDesign screen shown in Figure C-22.

FIGURE C-22

1. _____   4. _____
2. _____   5. _____
3. _____   6. _____

Match each term with the statement that best describes it.

7. **Live Distribute**
8. **Align**
9. **Group**
10. **Smart guide**

a. To position one or more objects in relation to other objects or page elements, such as margin guides

b. A good choice when you wish to manually distribute objects

c. A colorful guide that appears automatically when an object touches another object, a margin guide, or the center of the page

d. To combine two or more objects as one object

Select the best answer from the list of choices.

11. **Which of the following is a Transform command?**
    a. Type
    b. Rotate
    c. Effects
    d. Transparency

12. **Which InDesign element can you align an object to?**
    a. Ruler
    b. Page
    c. Column
    d. Gutter

13. **Which dialog box allows you to move and copy multiple objects?**
    a. Move
    b. Move and Copy
    c. Transform
    d. Step and Repeat

14. **Which of the following is not an alignment choice for a stroke?**
    a. Inside
    b. Center
    c. Middle
    d. Outside

Skills Review

1. **Work with smart guides.**
    a. Start InDesign, navigate to the drive and folder where you store your Data Files, then open ID C-2.indd.
    b. Save the document as **Holiday**, then reset the Essentials workspace.
    c. Click View on the Application bar, point to Grids & Guides, then, if there is not a check mark next to Smart Guides, click Smart Guides to select it. (*Hint*: If there is a check mark next to Smart Guides, the feature is on.)
    d. Click the Selection tool on the Tools panel, if necessary.
    e. Click the photo, slowly drag it to the right until you see a vertical green guide, then release the mouse button. (*Hint*: The green smart guide indicates that the horizontal center of the photo is aligned with the horizontal center of the text box.)
    f. Continue to drag the photo to the right until you see a vertical pink guide, then release the mouse button. (*Hint*: The pink smart guide indicates that the horizontal center of the photo is aligned with the horizontal center of the page.)
    g. Slowly drag the photo upward until you see a smart guide appear showing the vertical center of the page, keep adjusting the position of the photo until you see both the horizontal and vertical center smart guides, then release the mouse button. (*Hint*: The photo is perfectly centered horizontally and vertically on the page.)
    h. Save your work.

2. **Create an object.**
    a. Click the Rectangle tool on the Tools panel.
    b. Position the Rectangle tool pointer on the left side of the page anywhere next to the left side of the photo and inside the left margin guide.
    c. Drag to create a small rectangle, then release the mouse button.
    d. Verify that the rectangle is still selected, then click the Swatches panel tab on the right to open the Swatches panel.
    e. Click the Fill button on the Tools panel, if necessary, then click [Black] on the Swatches panel.
    f. Click the Stroke button on the Tools panel, then click [None] on the Swatches panel.
    g. Save your work.

3. **Transform an object.**
    a. Make sure the black rectangle is selected.
    b. Click the upper-left reference point on the Control panel, double-click the X Location value if necessary, type **0**, then press [Tab].
    c. Type **0** in the Y Location box, then press [Enter] (Win) or [return] (Mac).
    d. Double-click the value in the W (Width) text box in the Control panel, type **8.5**, then press [Tab].
    e. Type **5.5** in the H (Height) text box, then press [Enter] (Win) or [return] (Mac).
    f. Save your work.

Skills Review (continued)

4. Arrange and lock an object.

  a. Click the Selection tool, then verify that the black rectangle is still selected.

  b. Click Object on the Application bar, point to Arrange, then click Send Backward.

  c. Verify that the black rectangle is still selected, click Object on the Application bar, then click Lock.

  d. Click the photo, then lock it.

  e. Deselect all, press [W] to view your work without guides, then save your work.

  f. Press [W] to return to Normal view.

5. Step and repeat an object.

  a. Click and hold the Rectangle tool on the Tools panel, click the Ellipse tool, then click to the left of the upper-left corner of the photo and inside the left margin.

  b. Type **.25** in the Width text box, press [Tab], type **.25** in the Height text box, then click OK.

  c. Change the fill color of the circle to [None], then change the stroke color to [Paper] (white).

  d. Verify that the circle is still selected, click Edit on the Application bar, then click Step and Repeat.

  e. Click the Preview check box in the Step and Repeat dialog box.

  f. Type **14** in the Count text box, press [Tab] until the Vertical Offset text box is highlighted, type **.25**, press [Tab], then type **0** in the Horizontal Offset text box. (*Hint*: If you get a warning, change the Horizontal and/or Vertical text box values to 0, then enter the Count value again.)

  g. Click OK to close the Step and Repeat dialog box.

  h. Click Object on the Application bar, then click Group.

  i. Verify that the group is still selected, then open the Step and Repeat dialog box.

  j. Type **2** in the Count text box, press [Tab] until the Vertical Offset text box is highlighted, type **0.125**, press [Tab], type **0.3125** in the Horizontal text box, then click OK. (*Hint*: It is OK if any of your circle groups overlap the photo.)

  k. Save your work.

6. Use Live Distribute.

  a. Click the Selection tool on the Tools panel, if necessary.

  b. Click the first group of circles, press and hold [Shift], then click the second and third groups of circles so that all three groups are selected, if necessary.

  c. Position the mouse pointer over the bottom-right selection handle of the bounding box.

  d. Click the selection handle, press [Spacebar], drag the pointer slowly to the right, then drag to the left until the three groups of circles overlap to create an interesting pattern.

  e. Verify that the three groups are still selected, click Object on the Application bar, then click Group.

  f. Save your work.

7. Use the Align panel.

  a. If necessary, drag the group of circles so that they appear centered within the black area to the left of the photo and inside the left margin.

  b. Verify that the group of circles is still selected, press and hold [Alt] (Win) or [option] (Mac), drag a duplicate of the pattern to the right side of the page, then release the mouse button when the duplicate is positioned inside the right margin guide.

  c. Click Window on the Application bar, point to Object & Layout, then click Align.

  d. Click the Selection tool on the Tools panel, if necessary, click the pattern on the left, press and hold [Shift], then click the pattern on the right.

  e. On the Align panel, click the Align to list arrow, then click Align to Selection if necessary.

  f. On the Align panel, click the Align top edges button.

  g. Deselect all, click the edge of the text box, then drag it left until it aligns with the left side of the photo and the bottom margin guide.

  h. Save your work.

Skills Review (continued)

8. Modify corners and strokes.

  a. Click Window on the Application bar, point to Workspace, then click Reset Essentials.

  b. Click Object on the Application bar, then click Unlock All on Spread.

  c. Deselect all, click the Selection tool on the Tools panel, then click the photo.

  d. Show the Swatches panel, click the Stroke icon on the Tools panel, then click [Paper] on the Swatches panel.

  e. Show the Stroke panel, click the Weight list arrow, then click 10 pt.

  f. Click Object on the Application bar, then click Corner Options.

  g. Click the top-left down arrow, then click Bevel.

  h. Click OK, deselect all, press [W] to view the document without guides, then compare your screen to Figure C-23.

  i. Save your work, then exit InDesign.

FIGURE C-23

Independent Challenge 1

You are applying for a job as a fabric designer for a teen furniture store. As part of the interview process, you've been asked to pick six colors for furniture and accessories that would appeal to teenagers, and provide a printout of them to the human resources manager. You've decided to use InDesign to create the color set.

  a. Open ID C-3.indd, then save it as **Color Samples**.

  b. Select the rectangle, then open the Step and Repeat dialog box.

  c. Step and repeat four copies of the square that have a 2" vertical offset and a 0" horizontal offset.

  d. Fill the five rectangles with colors and tints of colors from the Swatches panel. Use the Color panel to create new swatches and add them to the Swatches panel. (*Hint*: When you create a color, right-click the Swatch button on the Color panel and then click Add to Swatches.)

  e. Do not apply a stroke to the rectangles.

  f. Group the five rectangles.

  g. Deselect all objects, press [W] to switch to Preview mode, then compare your screen to Figure C-24. (*Hint*: The colors of the rectangles on your screen will be different.)

  h. Save the document, then exit InDesign.

FIGURE C-24

Independent Challenge 2

You left your wallet at the movie theatre. A few days later, you receive it in the mail with a note from someone who found it. Everything you had in it is still there. You are so relieved and grateful that you compose a thank you note right away.

  a. Start InDesign.

  b. Open ID C-4.indd, then save it as **Thank you**.

  c. Create a rectangle that snaps to all four margin guides.

  d. Fill the rectangle with a color of your choice.

Independent Challenge 2 (continued)

e. Send the rectangle behind the flower graphic and text box.

f. Lock the rectangle.

g. Align the picture of the flowers horizontally and vertically with the center of the page.

h. Align the text box with the horizontal center of the page.

i. Place a 4-point stroke around the picture of the flowers using a stroke color of your choice.

Advanced Challenge Exercise

■ Click the Selection tool, then click the picture of the flowers.

■ Click the yellow square on the bounding box of the picture's frame.

■ Click and drag one of the yellow diamonds to round the four corners to your liking.

■ Click the page to deselect.

j. Switch to Preview mode, then compare your document to Figure C-25.

k. Save the document, then exit InDesign.

FIGURE C-25

Thank You

Independent Challenge 3

Your design class at school is having a contest to design a logo for a non-profit organization that provides three services for the homeless: food, shelter, and medical care. You decide to use three colors to represent the three services and your knowledge of working with objects to create a winning logo.

a. Start InDesign, create a new document, then save it as **Services**.

b. Create a .5" square, then step and repeat two copies of it.

c. Fill the squares with three different colors of your choice, and remove the stroke colors, if necessary.

d. Position the three squares vertically, leaving some room between them.

e. Using the Align panel, align the three objects by their left edges.

f. Click the Distribute vertical centers button to create the same amount of space between the three squares.

g. Select the first square, then change the style of two corners of the square using the Corner Options dialog box. (*Hint*: Be sure to deactivate the Make all settings the same button in the Corner Options dialog box.)

h. Repeat Step g for the second and third squares.

i. Step and repeat two copies of the group with a Vertical offset of 0 and a Horizontal offset of 0.625. (*Hint*: You should have three columns of three shapes for a total of nine shapes.)

j. Place a 1-point black stroke on all nine shapes, then deselect all.

k. Group each column of shapes so that you have three groups and then apply a different fill color to each group.

l. Select the three groups of shapes, then use the Live Distribute feature to overlap the groups to make an interesting logo. Figure C-26 shows one example.

FIGURE C-26

Independent Challenge 3 (continued)

Advanced Challenge Exercise

- Display the Stroke panel.
- Select the nine shapes that make up the logo.
- Click the Align Stroke to Inside button on the Stroke panel.
- Increase the stroke weight to 3 pt.

m. Save the document, then exit InDesign.

Real Life Independent Challenge

InDesign is a great program for creating your own professional-looking printed materials. Design a simple business card with your name and a service that you provide (for example, dog walking or house sitting). Include your telephone number and an e-mail address. Use the shape tools and the Step and Repeat command to create a simple but interesting pattern for your card.

a. Start InDesign, then create a new document that is 3" wide by 2.5" tall, without facing pages and with 0" margins.

b. Save the document as **Business Card**.

c. Create a rectangle that is the same size as the document and that snaps to all four edges of the document.

d. Create a text box, then type your name, a fictitious profession and/or company name, phone number, and e-mail address.

e. Format the text to your liking.

f. Create your pattern using one or more of the shape tools, the Swatches panel, and the Step and Repeat command.

g. Use any of the Transform, Arrange, and Align commands to further design your pattern. Be creative.

h. Group and lock objects as you deem necessary.

i. Switch to Preview mode. A sample business card is shown in Figure C-27.

j. Save the document, then exit InDesign.

FIGURE C-27

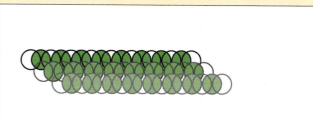

UNDER CONTROL
Ann Fisher
Professional Organizer
555-555-1222
yourname@organize.net

Visual Workshop

Create a new 8.5" x 11" document that has .5" margins and does not have facing pages. Save it as **Bars**. Using Figure C-28 as a guide, recreate the image. Start by creating a rectangle that is 7.5" wide and 1" tall, and then fill it with red. Snap it to the top and left margin guides. Step and repeat the rectangle. The black rectangle should snap to the top margin guide and should be .5" wide and 8.875" tall. Once the bars are layered correctly, group and lock all of the bars. Switch to Preview mode, save the document, then exit InDesign.

FIGURE C-28

Working with Graphics

In addition to creating your own graphics in InDesign, you can also place graphics from other programs, such as Adobe Illustrator and Photoshop, in InDesign documents. InDesign places graphics into frames; there are many ways that you can manipulate the graphic and the frame to fit your layout needs. Placed graphics are known as **links** because the placed graphic that appears in the document is actually a link to the original graphic file on your computer. Information about placed graphics appears on the Links panel. You can use the Links panel to replace one placed object with another, find a placed object in a document, and even edit a placed object by launching the software program that created it. Your client, The Happy Apple, creates a newspaper advertisement each week promoting its weekly specials. You work with your contact, Ted, to place the images that are needed into the InDesign document.

OBJECTIVES

Understand bitmap and vector graphics

Place a graphic into a frame

Work with the content indicator

Transform frame contents

Use the Links panel

Replace a linked image and embed a file

Add graphics to a library

Understanding Bitmap and Vector Graphics

Graphic files come in many formats. Two formats that are commonly placed into InDesign documents are bitmap and vector. A **bitmap graphic** is a graphic that is made up of **pixels**: tiny color squares arranged in a grid that are used to display graphics shown on a monitor or television screen. Scanned photographs and photographs taken from a digital camera are bitmap graphics. Files created in an image-editing software program, such as Adobe Photoshop, are another example of bitmap graphics. If you zoom in on a bitmap graphic or greatly increase its size, you can see its pixels. A **vector graphic** is a graphic that is made up of **vectors**, which are straight or curved line segments connected by **anchor points** (small dots), much like a completed connect-the-dots drawing. Vector graphics are created in drawing programs such as Adobe Illustrator. They are an ideal format for illustrations and logos because they can be resized in page layouts without losing image quality. Vector graphics can be manipulated in InDesign using the Pen tool and the Direct Selection tool. You can add, move, and delete anchor points and line segments to change the shape of the vector. Before working with the images you'll use in the advertisement, you review the properties of bitmap and vector graphics.

STEPS

1. **Start InDesign, open ID D-1.indd from the drive and folder where you store your Data Files, then save it as Graphics**

   The file includes one bitmap image of papayas and one vector image of an apple.

2. **Click the workspace switcher on the Application bar, then click Essentials**

3. **Click the Zoom tool 🔍 on the Tools panel**

   You will use the Zoom tool to enlarge your view of the bitmap image to view the pixels.

4. **Drag a small rectangle with the Zoom tool pointer ⊕ over the papayas image in the approximate location shown in Figure D-1, then release the mouse button**

   The dotted rectangle that appears as you drag the Zoom tool pointer is called a **marquee**. Everything inside the marquee will be enlarged on the screen when you release the mouse pointer. At a high zoom percentage, you can easily see the pixels that make up the image.

5. **Click View on the Application bar, then click Fit Page in Window**

6. **Click the Direct Selection tool ▸ on the Tools panel, then position the Direct Selection tool pointer ▸ near the upper-right edge of the red apple until it appears with a small line segment next to it ▸**

   When the Direct Selection tool pointer is positioned over the edge of an unselected vector graphic, the anchor points and line segments become visible. As shown in Figure D-2, the pointer is over a line segment, indicated by the tiny line segment icon next to the arrow pointer.

   > **QUICK TIP**
   > In order to manipulate a vector graphic's anchor points and line segments in InDesign, you must copy and paste it from Illustrator to InDesign. If you use the Place command, the vector graphic will not be editable.

7. **Click any one of the anchor points on either side of the line segment, then drag slowly in any direction to change the location of the anchor point and the shape of the apple, as shown in Figure D-3**

   Most vector graphics are created in Adobe Illustrator but they can be manipulated in Adobe InDesign using the same tools.

8. **Save your work, then close the Graphics file**

Marquee

Pixels

Bitmap graphic

FIGURE D-2: Viewing the parts of a vector

Anchor point

Line segment

Pointer indicates it is over a line segment

the h

FIGURE D-3: Moving an anchor point

Anchor point relocated

the h

X: 3.91 in
Y: 7.76 in

InDesign CS5

Understanding resolution issues

Resolution, also known as screen resolution, is the number of pixels per inch (ppi) used to display computer graphics on a monitor. There should be at least 72 pixels per inch in order for a graphic to display correctly. The resolution required for printed materials, also known as the number of lines per inch (lpi) or dots per inch (dpi), is much higher. This is because pixels are converted to dots when graphics are printed. The number of dots per inch determines the quality of the print job. For example, printed newspapers have a lower lpi than a glossy magazine. When working in InDesign, it is important that you avoid resizing bitmap graphics. When you resize a graphic to make it larger, the same number of pixels is forced to fill a larger area. The pixels are spread farther away from each other, resulting in poor print quality. This is why bitmap images are known as being "resolution dependent." Vector graphics, on the other hand, are not made of pixels and are "resolution independent," meaning that you can greatly reduce or increase their size and they will print with the same level of quality.

Placing a Graphic into a Frame

Graphics are placed into frames. Frames are created using any of the frame tools: the Rectangle, Ellipse, and Polygon tools. After you create a frame, you place a graphic into it using the Place command on the File menu. When you place a graphic into a frame, the upper-left corner of the graphic snaps to the upper-left corner of the frame and then fills the remainder of the frame. If the frame is larger than the graphic, not all of the frame will be filled with the graphic. If the graphic is larger than the frame, part of the graphic will not be seen; it will be cropped by the frame. InDesign offers many solutions for fitting frame contents. Ted has sent over photos of this week's deli specials for the newsletter. You create a frame for the first one and then place a bitmap graphic into it.

STEPS

1. Open ID D-2.indd from the drive and folder where you store your Data Files, then save it as Specials

2. Make sure that the Essentials workspace is selected and that the guides are visible

3. Click the Rectangle Frame tool ⊠ on the Tools panel, then click the page
   The Rectangle dialog box opens.

4. Type 4 in the Width text box, press [Tab], type 4 in the Height text box, then click OK

5. Click the Selection tool ▶ on the Tools panel, then drag the edge of the frame so that it is aligned with the left margin and the bottom guide, as shown in Figure D-4
   The smart guides appear green when the frame is touching both the left margin guide and the horizontal guide.

> **QUICK TIP**
> You can also place a graphic without first creating a frame. A frame is automatically created for the graphic when it is placed on the page. The frame is the same size as the graphic.

6. Verify that the frame is still selected, click File on the Application bar, then click Place
   The Place dialog box opens.

7. In the Place dialog box, navigate to the drive and folder where you store your Data Files, click Pizza 1.psd as shown in Figure D-5, then click Open
   An image of a pizza against a white background fills the frame from the upper-left corner of the frame, as shown in Figure D-6. The bounding box surrounds the frame.

8. Save your work, then keep the Specials document open

Placing multiple images

Some types of documents require many pictures. A clothing catalog is a good example. When you have many pictures that you plan to place in InDesign, you can select them for placement all at once instead of one at a time. You do this by pressing and holding [Ctrl] (Win) or ⌘ (Mac) as you select multiple graphics in the Place dialog box when placing graphics. The cursor becomes a loaded graphics pointer. It displays the thumbnail of the first selected graphic and the number of total graphics to be placed. Each time you click, a graphic is placed in the document in the order that it was selected in the Place dialog box.

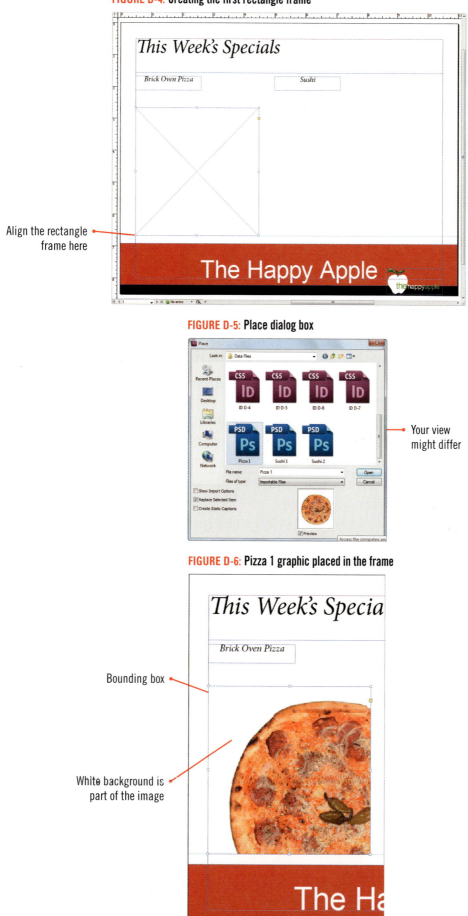

FIGURE D-4: Creating the first rectangle frame

This Week's Specials

Brick Oven Pizza   Sushi

Align the rectangle frame here

The Happy Apple

FIGURE D-5: Place dialog box

Your view might differ

FIGURE D-6: Pizza 1 graphic placed in the frame

This Week's Specia

Brick Oven Pizza

Bounding box

White background is part of the image

The Ha

InDesign CS5

Working with the Content Indicator

When you place a graphic into a frame, you only see the part of the graphic that fits inside the frame. You may want to show a different view of the graphic without changing the frame size. The **content indicator**, a donut-shaped icon, appears over a placed graphic when you move the Selection tool over the graphic. The content indicator allows you to move a graphic in a frame without moving the frame. Once you begin dragging the content indicator, you will see the part of the image that lies outside the frame borders and the part of the image inside the frame borders. You can drag the image until it is cropped to your liking. **Cropping** an image in InDesign means hiding part of it without permanently removing it. You use the content indicator to move the pizza image so that it is more centered in the frame.

STEPS

1. **Verify that the frame is still selected with the Selection tool**

2. **Position the mouse pointer over the pizza image until the content indicator is visible**

3. **Position the mouse pointer over ⊙ so that you see a hand pointer, as shown in Figure D-7**

   You use the hand pointer to drag the graphic.

4. **Drag ⊙ slowly up and to the left until your screen resembles Figure D-8, then release the mouse**

   The area of the graphic outside of the frame appears ghosted. The brown frame represents the borders of the graphic file, not the InDesign frame that the graphic is placed in.

5. **Double-click the pizza image**

   The frame becomes selected, indicated by the bounding box.

6. **Double-click the pizza image again**

   The image becomes selected, indicated by the brown outline that appears surrounding the pizza image.

7. **Save your work**

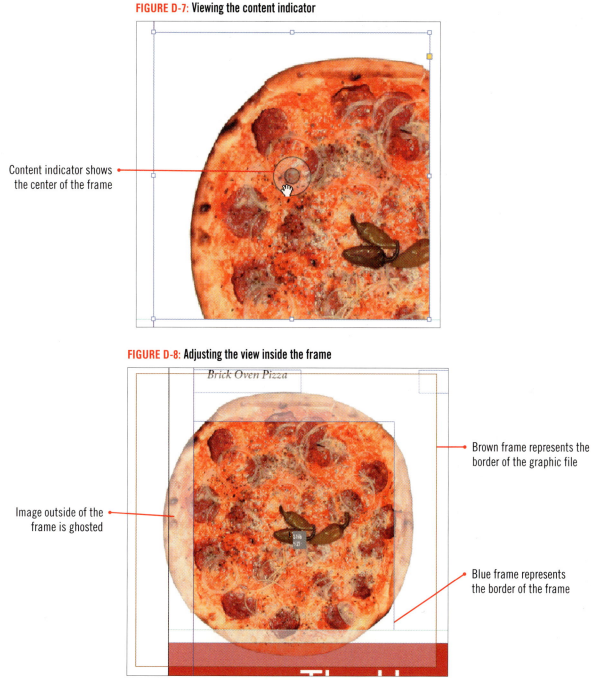

FIGURE D-7: Viewing the content indicator

Content indicator shows
the center of the frame

FIGURE D-8: Adjusting the view inside the frame

Brick Oven Pizza

Brown frame represents the
border of the graphic file

Image outside of the
frame is ghosted

Blue frame represents
the border of the frame

Other uses of the Direct Selection tool

The Direct Selection tool has many uses in addition to selecting a placed object separately from its frame. You can use it to select the individual anchor points and line segments of vector graphics, such as rectangles and rectangle frames that you create with InDesign. To select an anchor point or line segment in a graphic, make sure that the graphic is not selected, then click the point or segment you wish to select with the Direct Selection tool. You can then edit the graphic to make a subtle change to the object or to create an entirely new shape. When anchor points are selected and editable, you can drag either the point or one of its adjoining line segments. Dragging an anchor point changes the shape of the object because the line segments attached to either side of it change when the anchor point is moved. Dragging a line segment is one way to resize a shape by moving only one side of it. Press and hold [Shift] while you drag to constrain the shape without changing its horizontal or vertical axis.

You can also use the Direct Selection tool to select just one of the items in a set of objects that are grouped together. You may want to do this in order to make a small change to one of the items in the group without ungrouping the group of items. To select one item in a group, make sure that the grouped object is not selected, then click the item you wish to select with the Direct Selection tool. Make changes as necessary to the item, then deselect it.

Transforming Frame Contents

When the image inside a frame is selected, the Control panel displays options for transforming the frame contents. For example, you can scale an image, rotate it, center it, or flip it. There are also buttons for fitting the image to match the size of the frame and vice versa. Table D-1 describes the fitting options in more detail. Although you and Ted like how the pizza is framed, you want to scale the pizza image and then center it inside the frame.

STEPS

1. **Click the Selection tool on the Tools panel, click the top-left reference point on the Control panel, then double-click the pizza image**

   The image of the pizza is selected. The Control panel displays options for modifying the image, as shown in Figure D-9. Notice the X and Y values change to X+ and Y+. They represent the horizontal and vertical locations of the upper-left corner of the pizza image in relation to the upper-left corner of the frame. They are both negative numbers because they are located above and beyond the upper-left corner of the frame.

2. **Double-click the Scale X Percentage text box on the Control panel, as shown in Figure D-10, type 75, then press [Enter] (Win) or [return] (Mac)**

   The Scale Y Percentage text box value changes to 75% automatically because the Make all settings the same button is selected. The pizza image is scaled 75%, as shown in Figure D-11.

   QUICK TIP
   The Control panel has many effects that you can add to frames and images. Select an image or a frame, click the Add an object effect to the selected target button fx, then select an effect.

3. **Click the Center content button on the Control panel**

   The pizza image is centered inside the frame.

4. **Click the Select container button on the Control panel**

   The frame is selected. Clicking the Select container button on the Control panel is equivalent to double-clicking the image to select the frame.

5. **Save your work**

TABLE D-1: Fitting commands

command	button	description	use when
Fit content to frame		Image is resized to fit the exact size of the frame	Frame size must remain the same and it is OK if the image is distorted when stretched or shrunk to fit the frame
Fit frame to content		Frame is resized to the exact size of the image	Picture size must remain at 100% and the frame size does not matter
Center content		Image is centered in the frame without any reduction in image or frame size; if image is larger than the frame, some of the image will be cropped	The image and frame are similar in size and you want to center the content quickly
Fit content proportionally		Image is resized to fit the frame while maintaining its proportion; if the frame and the image are different sizes, some empty space may appear inside the frame	Frame size cannot change and all of the image must be visible; only works well when the frame and image are similar in size
Fill frame proportionally		Entire frame is filled with the image and the image's proportions are preserved; if the image is larger than the frame, some of it will be cropped by the frame border	Frame size cannot change and not all of the image needs to be visible; only works well when the frame and image are similar in size

Working with Graphics

FIGURE D-9: Viewing the Control panel

Horizontal and vertical locations of the upper-left corner of pizza image in relation to the upper-left corner of the frame

Width and height of pizza image

Upper-left corner of pizza image

Upper-left corner of frame

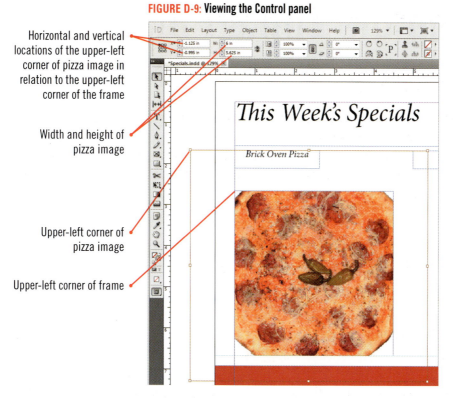

FIGURE D-10: Highlighting the Scale X Percentage value

| X+ | -1.125 in | W: | 6 in | | | 100% | | | 0° | |
| Y+ | -0.995 in | H: | 5.625 in | | | 100% | | | 0° | |

Scale X Percentage text box

FIGURE D-11: The scaled image

Using the Links Panel

When you place an image in a frame, the frame displays a **preview**, which is a graphical representation of the original image file and not the file itself. A link is automatically established between the preview and the actual image file, which remains in its original location on the local internal hard drive or storage device. Linking images helps to keep an InDesign file size manageable because the size of the placed image files is not added to the InDesign file size. Once images are placed in a document, information about each placed file, such as its name, size, and the page where it appears in the document, is displayed on the Links panel. See Table D-2 on page 88 for more information about each link status. ▨▨▨▨ You place another graphic in the document and then view three links on the Links panel.

STEPS

1. Click the **Rectangle Frame tool** ⊠ on the Tools panel, then click an empty part of the page

2. Type **5.5** in the Width text box, press **[Tab]**, type **4** in the Height text box, then click **OK**

3. Position the new frame in the location shown in Figure D-12

4. Verify that the frame is still selected, click **File** on the Application bar, click **Place**, click **Sushi 1.psd**, then click **Open**

   A photo of sushi fills the frame, but the image is very large. You want the image to appear proportional to the frame.

QUICK TIP

Click the Show/Hide Link Information button in the lower-left corner of the top section of the Links panel to hide the Link Info section of the Links panel.

5. Click the **Fill frame proportionally button** ▣ on the Control panel

   The image fills the entire frame and maintains its proportion.

6. Click the **Links panel icon** 🔗, if necessary, then compare your screen to Figure D-13

   The Links panel lists the three images placed in the document: logoWhite.ai, Pizza 1.psd, and Sushi 1.psd. Sushi 1.psd is highlighted on the panel because it is still selected on the page. The Links panel includes three information columns—Status, Name, and Page—and a row of buttons for working with links. The bottom section of the Links panel is called the Link Info section. It displays detailed information about the highlighted link. You can view the next link or the previous link in the list by clicking the Select next link in the list button or the Select previous link in the list button.

QUICK TIP

The links are sorted by page number from lowest to highest. You can change the sort order of links by clicking a column name. For example, click the Name column to sort links alphabetically.

7. On the Links panel, move the pointer along the blue highlighted area for **Sushi 1.psd** until you see a tooltip stating the path of the file, then continue to move the pointer until you see a ScreenTip that reads **OK** under the Status column, as shown in Figure D-14

   There are four possible statuses for each link: OK, Missing, Modified, and Embedded. The OK status indicates that the linked file has not been moved or modified since it was placed in the document.

8. Click **logoWhite.ai** on the Links panel, then click the **Go to Link button** ⤴ on the Links panel

   The Happy Apple logo (logoWhite.ai) fills the document window and is selected. The Go to Link button helps you identify a link when you are not sure what it is or where it is in the document.

QUICK TIP

A number indicating how many times a link is used in a document appears in parentheses next to its name on the Links panel.

Printing an InDesign document with linked files

When you print an InDesign document that contains linked files, the original files that are linked to the document must be present on the same computer in order for the document to print correctly. If you send your InDesign document to a printer or a service bureau for printing, you must send not only the InDesign document, but also all of the linked files in one folder. When an InDesign file and its linked files move from one computer to another, occasionally the InDesign file opens with a warning that the linked images cannot be found. The files are there; the links just need to be re-established to the files in their location on the new computer. A warning dialog box will appear with the name of the first linked file that InDesign cannot find. All you need to do is to re-establish the links by locating the first linked file in the folder that contains it, and the rest of the files in that folder will update automatically.

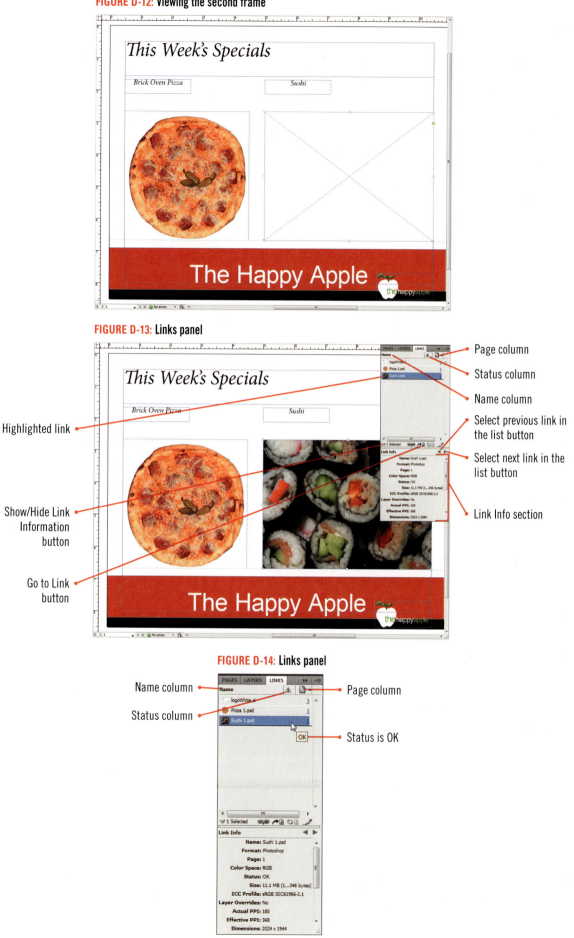

Page column

Status column

Name column

Select previous link in the list button

Select next link in the list button

Link Info section

Highlighted link

Show/Hide Link Information button

Go to Link button

FIGURE D-14: Links panel

Name column

Page column

Status column

Status is OK

InDesign CS5

Replacing a Linked Image and Embedding a File

When working with an InDesign publication, it is very likely that you will replace one image with another. To replace a placed image in InDesign, click the image on the Links panel, click the Relink button on the Links panel, then choose a new file in the Relink dialog box. The new image replaces the original image and inherits any fitting commands and transformations that were made to it. For example, if you place an image, rotate it 15°, then replace it with a new image, the new image will be automatically rotated 15°. Small images that do not have a large file size can be embedded in the document. Embedding a file makes it a permanent part of the InDesign file; it is no longer linked. Embedded files remain on the Links panel with an Embedded icon. Embedding a file is a great way to protect it from being changed, moved, or deleted. Ted would prefer that you use a different sushi image. You use the Links panel to replace the sushi image with a new and improved image. You then embed the Happy Apple logo.

STEPS

1. Click **View** on the Application bar, then click **Fit Page in Window**

2. Click the **Selection tool** ▶ on the Tools panel, then click the **sushi image**

QUICK TIP
To relink an image without inheriting any previously applied fitting commands and transformations, click Edit (Win) or InDesign (Mac) on the Application bar, point to Preferences, click File Handling, then remove the check mark in the Preserve Image Dimensions When Relinking check box.

3. Click the **Relink button** 🔗 on the Links panel

   The Relink dialog box opens.

4. Navigate to the drive and folder where you store your Data Files, click **Sushi 2.psd**, as shown in Figure D-15, then click **Open**

   Sushi 2.psd replaces Sushi 1.psd in the document and on the Links panel. The image is automatically resized to fill the frame proportionally because you had previously applied this command to Sushi 1.psd. You want to embed the Happy Apple logo so that it will not be affected by anyone else moving or modifying it.

5. Click **logoWhite.ai** on the Links panel

   To embed the logo, you must first select it.

6. Click the **Panel options button** ▾☰, click **Embed Link**, then save your work

   The logo is now embedded into the InDesign file. The status changes to Embedded on the Links panel, as shown in Figure D-16. If the Embed Link command is not available you may need to update the link first.

TABLE D-2: Link status

status and icon	indicates	to change status to OK
OK	Linked file has not been changed or moved from its location on the computer since it was placed into InDesign	N/A
Missing ❓	Linked file has been moved from its location on the computer when it was placed into InDesign	Click the Relink button on the Links panel or double-click the Missing icon; navigate to and select the linked file in the Relink dialog box, then click Open to relink the file and change the status of the missing link back to OK
Modified ⚠	The linked file was modified after it was placed into InDesign	Double-click the Modified icon in the Status column next to the link in question, which updates automatically
Embedded 🖼	The file is embedded instead of linked	N/A

FIGURE D-15: Relink dialog box

FIGURE D-16: Embedding the logo file

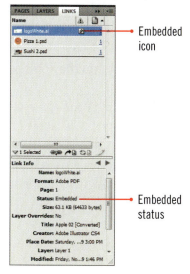

Embedded icon

Embedded status

Changing Links panel options

By default, the Links panel displays three columns of information: Name, Status, and Page. This information is enough for most people to have when creating simple documents. However, depending on how you use InDesign, you may want to display more information about placed files on the Links panel. For example, you may want to view the Dimensions column to view the size of an image. There are 44 possible columns of information available, ranging from Author to Transparency. You can customize the Links panel by adding or removing columns using the Panel Options dialog box. At the top of the Panel Options dialog box, you can choose the row size and whether you want to view image thumbnails in the Name column, the Link Info section, or both.

Editing a link

You can edit a linked file in InDesign using the Edit Original button on the Links panel or the Edit Original command on the Links panel menu. Click a link in the Links panel that you wish to edit, then click the Edit Original button. The file opens in the software program that it was created in. For example, if you edit a photograph, it will open in the photo-editing program that it originated from. If you edit a file that you did not create, InDesign will open the program on your computer that is associated with the file type. If you want to use a specific program to edit a file, select the file in the Links panel, click the Links panel list arrow, point to Edit With, then click the name of the program you want to use to edit the file on the menu that opens. When you edit a file, InDesign remains open. When you finish editing the file, close the software program you are using. You'll see the updated file with the edits made to it in InDesign.

Adding Graphics to a Library

A **library** is a type of InDesign file that is strictly for storing often-used text, graphics, and even InDesign pages for use in any InDesign document you create. Libraries are very convenient because they store all the formatting that you have applied to objects and text. For example, if you place in a library a graphic that has been resized or centered in its frame, those settings are stored with the graphic. When you use the graphic again in a new document, you won't have to resize or center it. Libraries are easy to work with in InDesign because they are InDesign files (with an .indl extension) that look and work like InDesign panels. Ted wants to use the pizza and sushi graphics and the logo again in future InDesign documents, so you create a library file to store them in.

STEPS

1. **Close the Links panel**

2. **Click File on the Application bar, point to New, then click Library**

   The New Library dialog box opens.

3. **Navigate to the drive and folder where you store your Data Files, then type Specials Library in the File name text box, as shown in Figure D-17**

   Anyone working on the weekly specials advertisements will be able to access items in the library.

4. **Click Save to close the New Library dialog box**

   The Specials Library appears in the document window. Now you're ready to add items to the library.

5. **Click the Selection tool ▶ on the Tools panel, click the pizza image, then drag it to the library**

   As you drag an item to a library, a plus sign appears next to the pointer indicating that the item is being dragged to the library.

6. **Compare your library to Figure D-18**

   A copy of the pizza image is added to the Specials Library. Notice that the original pizza image remains in the document. The library item displays the entire image, not the way it is cropped in the document.

7. **Add the Sushi 2.psd graphic and the Happy Apple logo to the library so that it contains three items**

   The library items are listed alphabetically.

8. **Drag Pizza 1.psd from the library to anywhere on the page**

   Notice that the image is identical to the original pizza image. The image is scaled 75% and centered.

9. **Undo your last step, reset the Essentials workspace, save your work, close the Specials Library, press [W] to preview your work without guides, deselect any images if necessary, then compare your screen to Figure D-19**

10. **Close the Specials.indd file, then exit InDesign**

> **QUICK TIP**
>
> To add an entire page of objects to a library as a single item, click the Panel options button ▣, then click Add Items on Page 1. To add all objects on a page as separate library items, click Add Items on Page 1 as Separate Objects.

> **QUICK TIP**
>
> You can change a library item by selecting it in the library, selecting one or more items in the document, clicking the Panel options button ▣, then clicking Update Library Item.

Viewing and sorting library items

There are three ways to view library items within the library. You can view them as a list, as thumbnails, or as large thumbnails. To change the view of library items, click the Panel list arrow, then click List View, Thumbnail View, or Large Thumbnail View. If you have multiple items in a library, it can be helpful to sort them. By default, libraries are sorted alphabetically by name; but you can also sort them by type or sort them so that the newest addition or oldest addition to the library appears first in the library. Sorting library items by type puts items of the same type, like text, together in the library. To sort library items, click the Library list arrow, point to Sort Items, then click by Name, by Newest, by Oldest, or by Type.

FIGURE D-17: New Library dialog box

Name of
library file

FIGURE D-18: Pizza 1.psd added to the Specials Library

FIGURE D-19: Finished project

Practice

For current SAM information, including versions and content details, visit SAM Central (http://www.cengage.com/samcentral). If you have a SAM user profile, you may have access to hands-on instruction, practice, and assessment of the skills covered in this unit. Since various versions of SAM are supported throughout the life of this text, check with your instructor for the correct instructions and URL/Web site for accessing assignments.

Concepts Review

Label the elements of the InDesign screen shown in Figure D-20.

FIGURE D-20

1. _____   4. _____

2. _____   5. _____

3. _____

Match each term with the statement that best describes it.

6. **X+**

7. **Library**

8. **Pixels**

9. **Preview**

10. **Direct Selection tool**

a. Tiny colored squares arranged in a grid that are used to display graphics shown on a monitor or television screen

b. Horizontal location of image inside a frame

c. Used with vector graphics

d. Stores images without removing formatting

e. Appears in a frame

Select the best answer from the list of choices.

11. Which term refers to hiding part of an image without removing it?

    a. Resize   **c.** Crop

    b. Place   **d.** Preview

12. Which text boxes on the Control panel would you choose to change the size of a photo in a frame?

    a. X and Y   **c.** Scale X Percentage and Scale Y Percentage

    b. X+ and Y   **d.** X% and Y%

13. Which of the following items could you place in an InDesign library?

    a. Graphic   **c.** Content indicator

    b. Dialog box   **d.** Panel

14. What type of graphic file is not linked to an InDesign document?

    a. Embedded   **c.** Vector

    b. Linked   **d.** Cropped

Skills Review

1. Understand bitmap and vector graphics.

  a. Start InDesign, open ID D-3.indd from the drive and folder where you store your Data Files, then save it as **Examples**.

  b. Click the workspace switcher on the Application bar, then click Essentials.

  c. Click the Zoom tool on the Tools panel.

  d. Drag a small rectangle with the Zoom tool pointer over a section of the lollipops image, then release the mouse button.

  e. Click View on the Application bar, then click Fit Page in Window.

  f. Click the Direct Selection tool on the Tools panel, then position the Direct Selection tool pointer over the bottom right leaf of the flower.

  g. Click any one of the anchor points on either side of the line segment, then drag slowly in any direction to change the location of the anchor point and the shape of the leaf.

  h. Save your work, then close the Examples file.

2. Place a graphic into a frame.

  a. Start InDesign, open ID D-4.indd from the drive and folder where you store your Data Files, then save it as **Organic Fruit**.

  b. Make sure the Essentials workspace is selected.

  c. Click the Rectangle Frame tool on the Tools panel, then click the page.

  d. Type **3.5** in the Width text box, press [Tab], type **4** in the Height text box, then click OK.

  e. Click the Selection tool on the Tools panel, then drag the edge of the frame so that it is left-aligned with the left margin and bottom-aligned with the horizontal guide.

  f. Verify that the frame is still selected, click File on the Application bar, then click Place.

  g. Navigate to the drive and folder where you store your Data Files, open the Fruit folder, click oranges.psd, then click Open.

  h. Save your work and keep the Organic Fruit document open.

3. Work with the content indicator.

  a. Verify that the frame is still selected with the Selection tool.

  b. Position the mouse pointer over the image of the oranges so that you see the content indicator.

  c. Position the mouse pointer over the content indicator so that you see a hand pointer.

  d. Drag the content indicator slowly to the left and upward, then release the mouse pointer.

  e. Double-click the image of the oranges to see the brown frame which represents the borders of the oranges image.

  f. Double-click the image of the oranges again to see the bounding box of the frame.

  g. Save your work.

Skills Review (continued)

4. Transform frame contents.

   a. Click the Selection tool on the Tools panel, then double-click the image of the oranges.

   b. Double-click the Scale X Percentage text box on the Control panel, type **125**, then press [Enter].

   c. Click the Center content button on the Control panel.

   d. Click the Select container button on the Control panel.

   e. Save your work.

5. Use the Links panel.

   a. Click the Rectangle Frame tool on the Tools panel, then click the page.

   b. Type **5** in the Width text box, press [Tab], type **4** in the Height text box, then click OK.

   c. Click the Selection tool on the Tools panel, then drag the new frame so that its right edge is snapped to the right margin guide and its bottom edge is snapped to the bottom guide.

   d. Verify that the frame is still selected, click File on the Application bar, click Place, navigate to the Fruit folder, click red grapes.psd, then click Open.

   e. Click the Fill frame proportionally button on the Control panel.

   f. Click the Links panel icon to open the Links panel.

   g. On the Links panel, position the pointer to the right of red grapes.psd under the Status column icon until you see a ScreenTip that reads OK.

   h. Click oranges.psd on the Links panel, then click the Go to Link button.

   i. Save your work.

6. Replace a linked image and embed a file.

   a. Click View on the Application bar, then click Fit Page in Window.

   b. Click the Selection tool on the Tools panel, then click the red grapes image.

   c. Click the Relink button on the Links panel.

   d. Navigate to the drive and folder where you store your Data Files, open the Fruit folder, click seedless grapes.psd, then click Open.

   e. Use the content indicator to crop the image so that you see most or all of the grapes in the frame.

   f. Select Organic logo.ai on the Links panel.

   g. Click the Links panel options button, then click Embed Link.

   h. Save your work.

7. Add graphics to a library.

   a. Close the Links panel.

   b. Click File on the Application bar, point to New, then click Library.

   c. If necessary, navigate to the drive and folder where you store your Data Files, then type **Fruit Library** in the File name text box.

   d. Click Save to close the New Library dialog box.

   e. Click the Selection tool on the Tools panel, click the oranges image, then drag it to the library.

   f. Release the mouse button.

   g. Add the seedless grapes.psd graphic and the Organic Source logo to the library so that your library contains three items.

   h. Drag oranges.psd from the library to anywhere on the page.

   i. Undo your last step, reset the Essentials workspace, then save your work.

Skills Review (continued)

j. Close the Fruit library, press [W] to preview your work without guides, deselect any images if necessary, then compare your screen to Figure D-21.

k. Close the Organic Fruit.indd file, then exit InDesign.

FIGURE D-21

Organic Fruit

Oranges

Grapes

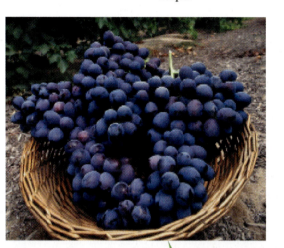

Organic Source

Independent Challenge 1

You work as a package designer for a pet care product company. You are currently working on a price tag that will be placed on a cat tree. Your last step is to place a picture of a cat and position it well in the space allotted.

a. Start InDesign, open ID D-5.indd, then save it as **Cat Tree**.

b. Create a rectangular frame a little larger than the oval in the middle of the price tag.

c. Place cat.jpg from the Animals folder into the frame.

d. Fill the frame proportionally.

e. Send the frame to the back.

f. Double-click the cat image with the Selection tool.

g. Make any size or location changes to the image on the Control panel.

h. Use the content indicator to move the image, if necessary.

i. When you are happy with the way that the frame crops the image, lock the image of the cat.

Independent Challenge 1 (continued)

j. Save your work, then compare your screen to Figure D-22.

k. Close the Cat Tree.indd file.

Independent Challenge 2

You volunteer two hours a week doing community service work for school credit at your local library. Each week, your supervisor assigns you different tasks. This week, she has asked you to create some fun pages to be distributed at the weekly story hour. The supervisor supplies you with an old version of fun pages and asks you to improve it with better images.

a. Start InDesign, open ID D-6.indd, then save it as **Fun Pages**.

b. Using artwork in your Data Files folder, fill five squares with images of fruit and one square with an image of candy. (*Hint*: Images are in the Fruit, Candy, Animals, and Toys folders.)

c. Use the content indicator and options on the Control panel to crop each picture in an interesting way.

d. Repeat Steps b and c for the next six frames, filling them with five images of animals and one image of a toy.

e. Place a 3-point stroke around each frame in the first group using a stroke color of your choice, then do the same for the second set of six frames using a different stroke color.

f. Use the Links panel to swap images, if necessary.

Advanced Challenge Exercise

- Select the first set of six frames.
- Click the Add an object effect to the selected target button, then click Drop Shadow.
- Accept the default settings in the Effects dialog box, then click OK.
- Apply an Inner Bevel effect with default settings to the second set of six frames.

g. Deselect all, save your work, press [W] to hide guides, then compare your screen to Figure D-23.

h. Close the Fun Pages.indd file.

Purrfect Cat Tree

On Sale!
$129·99

Three levels of living space
Heavyweight design
Durable construction
Stain-resistant carpet

FIGURE D-23

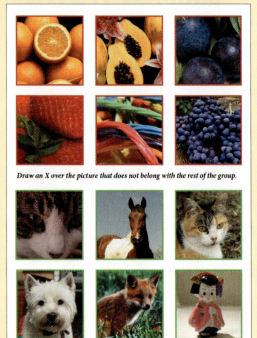

Draw an X over the picture that does not belong with the rest of the group.

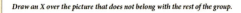

Draw an X over the picture that does not belong with the rest of the group.

Independent Challenge 3

You're writing a cookbook and starting to collect images to use in your chapter on smoothies. You decide to place your artwork in an InDesign library because you have spent a lot of time cropping the images carefully. You also add the entire page of images as a new library item and update a library item.

a. Start InDesign, open ID D-7.indd, then save it as **Smoothies**.

b. Create a new library and name it **Cookbook Images**.

c. Drag each item from the InDesign document to the library.

d. Click the Panel options button, then click Large Thumbnail View.

e. Click the Panel options button, then click Add Items on Page 1.

f. Rename the new library item **Smoothie Chapter Opener Art**.

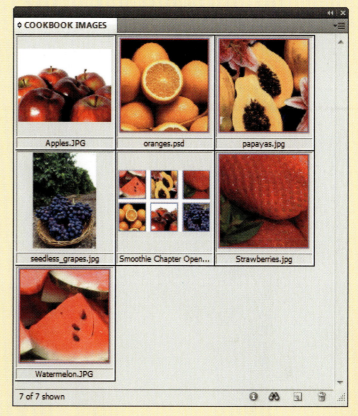

Advanced Challenge Exercise

- Drag the image of the strawberries to the library so that there are two strawberry items in the library.
- Select one of the Strawberry library items.
- Deselect the image of the strawberries in the document.
- Select the image of the oranges, press [Shift], then select the image of the apples.
- Click the Cookbook Images panel options button, then click Update Library Item.
- Double-click the new library item and then rename it **Fruit** in the Item Information dialog box.

g. Compare your library to Figure D-24, then close the Smoothies.indd file and the Cookbook Images library.

Real Life Independent Challenge

Start InDesign and create a new document using the Compact Disc page size option in the New Document dialog box. Name the document **CD Cover**. Create a CD cover for a band: real or fictitious. Create a frame and then place one of your favorite pictures in the frame. Crop the picture in an interesting way. Add a border to the frame, and then experiment with effects for the frame and the image. Add a title to the CD cover. Save the picture in a library called **My Library** for future use. Save your work, and then close the CD Cover.indd file.

Visual Workshop

Start InDesign, then create a new 8.5" x 11" document with a landscape orientation. Save the document as **Horse**. Create a rectangular graphics frame that is 7.85 inches wide and 7.50 inches tall. Position the frame as shown in Figure D-25. Place the Horse.jpg image from the Animals folder and then crop the image in the frame exactly how it is cropped in the figure. Show the Links panel and change the Links panel options so that the thumbnail of the horse is displayed in the Link Info section. Save your work, then close Horse.indd.

Using Master Pages

Most of the pages in multiple-page documents such as magazines and catalogs usually share a similar look. For example, catalog pages are filled with pictures of items for sale and descriptions of those items, and the pictures and descriptions are often in the same location on each page. Imagine if you were creating a 100-page catalog and you had to make sure that all graphics frames and text boxes were in the same locations on all 100 pages. Arranging each page, one at a time, would be time consuming and would likely result in some inconsistencies between pages. The master pages feature in InDesign enables you to apply the same design to multiple pages. Master pages are page designs that are available to be applied to pages in the same way that character styles are available to be applied to text. For example, if you need to create 100 pages that all look the same, you can create that look on a master page and then apply the master page to your 100 blank pages. Think of all the time you can save! Your next project is to work with the marketing director, Kate, at BreakTime on a booklet announcing its high school summer camp program. The booklet will contain photos and brief descriptions of six new themed camps. You plan to create and use master pages to format the booklet pages consistently.

OBJECTIVES

Create a multipage document
Create master items
Override master items
Modify a master page
Create a new master page
Apply master pages
Work with master pages

Creating a Multipage Document

Most publications that require master pages have left and right pages, such as books, magazines, newspapers, and catalogs. Once you've created a multiple-page document in InDesign, you'll be ready to work with master pages on the Pages panel. The Pages panel displays master page icons and document page icons, which represent the master pages and document pages in your publication, respectively. Kate would like you to create the camp brochure. You start by creating a new, custom-sized, eight-page document with facing pages and then open the Pages panel to view the master pages and pages.

STEPS

1. Start InDesign, click **File** on the Application bar, point to **New**, then click **Document**

2. Type **8** in the Number of Pages text box, then verify that the Facing Pages check box is checked

   You are creating an eight-page document with left and right pages.

3. Double-click the **Width value**, type **6**, press **[Tab]**, type **4** as the Height value, press **[Tab]**, verify that the **Landscape button** to the right of Orientation is selected, then compare your New Document dialog box to Figure E-1

   The width of the booklet is greater than the height, so the Landscape button is automatically selected after you enter the Width and Height values. If necessary, change the ruler units to inches in the Units & Increments window of the Preferences dialog box.

4. Click **OK** to close the New Document dialog box, then if necessary, change the Ruler Units to inches in the Preferences dialog box

5. Click the **workspace switcher** on the Application bar, then click **Reset Essentials**

   The workspace returns to the Essentials workspace.

6. Click the **Pages panel button** on the right side of the workspace to open the Pages panel

   The Pages panel opens, as shown in Figure E-2. The Pages panel is divided into two sections. The top section displays the available master pages, and the lower section displays the document pages. The default A-Master appears in each new document. It is blank. All new pages in a document have the A-Master applied to them by default. Page 1 is highlighted in blue on the Pages panel because it is the active page in the document window.

7. Double-click **A-Master** on the Pages panel

   As shown in Figure E-3, the left and right pages of the A-Master fill the screen. Notice that "A-Master" appears on the left side of the status bar, indicating that the A-Master master page is open in the document window.

8. Double-click the **Page 1 icon** on the Pages panel

   Page 1 appears in the document window. Notice "1" replaces "A-Master" in the page menu on the status bar.

9. Double-click **A-Master** on the Pages panel again, then save the document as **Camp Booklet**

QUICK TIP
Click the Facing Pages check box to remove the check mark if you want to create a multipage document that does not require facing pages, such as flash cards.

TROUBLE
If you do not see all eight pages in the Pages panel, drag the lower-right corner of the panel down until all eight pages are visible.

QUICK TIP
The page icon named [None] in the top section of the Pages panel is used for inserting blank pages into a document.

QUICK TIP
You can also click the arrow next to A-Master in the status bar, and then click the number 1 on the menu to show Page 1 in the document window.

Inserting pages

To add new pages to a document after it has been created, click the Pages Panel options button, click Insert Pages to open the Insert Pages dialog box, and then choose how many pages you would like to insert and their locations. For example, you can choose to insert pages at the beginning or end of the document, or before or after a specific page number. To choose which master page should be applied to the newly inserted pages, click the Master list arrow and then choose the name of a master page before closing the Insert Pages dialog box.

Facing Pages
check box

Landscape
button

FIGURE E-2: Pages panel

Default A-Master

Available master pages

Page 1 selected

Eight document pages

Drag to resize panel, if needed

FIGURE E-3: A-Master in the document window

A-Master is
selected

Left and right
master pages

A-Master
is active

Using Master Pages

Creating Master Items

The objects that you place on master pages are called **master items**. Master items appear on every document page to which the master page is applied. Company logos, page numbers, and empty frames reserved for text and pictures are good examples of master items. If you remove or change a master item on a master page, that item is removed from or changed on the corresponding document pages, as well. Kate would like each page in the booklet to contain a photo and a camp theme title. You add a text box, a graphics frame, and a page number as master items to the left page of the A-Master and then copy them to the right page of the master.

STEPS

1. Click the **Type tool** T. on the Tools panel, create a text box on the left page that is .5 inches wide and .3125 inches in height, click the **Selection tool** , then drag the text box to the location shown in Figure E-4

2. Click T., click inside the text box, click **Type** on the Application bar, point to **Insert Special Character**, point to **Markers**, then click **Current Page Number**

   As shown in Figure E-5, the letter "A" appears in the text box as a placeholder for the page number that will appear on all left document pages. The letter "A" is in the default font and point size, Minion Pro, 12 pt. When the current page number marker is placed on a master, InDesign places consecutive page numbers on each document page to which the master is applied. The dotted line surrounding the text box indicates that it is a master item. You format and align the marker.

3. Double-click the **A** on the left master page to select it, then click the **Align center button** on the Control panel

4. Click **Object** on the Application bar, then click **Text Frame Options**

   The Text Frame Options dialog box opens.

5. Click the **Align list arrow**, click **Center**, then click **OK**

   The text is vertically centered within the text box.

6. Click the **Rectangle Frame tool** on the Tools panel, then create a frame that snaps to the inside of the four margin guides on the left master page (W: 5, H: 3)

   This frame is also a master item. It will be used for the photos that will be placed on each individual page in the booklet.

7. Click on the Tools panel, click the **page number text box**, press and hold **[Shift][Alt]** (Win) or **[Shift][option]** (Mac), click the **rectangle frame**, then drag the **two items** to the right master page, snapping the frame to the four margin guides

   A copy of the page number text box is placed on the right page. Pressing [Alt] (Win) or [option] (Mac) as you drag makes a copy of the object, and pressing [Shift] as you drag constrains an object along its horizontal or vertical axis.

8. Deselect the objects, click the **page number text box** on the right master page, then position it as shown in Figure E-6

   The master items created on the A-Master are automatically placed on all document pages. Notice the dotted outlines on the page icons on the Pages panel. They represent the page number and rectangle frame on each page.

9. **Save your work**

Text box

Page number
placeholder

Dotted line
indicates a
master item

FIGURE E-6: A-Master spread

Dotted outlines of
master items
appear on each
page thumbnail

Move the page
number text
box here

InDesign CS5

Numbering options

You can change the InDesign page numbering style using the Numbering & Section Options dialog box. To open the dialog box, click the Pages Panel options button, then click Numbering & Section Options. Click the Style list arrow, then click a new style, such as a, b, c, d, or 01, 02, 03, and so on. You can also enter a prefix for each page number in the Section Prefix text box, such as "page" or "Page."

You can also have more than one page numbering system in a document. For example, some books begin with a preface section using lowercase Roman numerals (i, ii, iii, and so on), followed by

Chapter 1, which starts on page 1 and uses the numbers 1, 2, 3, and so on. To define a new page numbering section, first activate the document page where the new section should start, click the Pages Panel options button, then click Numbering & Section Options. In the New Section dialog box, click the Start Section check box if necessary, click the Start Page Numbering at option button, and then type a page number. For example, if you choose page 5 in the Pages panel to start a new section, type 1 in the Start Page Numbering at text box to force page 5 to be numbered as page 1.

Overriding Master Items

Some master items do not need to be modified on the document pages on which they're placed. A company logo placed in the corner of a master page is a good example; it would look the same on each page. However, empty text boxes and graphics frames placed on master pages need to be modified on document pages when you type text or place items in them. To modify master items on document pages, you must override them. Overriding a master item is how you unlock the master item on the current page so that you can work with it. You are ready to place pictures of camp activities that Kate has provided for you on the first seven pages of the booklet. The eighth page will serve as the back cover of the booklet and will not include a photo.

STEPS

1. **Double-click 2-3 below the pages 2 and 3 icons on the Pages panel**

   Note that 2-3 is a spread number. Double-clicking a spread number displays the left and right page of a spread in the document window.

2. **Press and hold [Shift][Ctrl] (Win) or [Shift]⌘ (Mac), then click the left frame**

   The frame is selected and ready for editing. Pressing and holding [Shift][Ctrl] (Win) or [Shift]⌘ (Mac) when clicking a master item overrides it.

3. **Click File on the Application bar, click Place, navigate to the drive and folder where you store your Data Files, click Animal Care.jpg, then click Open**

4. **Click the Fill frame proportionally button on the Control panel, click the image, then drag the content indicator to move the image in the frame until your screen resembles Figure E-7**

5. **Double-click the Page 3 icon on the Pages panel, click the Pages Panel options button , then click Override All Master Page Items**

   The master items on the current document page are overridden. The dotted lines around the text box and the rectangle frame on page 3 disappear. Using the Override All Master Page Items command is equivalent to pressing and holding [Shift][Ctrl] (Win) or [Shift]⌘ (Mac) to override a master item.

6. **Place the file Equestrian.jpg in the frame on page 3, then fit and crop the image inside the frame to your liking**

7. **Using the Override All Master Page Items command, place the following images in the frames on each page, then fit and crop the images as necessary for pages 4–7:**

page number	name of picture
4	Hiking.jpg
5	Farming.jpg
6	Ocean.jpg
7	Theatre.jpg

8. **Compare your pages 4–5 to Figure E-8, then save your work**

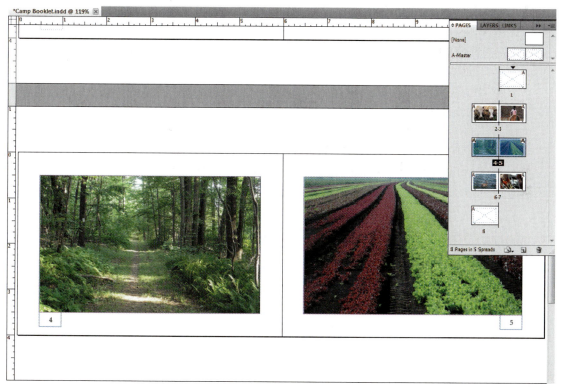

Removing local overrides

Adding a non-master item to a document page that has a master applied, and overriding a master item on a document page, are known as local changes or local overrides. No matter which local overrides you've made on a document page, you can always return to the look of the original master page by removing the local changes. To do so, select the page on the Pages panel from which you want to remove local overrides, click the Pages Panel options button, then click Remove All Local Overrides. All local items disappear and any modifications you made to master items are undone. For example, if you had placed an image in a graphics frame master item, InDesign removes it from the frame.

InDesign CS5

Modifying a Master Page

One of the real benefits of using master pages is that it is easy to change them at any time in the production process. For example, you can change the size of a frame or remove a text box. The changes you make on the master pages are reflected on the document pages. You can also add new master items to the left and right master pages on the A-Master, format the text, and then add titles to each document page that the master page has been assigned. Kate would like the photos to have a caption. You add a guide and a text box to the left and right master pages on the A-Master, format the text and then add titles to each document page.

STEPS

1. **Double-click A-Master on the Pages panel**
   The left and right master pages appear in the workspace.

2. **Place the mouse pointer over the horizontal ruler, press and hold [Ctrl] (Win) or ⌘ (Mac), then click and drag a horizontal guide to the 0.125 in mark on the vertical ruler**
   You'll use the guide to position text boxes on each page. Pressing [Ctrl] (Win) or ⌘ (Mac) creates a spread guide, covering both left and right pages.

3. **Click the Type tool T, on the Tools panel, create a text box that is 3.25 inches wide and 0.35 inches tall, click the Selection tool ▶ on the Tools panel, then drag the text box so that its top snaps to the guide and is located on the left page, as shown in Figure E-9**

4. **Click T, click inside the text box, click the Font style list arrow, click Bold Italic, click the Font size list arrow, click 24 pt, then type Camp Theme**
   Your Control panel should match Figure E-10.

5. **Click ▶, press and hold [Alt] (Win) or [option] (Mac), then drag a copy of the text box so that it snaps to the upper-left corner of the right page**
   The two text boxes will be used on each document page to display the camp theme. Each description will be in the same location and have the same formatting applied.

6. **Double-click 2-3 on the Pages panel**
   Pages 2 and 3 of the document open in the workspace. Each page has the Camp Theme text box applied to it.

7. **Click the Pages Panel options button ▼≡, click Override All Master Page Items, double-click inside the Camp Theme text box on the left to switch to the Type tool, then type Moovin on the Farm**

QUICK TIP
The keyboard short-cut for Override All Master Page Items is [Alt][Shift][Ctrl][L] (Win) or [option] [shift] ⌘[L] (Mac).

8. **Repeat Step 7 to add the following titles to pages 3–7:**

page number	text
3	Horseback Riding
4	The Mighty Hike
5	Garden Greatness
6	Oceanography
7	Performing Arts

9. **Compare pages 6 and 7 to Figure E-11, then save your work**

FIGURE E-9: Positioning the text box

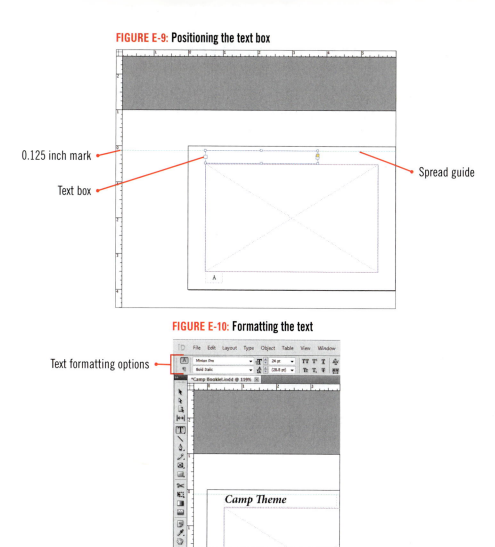

0.125 inch mark

Text box

Spread guide

FIGURE E-10: Formatting the text

Text formatting options

Camp Theme

FIGURE E-11: Pages 6 and 7 of the Camp booklet

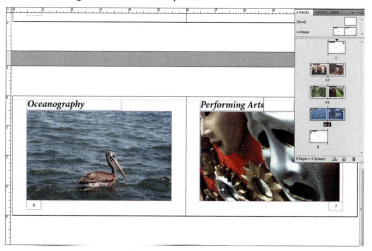

Oceanography

Performing Arts

Moving document pages

Often, you will need to change the order of pages in a document. Moving a page in a document shuffles the pages between the moved page's previous and new locations. For example, if you move page 2 into the page 4 position, page 2 becomes page 4, and pages 3 and 4 are shuffled to become pages 2 and 3. You can move pages in a document by dragging page icons on the Pages panel to new locations on the panel. This works well for short documents; but when you have hundreds of pages in a document, you won't want to scroll through them all to move one or two pages. Instead, you can use the Move Pages command on the Pages Panel options menu. The Move Pages dialog box lets you indicate which pages to move and where to move them.

Creating a New Master Page

InDesign documents can have many master pages for many styles of pages. Sometimes, a new master page is only slightly different from one that already exists. For example, in a magazine you have pages with text and photos, and pages with only text. When you create a new master page, you can base it on one that already exists in the document. When you base a new master on an existing master, you start off with an exact copy of the existing master with all of its master items. This allows you to keep the master items (such as page numbers) that you want, delete any master items that you do not want, and modify the master items as necessary. You create a new master page based on the A-Master, then modify the new master that Kate can use for the front cover of the booklet.

STEPS

1. Click the **Pages Panel options button** , then click **New Master**

   The New Master dialog box opens. The default prefix assigned to the master is B and the default name for the new master is Master.

2. Double-click **Master** in the Name text box, then type **Front Cover**

3. Click the **Based on Master list arrow**, then click **A-Master**

> **QUICK TIP**
> To view all of the master pages, drag the double-line between the master pages and the document pages on the Pages panel to resize the top section.

4. Press **[Tab]**, type **1** in the Number of Pages text box, compare your New Master dialog box to Figure E-12, then click **OK**

   Entering 1 in the Number of Pages text box creates a single-page master. The new B-Front Cover master page appears in the top section of the Pages panel, as shown in Figure E-13. The "A" on the B-Front Cover master page icon indicates that it is based on the A-Master. The B-Front Cover master page becomes the active page in the document window. You're ready to customize the B-Front Cover master.

5. Click the **Pages Panel options button** , then click **Override All Master Page Items**

   Like master items on document pages, master items on master pages that are based on another master page are locked and must be overridden to be deleted or modified.

> **QUICK TIP**
> The page number text box has the letter "B" in it as a page number placeholder.

6. Click the **Selection tool** on the Tools panel, click the **page number text box**, then press **[Delete]**

   The Front Cover master page no longer has a page number placeholder.

7. Drag the **Camp Theme text box** so that it snaps to the left and bottom margin guides, resize it so that it is as wide as the graphics frame, type **BreakTime – Summer 2014** in the text box, then click the **Align center button** on the Control panel

8. Click , click the **graphics frame**, drag the **bottom-middle selection handle** up until the height of the graphics frame is 2.5 inches, then compare your screen to Figure E-14

9. Save your work

Master text frames

If you are planning to create a document with text on every page, you want to create the document with a master text frame on every page. A **master text frame** is a text box master item added to the A-Master when a new document is created. The size of the master text frame is determined by the page size and margins defined in the New Document dialog box. The text box fills the entire page, snapping to the four margin guides. For example, if you create an 8.5" x 11" document with 1-inch page margins, the master text frame will be 6.5" x 9". To create a master text frame, click the Master Text Frame check box in the New Document dialog box when creating a new document. When the new document opens, the A-Master contains a master text frame and is applied to every page in the document.

FIGURE E-13: Pages panel with new B-Front Cover Master

New single master page

Drag to resize sections

"A" indicates that the B-Front Cover master page is based on the A-Master

FIGURE E-14: Modified Front Cover master page

Height of frame

Drag handle to resize frame

BreakTime - Summer 2014

InDesign CS5

Applying Master Pages

All new pages in a document have the A-Master applied to them by default, but it is simple to apply a master page other than the A-Master to a document page. To do this, drag the master page icon on the Pages panel to the document page icon on the Pages panel. You can also apply master pages to document pages using the Apply Master to Pages command on the Pages panel menu. To finish formatting the pages in the Camp booklet, you apply the B-Front Cover master page to page 1 of the booklet and then apply a blank master (None) to the last page of the booklet.

STEPS

1. **Double-click the page 1 icon on the Pages panel**

   Page 1 has the right page of the A-Master applied to it by default.

2. **Drag the B-Front Cover master page icon from the top section of the Pages panel over the page 1 icon in the lower section of the Pages panel until the page 1 icon is outlined in black, as shown in Figure E-16, then release the mouse button**

   Page 1 has the B-Front Cover master page applied to it, as indicated by the "B" on its page icon, and the B-Front Cover text.

3. **Click the Selection tool ▶ on the Tools panel, press and hold [Shift][Ctrl] (Win) or [Shift] ⌘(Mac), then click the frame to select it**

4. **Click File on the Application bar, click Place, click Camp.jpg, then click Open**

5. **Fit and center the image in the frame so that it resembles the placement shown in Figure E-17**

6. **Drag the [None] page icon from the top section of the Pages panel over the page 8 icon in the lower section of the Pages panel, then release the mouse button**

   The last page of the booklet becomes a blank page.

7. **Save your work**

Using options on the Pages Panel menu

To customize the Pages panel, click the Pages Panel options button, then click Panel Options to open the Panel Options dialog box, as shown in Figure E-15. In the Pages and Masters sections of the dialog box, choose a size for page and master icons by clicking the Size list arrow, then clicking a size. The Show Vertically and Show Thumbnails check boxes in the Pages and Masters sections control how the icons in the panel are displayed. If you remove the Show Vertically check mark, the page icons in the Pages panel will be displayed horizontally; you will only be able to resize the width of the Pages panel, not the height. If you remove the Show Thumbnails check mark, the page icons will be blank in the Pages panel. The Icons section of the dialog box defines which additional icons appear next to the page icons. For example, if the Transparency check box is checked, a small checkerboard icon appears next to the page icon where transparency has been applied to master items. Finally, in the Panel Layout section, you can choose whether you want masters or document pages on top of the panel.

FIGURE E-15: Panel Options dialog box

FIGURE E-16: B-Front Cover master applied to page 1

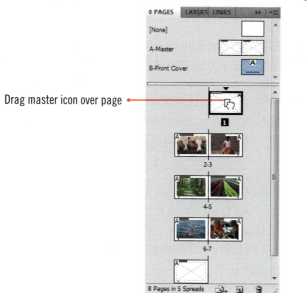

Drag master icon over page

FIGURE E-17: Front cover of Camp booklet

BreakTime - Summer 2014

InDesign CS5

Detaching master items

When you make a change to a master item on a master page, the change is reflected on all document pages. For example, if you change a square graphics frame to a circular graphics frame on the master page, all of the square frames on the document pages will change to circles. However, you can **detach** a master item on a document page so that any changes made to the master item on the master page will not affect the detached master item on the document page. To detach a master item on a document page, select it, click the Pages Panel options button, then click Detach Selection from Master. Detaching a master item is not the same as overriding a master item. Unlike master items that are overridden, detached master items are no longer affected by any changes made to the master page.

UNIT E

InDesign CS5

Working with Master Pages

The Pages Panel options menu is loaded with commands for working with master pages. You can insert and delete master pages and document pages, move document pages, apply color labels to document pages, load master pages from other InDesign documents, find unused master pages, and even save document pages as master pages. You apply color labels to pages in the Pages panel to indicate to Kate which artwork is final and which artwork may change, and then save pages 2 and 3 as a new master page to use in future documents.

STEPS

1. **Click the page 1 icon on the Pages panel, press and hold [Ctrl] (Win) or ⌘ (Mac), click the page 5 icon, and then click the page 6 icon**

   The three page icons are selected on the Pages panel. The artwork on these three document pages may change and Kate would like you to apply a gold label to them as a reminder.

2. **Click the Pages Panel options button, point to Color Label, then click Gold**

   A gold label appears beneath page icons 1, 5, and 6, as shown in Figure E-18.

3. **Click the page 2 icon, press and hold [Ctrl] (Win) or ⌘ (Mac), then click pages 3, 4, and 7**

   Kate would like you to apply a blue label to these icons to indicate that these pages are final.

4. **Click, point to Color Label, then click Blue**

   The icons have a blue label applied to them.

5. **Double-click 2-3 on the Pages panel to open pages 2 and 3 in the document window**

   You are going to save pages 2 and 3 as a new master page that can be used in the future for similar documents.

6. **Click, then click Save as Master**

   A new master named C-Master appears at the top of the Pages panel, as shown in Figure E-19. To use the C-Master in the future, you would load the master page into a new InDesign document using the Load Master command on the Pages Panel options menu.

7. **Double-click 6-7 on the Pages panel, deselect all, then close the Pages panel**

8. **Press [W] to hide all guides, then compare your pages to Figure E-20**

9. **Save your work, then exit InDesign**

> **QUICK TIP**
>
> To delete a master page, select the master on the Pages panel, and then click the Delete selected pages button on the Pages panel.

Loading master pages

To load a master page from one document to another, create a new InDesign document with the same size dimensions as that of the master page you plan to load. In the new document, click the Pages Panel options button, then click Load Master Pages. The Open a File dialog box opens for you to navigate to and select the InDesign document that has the master page you wish to load. If the document has more than one master page, all of the master pages are loaded. After the master pages are loaded, you can delete those that you do not need by dragging them from the Pages panel to the Delete selected pages button on the panel. If any of the master pages in the new document and the document being opened share the same name, you will be prompted to replace the existing master page(s) in the new document with the masters that are being loaded or rename the existing master pages.

Gold color label

C-Master

Completed label colors

FIGURE E-20: Pages 6 and 7 of the Camp booklet

Oceanography

Performing Arts

6

7

Preventing shuffling

Some multipage documents have spreads that must not be shuffled when other pages are moved. To keep the pages in a spread from being shuffled, select the spread on the Pages panel, click the Pages Panel options button, then click Allow Selected Spread to Shuffle to remove the check mark. A set of brackets surrounds the page numbers of the spread, indicating that the spread will not be shuffled when pages are moved. If a page is moved before or after one of the pages in a spread, it will be added to the spread. These types of spreads are known as **island spreads**. Island spreads can include as many as 10 document pages.

Practice

For current SAM information, including versions and content details, visit SAM Central (http://www.cengage.com/samcentral). If you have a SAM user profile, you may have access to hands-on instruction, practice, and assessment of the skills covered in this unit. Since various versions of SAM are supported throughout the life of this text, check with your instructor for the correct instructions and URL/Web site for accessing assignments.

Concepts Review

Label the elements of the InDesign screen shown in Figure E-21.

FIGURE E-21

1. _____
2. _____
3. _____

4. _____
5. _____

Match each term with the statement that best describes it.

6. **Shuffle**
7. **Current page number**
8. **Override**
9. **Load**
10. **Spread number**

a. Unlock
b. 4-5
c. Get a master page from another document
d. A special character known as a marker
e. Change the order of pages

Select the best answer from the list of choices.

11. **What type of document would not require facing pages?**
    - **a.** Magazine
    - **b.** Business card
    - **c.** Catalog
    - **d.** Book

12. **Which keys do you use to override an individual master item?**
    - **a.** [Alt][Ctrl] (Win) or [option]⌘ (Mac)
    - **b.** [Shift][Ctrl] (Win) or [Shift]⌘ (Mac)
    - **c.** [Ctrl] (Win) or ⌘ (Mac)
    - **d.** [Alt] (Win) or [option] (Mac)

13. **Which punctuation marks appear around a spread that is not allowed to shuffle?**
    - **a.** Quotation marks
    - **b.** Parentheses
    - **c.** Asterisks
    - **d.** Brackets

Skills Review

1. **Create a multipage document.**
   - **a.** Start InDesign, click File on the Application bar, point to New, then click Document.
   - **b.** Type **6** in the Number of Pages text box, then verify that the Facing Pages check box is checked.
   - **c.** Double-click the Width value, type **6**, press [Tab], type **8** as the Height value, press [Tab], verify that the Portrait button is selected, then click OK to close the New Document dialog box.
   - **d.** Click the workspace switcher on the Application bar, then click Reset Essentials.
   - **e.** Click the Pages panel button on the right side of the workspace to open the Pages panel.
   - **f.** Double-click A-Master on the Pages panel.
   - **g.** Double-click the Page 1 icon on the Pages panel.
   - **h.** Double-click A-Master on the Pages panel again, then save the document as **Desserts**.

2. **Create master items.**
   - **a.** Click the Type tool on the Tools panel, create a text box on the left page that is 0.5 inches wide and 0.5 inches in height, click the Selection tool, then drag the text box so that its top snaps to the bottom margin guide. (*Hint*: Try to align the left side of the text box with the left margin guide.)
   - **b.** Click the Type tool, click inside the text box, click Type on the Application bar, point to Insert Special Character, point to Markers, then click Current Page Number.
   - **c.** Double-click the A on the left master page to select it, then click the Align center button on the Control panel.
   - **d.** Click Object on the Application bar, then click Text Frame Options.
   - **e.** Click the Align list arrow, click Center, then click OK.
   - **f.** Click the Rectangle Frame tool on the Tools panel, then create a frame that snaps to the inside of the four margin guides on the left master page (W: 5, H: 7). Click the Selection tool on the Tools panel, click the page number text box, press and hold [Shift][Alt] (Win) or [Shift][option] (Mac), click the rectangle frame, then drag the two items to the right master page, snapping the frame to the four margin guides.
   - **g.** Deselect the objects, click the page number text box on the right master page, then position it on the right side of the page so that its right edge aligns with the right margin guide.
   - **h.** Save your work.

3. **Override master items.**
   - **a.** Double-click 2-3 below the page 2 and 3 icons on the Pages panel.
   - **b.** Press and hold [Shift][Ctrl] (Win) or [Shift]⌘ (Mac), then click the left frame.
   - **c.** Click File on the Application bar, click Place, navigate to the drive and folder where you store your Data Files, open the Desserts folder, click Chocolate Caramel Pie.jpg, then click Open.
   - **d.** Click the Fill frame proportionally button on the Control panel, click the image, then drag the content to move the image in the frame until it is cropped to your liking.
   - **e.** Double-click the Page 3 icon on the Pages panel, click the Pages Panel options button, then click Override All Master Page Items.
   - **f.** Place the file Fruit Tart.jpg from the Desserts folder in the frame on page 3, then fit and crop the image inside the frame to your liking.

Skills Review (continued)

g. Using the Override All Master Page Items command, place the following images in the frames on each page, then fit and crop the images as necessary for pages 4–5:

page number	name of picture
4	Cupcakes.jpg
5	Strawberry Shortcake.jpg

h. Save your work.

4. Modify a master page.

a. Double-click A-Master on the Pages panel.

b. Click the Type tool on the Tools panel, then create a text box that is 3.25 inches wide and 0.35 inches tall.

c. Click the Selection tool on the Tools panel, then drag the text box so that it sits on the top margin guide and is located on the left page. (*Hint*: Try to align the left side of the text box with the left margin guide.)

d. Click the Type tool, click inside the text box, then type **Name of Dessert**.

e. Select all of the text, click the Font style list arrow, click Medium, click the Font size list arrow, then click 24 pt.

f. Click the Selection tool on the Tools panel, press and hold [Alt] (Win) or [option] (Mac), then drag a copy of the text box so that it snaps to the top-left corner of the right page.

g. Double-click 2-3 on the Pages panel.

h. Click the Pages Panel options button, then click Override All Master Page Items.

i. Double-click inside the Name of Dessert text box on page 2 to switch to the Type tool, then type **Chocolate Caramel Pie**.

j. Repeat Steps g–h to add the following titles to pages 3–5:

page number	text
3	Fruit Tart
4	Cupcakes
5	Strawberry Shortcake

k. Save your work.

5. Create a new master page.

a. Click the Pages Panel options button, then click New Master.

b. Double-click Master in the Name text box, then type **Front Cover**.

c. Click the Based on Master list arrow, then click A-Master.

d. Press [Tab], type 1 in the Number of Pages text box, then click OK.

e. Click the Pages Panel options button, then click Override All Master Page Items.

f. Click the Selection tool on the Tools panel, click the page number text box with the letter "B," then press [Delete].

g. Drag the Name of Dessert text box so that its top snaps to the left and bottom margin guides, resize it so that it is as wide as the graphics frame, then type **Dessert Menu** in the text box.

h. Click the Selection tool on the Tools panel, click the graphics frame, drag the bottom-middle selection handle up until the height of the graphics frame is 6.25 inches, then save your work.

6. Apply master pages.

a. Double-click the page 1 icon on the Pages panel.

b. Drag the B-Front Cover master page icon from the top section of the Pages panel over the page 1 icon in the lower section of the Pages panel until the page 1 icon is outlined in black, then release the mouse button.

c. Click the Pages Panel options button, then click Override All Master Page Items.

d. Click the Selection tool on the Tools panel, then click the frame to select it.

e. Click File on the Application bar, click Place, click Cheesecake.jpg, then click Open.

f. Fit and center the image in the frame to your liking.

g. Drag the [None] page icon from the top section of the Pages panel over the page 6 icon in the lower section of the Pages panel, then release the mouse button.

h. Save your work.

Skills Review (continued)

7. Work with master pages.

  a. Click the page 1 icon on the Pages panel, press and hold [Ctrl] (Win) or ⌘ (Mac), then click the page 4 icon.

  b. Click the Pages Panel options button, point to Color Label, then click Yellow.

FIGURE E-22

  c. Click the page 2 icon, press and hold [Ctrl] (Win) or ⌘ (Mac), then click pages 3 and 5.

  d. Click the Pages Panel options button, point to Color Label, then click Red.

  e. Double-click 2-3 on the Pages panel to open pages 2 and 3 in the document window.

  f. Click the Pages Panel options button, then click Save as Master.

  g. Double-click 4-5 on the Pages panel, deselect all, then press [W] to hide all guides.

  h. Close the Pages panel, then compare your pages to Figure E-22.

  i. Save your work, then exit InDesign.

Cupcakes Strawberry Shortcake

Independent Challenge 1

You are spending your senior year in Italy teaching English to young children. You want to create a set of flash cards with the alphabet on one side for your students to use. You use InDesign to create the flash cards.

  a. Start InDesign and open the New Document dialog box.

  b. In the New Document dialog box, deselect the Facing Pages check box, change the Number of Pages to **26**, change the Width to **4** inches and the Height to **6** inches, then click OK.

  c. Save the document as **Flash Cards**.

  d. Open the A-Master master page in the document window.

FIGURE E-23

  e. Create a text box on the A-Master master page that snaps to all four margin guides. (*Hint*: The width of the text box should be 3 inches and the height of the text box should be 5 inches.)

  f. Insert the Current Page Number placeholder into the text box on the master page.

  g. Format the letter "A" on the master page using any font and large font size that you think would be appropriate for a flash card. (*Hint*: The font size in Figure E-23 is 108 points.)

  h. Center the "A" horizontally in the text box, then center the "A" vertically in the text box using the Text Frame Options dialog box.

  i. Activate page 1 in the document window.

  j. Click the Pages Panel options button, then click Numbering & Section Options.

  k. In the Page Numbering area of the Numbering & Section Options dialog box, click the Style list arrow, then click A, B, C, D....

  l. Click OK to close the Numbering & Section Options dialog box.

  m. Double-click the page B icon, then compare your screen to Figure E-23.

  n. Save your work, then exit InDesign.

B

Independent Challenge 2

You work for a graphic design company and are preparing an annual report for a new client. The client would like to see samples of text styles using different fonts and leading amounts. You create three sample pages in InDesign, then save them as three master pages.

a. Start InDesign, then create a new 8.5" × 11", three-page document without facing pages.

b. Save the document as **Text Samples**.

c. Activate the A-Master in the document window.

d. Create a text box on the A-Master that snaps to all four margin guides.

e. Click the Type tool, click inside the text box, then change the font size to 11 pt.

f. Click Type on the Application bar, then click Fill with Placeholder Text.

g. Activate page 1 in the document window.

FIGURE E-24

h. Override the text box master item to select it, select all of the text in the text box on page 1, then change the font and the leading value. (*Hint*: Use the Character panel to change the leading value. Do not resize the text box if the overset text icon appears.)

i. Repeat Step h for page 2 and page 3 using different fonts and leading values.

j. Save each page as a master page and name each new master using the font name chosen for that page.

k. Apply the B-Master to page 1, the C-Master to page 2, and the D-Master to page 3.

l. Delete the A-Master by dragging it to the Delete selected pages button on the Pages panel.

m. Compare one of your pages and your Pages panel to Figure E-24.

Advanced Challenge Exercise

- Click the Pages Panel options button, then click Insert Pages.
- In the Insert Pages dialog box, insert two pages after page 3 and apply the C-Master to the two new pages.
- Click OK to close the Insert Pages dialog box.

n. Save your work, then exit InDesign.

Independent Challenge 3

You work for a gift shop and would like to sell your own product: a flip book of daily quotes and inspirations taken from movies. You use InDesign to create the prototype.

a. Start InDesign and create a new 4" × 3", 366-page document with facing pages and a landscape orientation. (*Hint*: One page will be used for the front cover.)

b. Save the document as **Quotes**.

c. Activate the A-Master in the document window.

d. Create two text boxes on the left page (one for the page number and one for the quote) and place them where you want.

e. Insert an automatic page number placeholder in the text box designated for the page number and then format the page number.

f. Create a title placeholder, such as "quote," in the quote text box, then format the text using the font, size, and style of your choice.

g. Copy the two text boxes to the right page.

h. Rename the A-Master as **Quote Master**.

i. Create a new master based on the Quote Master, name it **Cover**, and change it to a one-page master.

j. Remove the page number text box on the Cover master, then type **Famous Movie Quotes** in the text box.

k. Format the text to your liking, then apply the Cover master to page 1.

l. Add any design elements that you wish using the basic shape tools.

m. Apply a color label to page 1 to differentiate it from the other pages.

n. Compare your first page to Figure E-25, then save your work.

FIGURE E-25

Advanced Challenge Exercise

- Display page 1 in the document window, if necessary.
- Override the text box on page 1.
- Click the Pages Panel options button, then click Detach Selection from Master.

o. Close the Quotes document, then exit InDesign.

Real Life Independent Challenge

You have graduated from college with a degree in photography and have started looking for a job in your field. You decide to create a booklet that contains samples of your photography. You'll use this booklet as your portfolio when applying for jobs.

a. Start InDesign and create a new six-page document with facing pages and any page size that you like.

b. Save the document as **Portfolio**.

c. Format the left and right master pages with automatic page numbering, one graphics frame (any shape), and one text box that will serve as a title for each piece of artwork.

d. Format the text boxes and the graphics frame any way that you wish.

e. On pages 2 through 6 in the document, override the graphics frame on each page and place a picture in the frame using any of your own photographs. (If you do not have any photos, you can use pictures from your Data Files folders.)

f. On pages 2 through 6, override the text box on each page and type a descriptive title in it for each picture.

g. Create a new master based on the A-Master and name it **Cover**, then change it to a single-page master.

h. Delete the page number from the Cover master page, make any other changes that you want to the master, then apply it to page 1. A graphics frame on the Cover master page is optional.

i. Add any local formatting you wish, such as strokes around the frames, to the document pages.

j. View the document window without guides, save your work, then exit InDesign.

Visual Workshop

Create a new 8.5" 3 11", three-page document with facing pages and 1-inch margins, then save it as **Master Pages**. Activate the A-Master in the document and create the master items shown in Figure E-26 on the left and right pages of the master. The text box is 0.5 inches in height, and the font and font size used in the text box are Minion Pro, 30 pt. The frame on each page is 6.5" 3 8". Rename the A-Master Photo Pages, compare your screen to Figure E-26, save your work, then exit InDesign.

FIGURE E-26

Working with Layers

Layers are the levels within an InDesign document on which objects appear. You can organize InDesign objects of the same type onto separate layers. For example, you can place all text boxes on a layer named Text and all graphics on a different layer named Graphics. There are many benefits to using layers. You can hide and show layers, lock and unlock layers, and even suppress the printing of specific layers. To work with layers, you use the Layers panel. Ted, your client at the Happy Apple, needs a poster for an upcoming sales meeting that displays store locations across the United States. You create the poster in InDesign and use the Layers panel to organize the poster artwork.

OBJECTIVES

Place an object on a layer

Change layer options

Create a new layer

Duplicate a layer

Lock and hide a layer

Move an object to another layer

Change layer order

Placing an Object on a Layer

Each new InDesign document starts out with an empty layer, named Layer 1, on the Layers panel. When you add an item to the document, whether by placing it or by creating it in InDesign, it is automatically placed as a **page item** on Layer 1 on the Layers panel. Each additional item you place or create in InDesign is also placed on Layer 1 but on one level higher than the last page item. You can view all of the objects and the order that they are stacked on a layer by expanding the layer. You create a new InDesign document, place a map graphic and some text in the document, then view the two page items on Layer 1 in the Layers panel.

STEPS

1. **Start InDesign, create a new 8.5" × 11" document without facing pages and with a landscape orientation, then save it as Store Locations**

2. **Click the workspace switcher, click Reset Essentials, then click the Layers panel icon 🔷 to open the Layers panel**

   The Layers panel opens with the default layer, Layer 1, highlighted. The pen icon next to Layer 1 on the Layers panel is called the Indicates current drawing layer icon 🖉, and it indicates the active layer. Anything added to the InDesign document is added to whichever layer is active on the Layers panel.

3. **Click the Rectangle Frame tool ⊠ on the Tools panel, then create a rectangle frame that snaps to all four margin guides**

   Your rectangle frame should be 10 inches wide and 7.5 inches tall.

4. **On the Layers panel, click the expand layer arrow ▷ pointing to Layer 1 to expand Layer 1**

   As shown in Figure F-1, the rectangle is the first item on Layer 1. The name <rectangle> is assigned to the object.

5. **Click the Selection tool ▶ on the Tools panel, click File on the Application bar, click Place, navigate to the drive and folder where you store your Data Files, click USAmap.ai, then click Open**

   A map of the United States appears in the frame. You are going to resize the map so that it fits the frame proportionally and then improve its display performance.

6. **Click the Fit content proportionally button 🔳 on the Control panel, click Object on the Application bar, point to Display Performance, then click High Quality Display**

   The map fits the frame proportionally and is displayed at a higher quality. The name <USAmap.ai> replaces the name <rectangle> on the Layers panel because the map now fills the frame. The map and the frame are considered one item.

7. **Deselect the map frame, click File on the Application bar, click Place, click Legend.doc, then click Open**

   The loaded cursor appears showing a thumbnail view of the text that will be placed.

8. **Click in the approximate location shown in Figure F-2 to place the map legend text in the lower-left corner of the document window**

   The legend text is added to the top of Layer 1. The name assigned to the Legend.doc page item is "Legend," followed by the first few words in the document. It is one level higher than the USAmap.ai page item on Layer 1 because it was placed after the map artwork was placed. In the document window, the legend text box is above the rectangle frame.

9. **Save your work**

> **QUICK TIP**
> High Quality Display may require more system resources. Fast Display replaces each graphic with a gray fill in order to improve speed performance when working in InDesign. Display settings do not affect print quality.

> **TROUBLE**
> If you do not dese-lect the map frame before placing the text, the text will be placed into the map frame, replacing the map. If this hap-pens, undo your last step, deselect, and then repeat Steps 7 and 8.

FIGURE F-1: Viewing the rectangle frame on Layer 1

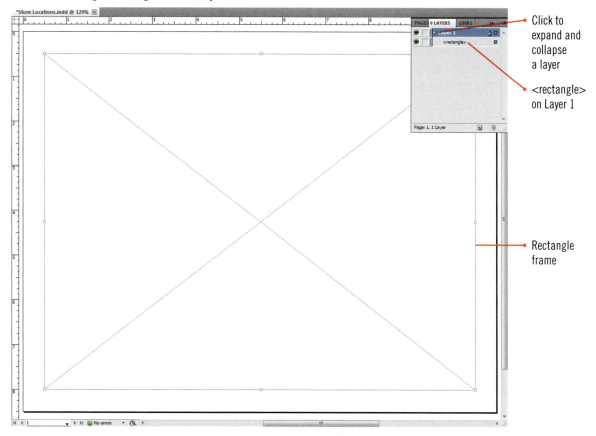

Click to expand and collapse a layer

<rectangle> on Layer 1

Rectangle frame

FIGURE F-2: Layers panel

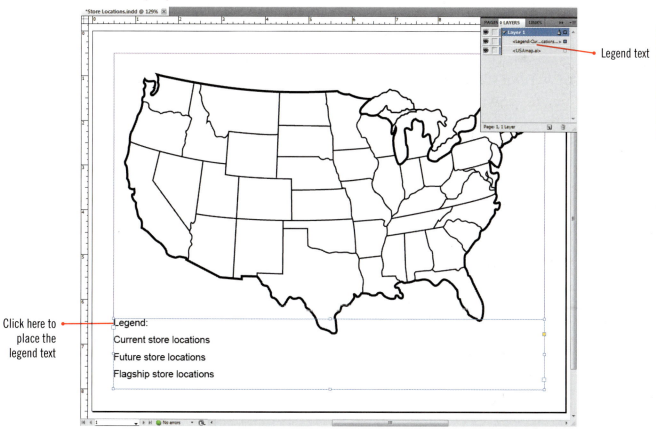

Legend text

Click here to place the legend text

InDesign CS5

Changing Layer Options

Each layer on the Layers panel has a unique selection color assigned to it. The **selection color** of a layer is the color of the bounding box that appears around selected objects on that layer. For example, the selection color for Layer 1 is Light Blue. When you select items on Layer 1, their selection color is Light Blue. You can change the selection color for a layer if you want to color-code your layers. You can also change the name of a layer. Naming layers is helpful to describe a layer's content, especially if you use layers to organize your document elements. For example, when creating a newsletter, you may want to place all text objects on a layer named Text. Ted asks you to name each layer and color-code it so that other employees will be able to easily identify the document items in your absence. You use the Layers panel to rename Layer 1 and change its selection color.

STEPS

1. **Click the Layers Panel options button** ▾≣**, then click Layer Options for "Layer 1"**
   The Layer Options dialog box opens. In this dialog box, you can change the name of Layer 1, change its selection color, and adjust other layer options. Layers are automatically named by InDesign using the next consecutive number: Layer 1, Layer 2, Layer 3, and so on.

> **QUICK TIP**
> You can also open the Layer Options dialog box by double-clicking a layer name on the Layers panel.

2. **Type United States Map in the Name text box**
   This layer will be for the map artwork and the legend. The name of the layer will make the layer easy to locate in the future after more layers are added.

3. **Click the Color list arrow, click Black, then compare your Layer Options dialog box to Figure F-3**
   The bounding box of selected objects on the United States Map layer will be Black instead of the default color, Light Blue. Because the map is black and the legend text is black, it makes sense to change the selection color to Black.

4. **Click OK to close the Layer Options dialog box**
   The changes made to Layer 1 appear on the Layers panel.

5. **Click the Selection tool** ▸ **on the Tools panel, if necessary, then click the map image**
   As shown in Figure F-4, the bounding box of the map has a black selection color. A small black square called the Indicates selected items icon ▪ appears filled in the layer color next to the Indicates current drawing layer icon ⬠ on the United States Map layer and next to <USAmap.ai> to indicate that the map is selected on the artboard.

6. **Click the Hand tool** ✋ **on the Tools panel, then drag the document window left so that the right side of the map is not blocked by the Layers panel**

7. **Deselect all, then save your work**

Selecting page items

When working on an InDesign document that you are unfamiliar with, it is likely that you will not know which items on the artboard correspond with a page item on the Layers panel. To find out what a page item is referring to, select the page item on the Layers panel, click the Layers Panel options button, then click Select Item(s). The object or objects become selected in the document window. To select items and fit them in the window to see them more clearly, choose Select and Fit Item instead. Selecting a layer is also referred to as **targeting** the layer.

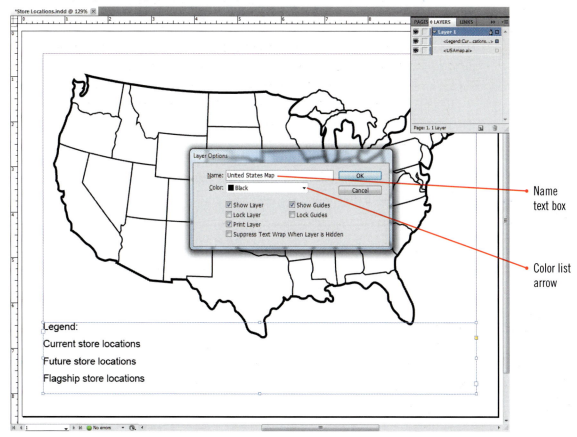

Name text box

Color list arrow

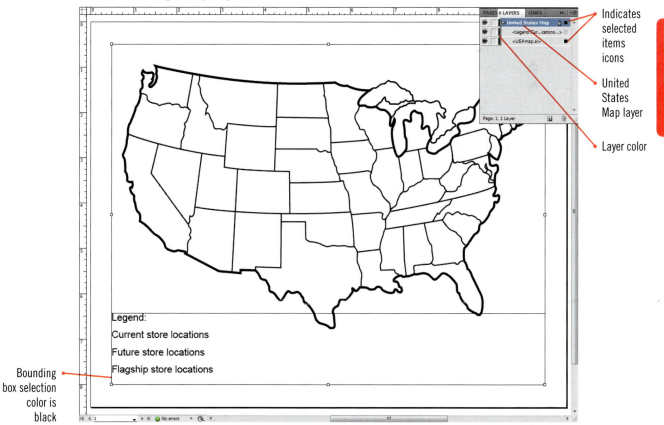

Indicates selected items icons

United States Map layer

Layer color

Bounding box selection color is black

Creating a New Layer

Having more than one layer in a document helps you keep your InDesign objects organized. Once items are on individual layers, you can hide and show those layers to view different versions of the same document. Placing items on individual layers also makes it easy to select those items in one step. If you press [Alt] (Win) or [option] (Mac) while clicking a layer on the Layers panel, all items on that layer are selected. There are two ways to create new layers. You can click the Create new layer button on the Layers panel or click the Layers Panel options button, then click New Layer. The New Layer dialog box is identical to the Layer Options dialog box. You create a new layer in the Store Locations document on which to put artwork that represents current Happy Apple store locations. By placing the current store artwork on its own layer, you'll be able to work with it as a unit.

STEPS

QUICK TIP

If you click the Create new layer button on the Layers panel to create a new layer, the New Layer dialog box does not open; instead, the new layer is automatically assigned a color, named with the next consecutive layer number, and placed at the top of the Layers panel.

1. **Click the Layers Panel options button ▼≡, then click New Layer**

   The New Layer dialog box opens, where you can choose a name and selection color for the layer before it appears on the Layers panel.

2. **Type Current Store Locations in the Name text box, click the Color list arrow, click Green, then click OK to close the New Layer dialog box**

   As shown in Figure F-5, the new layer is placed above the United States Map layer. New layers are automatically placed above the currently selected layer on the Layers panel. The order of layers on the Layers panel represents the same order of objects on those layers in the document window. Objects on the Current Store Locations layer will be on top of or "in front" of the objects on the United States Map layer in the document.

3. **Click and hold the Rectangle tool ▭ on the Tools panel until you see a menu of tools, then click the Ellipse tool ⬭.**

4. **Click the page to open the Ellipse dialog box, type .25 in the Width text box, press [Tab], type .25 in the Height text box, then click OK**

   A small circle appears on the page. The circle will represent current store locations on the map. The circle has a green selection color because it was created when the Current Store Locations layer was the active layer.

5. **Click the Zoom tool 🔍 on the Tools panel, then click the circle to enlarge your view**

6. **Click the Fill button ⬚ on the Tools panel, click the Swatches panel button ▦ on the right side of the workspace to open the Swatches panel, then scroll down and click C=75 M=5 Y=100 K=0 (green)**

   The circle's fill color changes to green.

7. **Click the Stroke button ⬚ on the Tools panel, then click [None] on the Swatches panel, if necessary**

QUICK TIP

Press [Alt] (Win) or [option] (Mac), then click a layer on the Layers panel to select all of the objects on that layer.

8. **Click the Selection tool ▸ on the Tools panel, then drag the circle to the approximate location shown in Figure F-6 (Maine)**

9. **Press and hold [Alt] (Win) or [option] (Mac), click and drag the circle in a downward direction to create a copy of it as shown in Figure F-7, create two more copies of the circle, and place them in the approximate locations in New England shown in Figure F-8**

   The four green circles represent the four current store locations in New England.

10. **Save your work**

Using the Arrange commands with multiple layers

When you have more than one layer in an InDesign document, the Arrange commands (Send to Back, Bring to Front, Send Backward, and Bring Forward) are applied only to the page items on the currently active layer on the Layers panel. For example, if you have three page items on Layer 3 and you send one of them to the back using the Send to Back command, it will go to the bottom of the stack of the three page items on Layer 3, rather than to the back of all of the objects in the document.

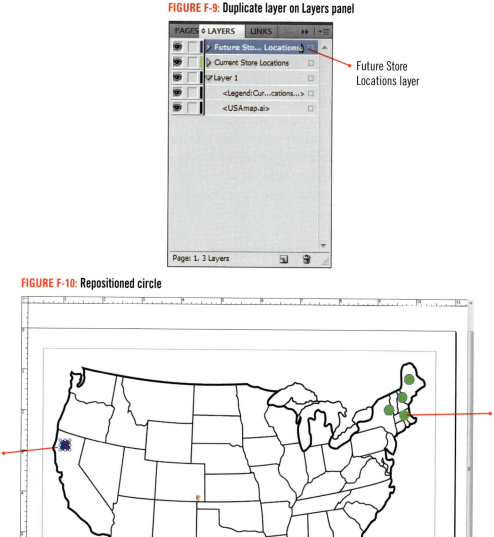

Future Store
Locations layer

Circle on the
Current Store
Locations layer
is now visible

Repositioned
circle on the
Future Store
Locations layer

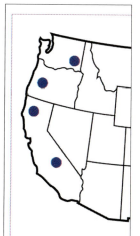

InDesign CS5

Locking and Hiding a Layer

You can lock and hide an entire layer or individual page items on a layer. Locking protects the entire layer or the page items on a layer from being moved, selected, or deleted accidently. InDesign documents can become complicated quickly, especially when you are creating a document with lots of detailed objects, such as a street map or a diagram. Objects on locked layers cannot be selected, so they also cannot be moved or deleted. You can also temporarily hide and show layers or page items on layers. Hiding layers can help you focus on one layer without being distracted by the objects on other layers. It also helps you to see what the document would look like without the objects on that layer, without having to delete those objects. You check the accuracy of your map by hiding and showing each layer, then you lock the United States Map page item to make sure that it does not get moved or deleted by accident.

STEPS

1. **Show the Layers panel, if necessary, then click the Toggles visibility icon 👁 to the left of the Future Store Locations layer on the Layers panel**

   As shown in Figure F-12, the Future Store Locations layer is hidden from view and the dark blue circles on the layer are no longer visible. When you hide the currently active layer, 👁 disappears and a red slash appears through the Indicates current drawing layer icon 🖊. Nothing can be placed or created on a hidden layer.

> **QUICK TIP**
> You can hide and lock guides on individual layers by opening the Layer Options dialog box for a layer, then clicking the Lock Guides and/or Show Guides check boxes.

2. **Click 👁 to the left of the Current Store Locations layer on the Layers panel**

   The green circles on the Current Store Locations layer are hidden from view in the document. Hiding multiple layers is a good way to check if InDesign objects are placed on the layers they are supposed to be placed on. For example, if one green circle was still in view after the Current Store Locations layer was hidden, that would indicate that the green circle was on the United States Map layer by mistake.

3. **Click 👁 to the left of the United States Map layer on the Layers panel**

   All three layers in the document are hidden and the document is blank.

> **QUICK TIP**
> Press and hold [Alt] (Win) or [option] (Mac), then click the Toggles visibility icon 👁 next to a layer to hide all other layers in the panel. Repeat to show all other layers again.

4. **Click the empty gray square where 👁 once was next to each of the three layers on the Layers panel**

   The 👁 icon reappears next to all three layers, and the map, green circles, and dark blue circles reappear.

5. **Click the empty gray square between 👁 and the <USAmap.ai> object on the United States Map layer on the Layers panel, as shown in Figure F-13**

   As shown in Figure F-14, the Toggles page item lock icon 🔒 appears, indicating that the layer is locked. If you wanted to lock the legend text, too, you would lock the United States Map layer. When you lock a layer, all page items on that layer are locked.

6. **Click the Selection tool ▸, if necessary, then click the map image on the page**

   As long as the United States Map layer is locked, the map image on the layer cannot be selected or changed.

> **QUICK TIP**
> Clicking the Toggles visibility icon 👁 and the Toggles page item lock icon 🔒 on the Layers panel is equivalent to selecting the Show Layer and Lock Layer check boxes, respectively, in the Layer Options dialog box.

7. **Double-click the United States Map layer on the Layers panel to open the Layer Options dialog box**

   As shown in Figure F-15, the check boxes in the Layer Options dialog box give you a quick rundown of what is happening with the layer. This layer is not hidden, it is not locked, and it will print. You can change layer settings by adding or removing check marks in the check boxes.

8. **Click OK, then save your work**

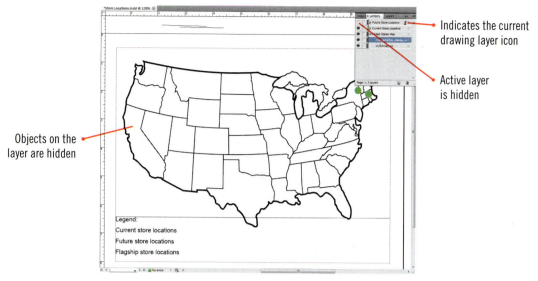

Indicates the current drawing layer icon

Active layer is hidden

Objects on the layer are hidden

FIGURE F-13: Locking the map item on the United States Map layer

Click to lock the item

FIGURE F-14: Viewing the locked page item

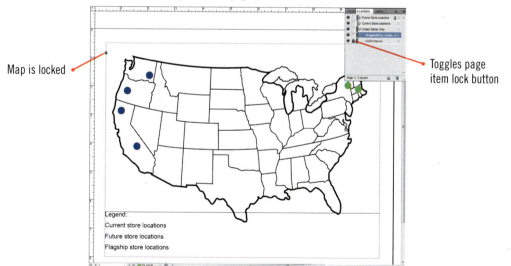

Map is locked

Toggles page item lock button

FIGURE F-15: Layer Options dialog box

Moving an Object to Another Layer

It is not unusual to realize that an object belongs on a different layer after you've created the object. Fortunately, it is possible to move an existing page item from one layer to another layer in a document. To move an InDesign object to a new layer, select the object on the page, then drag the Indicates selected items icon next to the page item being moved on the Layers panel to a new layer. Ted informs you that two of the future Happy Apple stores in California are going to be flagship stores that include a dining area, gardening center, and natural pharmacy in addition to the supermarket. To distinguish these two flagship stores from the two other future stores on the West Coast, you create a new layer, move two circles from the Future Store Locations layer to the new layer, and then apply a new fill color to the two circles.

STEPS

1. **Click the Future Store Locations layer at the top of the Layers panel, then click the Create new layer button 🔲 on the Layers panel**
   Layer 4 appears at the top of the Layers panel. New layers are placed above the selected layer in the panel.

2. **Double-click Layer 4 to open the Layer Options dialog box**

3. **Change the name of the layer to Flagship Store Locations and the selection color to Red, then click OK**

4. **Click the lowest dark blue circle on the state of California to select it, as shown in Figure F-16**
   The Future Store Locations layer becomes the active layer on the Layers panel, and the Indicates selected items icon ■ appears next to the Future Store Locations layer on the Layers panel. When you click an object in a document, the layer that the page item is on becomes the active layer.

5. **Click the expand layer arrow ▷ next to the Future Store Locations layer to expand the layer**
   ■ appears next to the <circle> object. You will move this item to the Flagship Store Locations layer.

6. **Drag ■ on the <circle> page item to the Flagship Store Locations layer on the Layers panel, as shown in Figure F-17, then release the mouse button**
   As you drag ■, the pointer becomes a fist icon 🖑 and a black line appears when the pointer is entering a new layer. The blue circle is now on the Flagship Store Locations layer and its selection color changed to red.

7. **Click the other dark blue circle on the state of California, then drag ■ from the Future Store Locations layer to the Flagship Store Locations layer on the Layers panel**

8. **Expand the Flagship Store Locations layer, then compare your Layers panel to Figure F-18**
   Both circles are on the new layer.

9. **Select both circles in the document, then change the fill color of the two circles on the Flagship Store Locations layer to C=15 M=100 Y=100 K=0 (red), deselect all, then save your work**

Merging layers

When creating an InDesign document, you may end up with more layers than you really need, or you may wish to consolidate, or **merge**, multiple layers into one general layer. When you merge layers together, the objects on each of the layers that are merged become objects on the single layer that results. To merge multiple layers into a single layer, press and hold [Ctrl] (Win) or ⌘ (Mac), then click all of the layers in the Layers panel that you wish to merge. Click the Layers Panel options button, then click Merge Layers. The name of first layer that was selected is retained as the name of the single merged layer. You may want to rename the merged layer so that it better describes its new contents.

FIGURE F-16: Selected circle

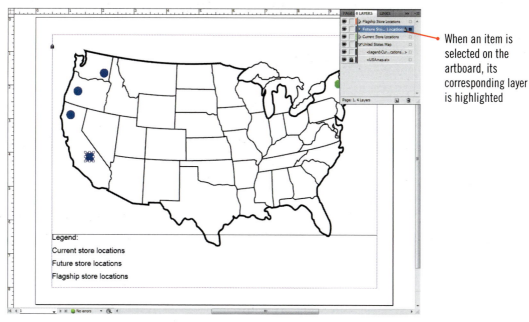

When an item is selected on the artboard, its corresponding layer is highlighted

FIGURE F-17: Moving the <circle> page item to the Flagship Store Locations layer

Fist pointer indicates the item is being moved

FIGURE F-18: Viewing the Flagship Store Locations layer

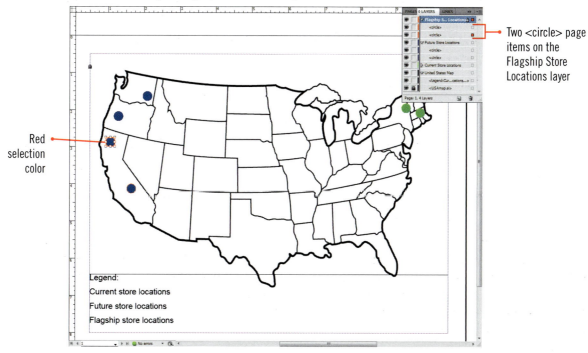

Two <circle> page items on the Flagship Store Locations layer

Red selection color

Changing Layer Order

The order of layers on the Layers panel is identical to the vertical stacking order of InDesign objects on the page. The top layer in the panel represents the top object(s) on the page and the bottom layer represents the bottom object(s) on the page. To change the order of layers on the Layers panel, you drag the layer to a new location in the panel, then release the mouse button when a black line appears above the layer you are dragging to. Ted asks you to add a starburst graphic to the map to announce the opening date of the two flagship stores. You place the starburst graphic on a new layer and then move the new layer beneath the Flagship Store Locations layer so that the starburst appears beneath the two red circles in the document.

STEPS

1. Verify that the Flagship Store Locations layer is targeted on the Layers panel, then click the Create new layer button ▣ on the Layers panel

   Layer 5 appears at the top of the Layers panel.

2. Double-click Layer 5 to open the Layer Options dialog box, rename the layer Opening, then click OK to accept the chosen selection color and close the dialog box

3. Click File on the Application bar, click Place, then double-click Starburst.ai

   The mouse pointer is loaded with Starburst.ai, an Adobe Illustrator file.

4. Click anywhere on the state of California, then compare your screen to Figure F-19

   The starburst graphic is placed on the currently active Opening layer, which is above the Flagship Store Locations layer on the Layers panel. The starburst graphic blocks or partially blocks the two red circles on the Flagship Store Locations layer.

5. Using Figure F-20 as a guide, drag the Opening layer below the Flagship Store Locations layer until you see a black line below the Flagship Store Locations layer, then release the mouse button

   The Opening layer is now below the Flagship Store Locations layer on the Layers panel and in the document. In the document, the red circles appear on top of the starburst and are no longer blocked by it.

6. Click the Selection tool ▶ on the Tools panel, if necessary, then drag the starburst graphic so that its location is approximately the same as that shown in Figure F-21

7. To finish the map, click the United States Map layer on the Layers panel, place the file named Legend dots.ai next to the legend text

8. Deselect all, press [W] to hide the guides, then compare your finished map and Layers panel to Figure F-22

9. Save your work, then exit InDesign

Pasting layers into a document

It is possible to paste objects and their corresponding layers from one InDesign document into another using the Paste Remembers Layers command on the Panel options menu. Pasting layers is very useful if you have spent a lot of time and energy creating layers in one document and plan on using the same layer structure in another document. Rather than recreating layers in a new document, you can copy and paste the objects and their layers into the new document and then make any necessary changes. To paste layers, click the Layers Panel options button, then click Paste Remembers Layers to add a check mark before the command. Next, copy or cut the InDesign objects and paste them into the new document. The pasted objects' layers will automatically be pasted into the Layers panel of the new document.

Artwork is blocking items on the Flagship Store Locations layer

FIGURE F-20: Moving the Opening layer

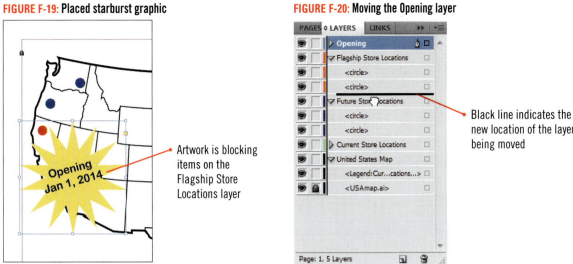

Black line indicates the new location of the layer being moved

FIGURE F-21: Repositioned starburst

FIGURE F-22: The finished map

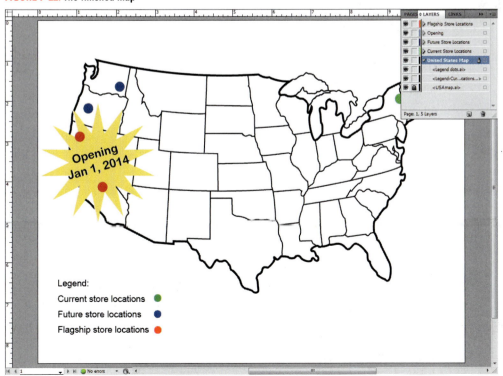

Legend:
Current store locations ●
Future store locations ●
Flagship store locations ●

Working with Layers

Practice

For current SAM information, including versions and content details, visit SAM Central (http://www.cengage.com/samcentral). If you have a SAM user profile, you may have access to hands-on instruction, practice, and assessment of the skills covered in this unit. Since various versions of SAM are supported throughout the life of this text, check with your instructor for the correct instructions and URL/Web site for accessing assignments.

Concepts Review

Label the elements of the InDesign screen shown in Figure F-23.

FIGURE F-23

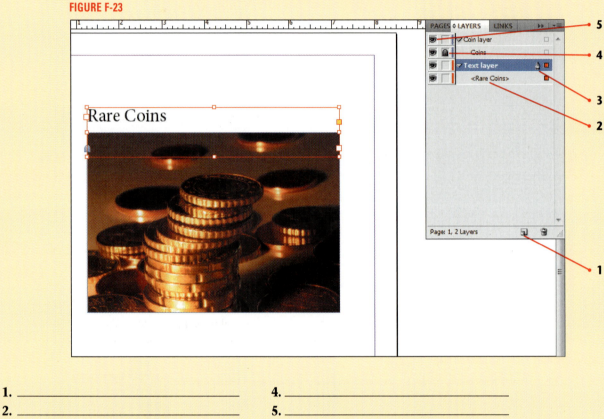

1. _____   4. _____

2. _____   5. _____

3. _____

Match each term with the statement that best describes it.

6. **Locked layer**
7. **Page item**
8. **Newly created layer**
9. **Indicates selected items icon** ■
10. **Indicates current drawing layer icon** 🖊

a. Used to move an object to a new layer
b. Objects on it cannot be selected
c. Indicates the active layer
d. Name given to an object on a layer
e. Appears above the selected layer on the Layers panel

Select the best answer from the list of choices.

11. In the Layers panel, what do you click to unlock a layer?

    a. 🔒   **c.** ▪

    b. 👁   **d.** ◿

12. Which of the following moves a layer to a new location on the Layers panel?

    a. Use the Move Layer command.

    b. Drag the layer in the panel.

    c. Press and hold [Alt] (Win) or [option] (Mac), then drag the layer in the panel.

    d. Drag the Indicates selected items icon ▪ on the layer you want to move.

13. When does the word "copy" appear after a layer name on the Layers panel?

    a. When the layer has been duplicated   **c.** When an object has been moved to the layer

    b. When an object on the layer has been copied   **d.** When the layer has been moved

Skills Review

1. **Place an object on a layer.**

    a. Start InDesign, create a new 8.5" × 11" document without facing pages and with a portrait orientation, then save it as **New York Coffee**.

    b. Click the workspace switcher, click Reset Essentials, then click the Layers panel icon to open the Layers panel.

    c. Click the Rectangle tool on the Tools panel, then create a rectangle frame that snaps to all four margin guides.

    d. On the Layers panel, click the expand layer arrow to expand Layer 1.

    e. Click the Selection tool on the Tools panel, click File on the Application bar, click Place, navigate to where you store your Data Files, click New York.tif, then click Open.

    f. Click the Fit content proportionally button on the Control panel, then click the Center content button on the Control panel.

    g. Click Object on the Application bar, point to Display Performance, then click High Quality Display.

    h. Deselect the map frame, click File on the Application bar, click Place, click New York Legend.doc, then click Open.

    i. Align the loaded cursor with approximately the 9-inch mark on the vertical ruler, then click to place the New York legend text in the lower-left corner of the document window. (*Hint*: Be sure all four lines of the legend are visible.)

    j. Save your work.

2. **Change layer options.**

    a. Click the Layers Panel options button, then click Layer Options for "Layer 1".

    b. Type **New York Map** in the Name text box.

    c. Click the Color list arrow, then click Black.

    d. Click OK to close the Layer Options dialog box.

    e. Click the Selection tool on the Tools panel, if necessary, then click the map image.

    f. Deselect all, then save your work.

3. **Create a new layer.**

    a. Click the Layers Panel options button, then click New Layer.

    b. Type **Current Locations** in the Name text box, click the Color list arrow, click Yellow, then click OK to close the New Layer dialog box.

    c. Click the Rectangle tool on the Tools panel. (*Hint*: The Rectangle tool may be hidden beneath the Ellipse tool.)

    d. Click the page to open the Rectangle dialog box, type **.25** in the Width text box, press [Tab], type **.25** in the Height text box, then click OK.

    e. Click the Zoom tool on the Tools panel, then click the square to enlarge your view as necessary.

    f. Click the Fill tool on the Tools panel, open the Swatches panel, then scroll down and click C=0 M=0 Y=100 K=0 (yellow).

    g. Click the Stroke button on the Tools panel, then click [None] on the Swatches panel, if necessary.

    h. Click the Selection tool on the Tools panel, then drag the square to just inside the upper-right corner of the map of New York.

i. Press and hold [Alt] (Win) or [option] (Mac), click and drag the square in a downward direction to create a copy of it as shown in Figure F-24, then create two more copies of the square, and place them in the approximate locations shown in the figure.

j. Save your work.

4. **Duplicate a layer.**

a. Show the Layers panel, then verify that the Current Locations layer is still active on the Layers panel.

b. Click the Layers Panel options button, then click Duplicate Layer "Current Locations".

c. Double-click the Current Locations copy layer on the Layers panel to open the Layer Options dialog box.

d. Type **Future Locations** in the Name text box, click the Color list arrow, click Dark Blue, then click OK.

e. Click the Selection tool on the Tools panel, if necessary, then click the yellow square near the bottom of the map.

f. Change the fill color of the selected square to C=100 M=90 Y=10 K=0 (dark blue), drag the square approximately 1 inch to the left, then deselect.

g. Press [Alt] (Win) or [option] (Mac), click the Future Locations layer on the Layers panel to select all of the objects on the layer, then click C=100 M=90 Y=10 K=0 (dark blue) on the Swatches panel.

h. Drag the blue squares to the approximate locations shown in Figure F-25, deselect, then save your work.

5. **Lock and hide a layer.**

a. Open the Layers panel, if necessary, then click the Toggles visibility button to the left of the Future Locations layer on the Layers panel.

b. Click the Toggles visibility button to the left of the Current Locations layer on the Layers panel.

c. Click the Toggles visibility button to the left of the New York Map layer on the Layers panel.

d. Click the empty gray square where the Toggles visibility icon once was next to each of the three layers on the Layers panel.

e. Click the empty gray square between the Toggles visibility icon and the <New York.tif> object on the Layers panel.

f. Double-click the New York Map layer on the Layers panel to open the Layer Options dialog box, then view the settings for the New York layer.

g. Click OK, then save your work.

6. **Move an object to another layer.**

a. Click the Future Locations layer at the top of the Layers panel, then click the Create new layer button on the Layers panel.

b. Double-click Layer 4 to open the Layer Options dialog box.

c. Change the name of the layer to **Café/Bookstore Locations** and the selection color to Grass Green, then click OK.

d. Click the blue square on the far left to select it.

e. Click the triangle next to the Future Locations layer to expand the layer.

FIGURE F-24

FIGURE F-25

    f. Drag the Indicates selected items icon on the <rectangle> page item to the Café/Bookstore Locations layer on the Layers panel, then release the mouse button.

    g. Click the next, left-most blue square on the state of New York, then drag the Indicates selected items icon from the Future Locations layer to the Café/Bookstore Locations layer on the Layers panel.

    h. Expand the Café/Bookstore Locations layer to view both squares on the Café/Bookstores layer.

    i. Change the fill color of the two squares on the Café/Bookstore Locations layer to C=75 M=5 Y=100 K=0 (green).

    j. Deselect all, then save your work.

7. Change layer order.

    a. Verify that the Café/Bookstore Locations layer is targeted on the Layers panel, then click the Create new layer button on the Layers panel.

    b. Double-click Layer 5 to open the Layer Options dialog box, rename the layer **New Store**, then click OK to accept the chosen selection color and close the dialog box.

    c. Click File on the Application bar, click Place, then double-click Opening Soon.ai.

FIGURE F-26

    d. Click the loaded cursor anywhere on the far-left green square on the map to place the Opening Soon graphic.

    e. Drag the New Store layer below the Café/Bookstore Locations layer until you see a black line below the Café/Bookstore Locations layer, then release the mouse button.

    f. Click the Selection tool on the Tools panel, if necessary, then drag the Opening Soon graphic so that the word "Soon" is slightly above the green square.

    g. To finish the map, click the New York Map layer on the Layers panel, place the file named Legend squares.ai, then move the legend squares into position next to the legend text.

    h. Deselect all, press [W] to hide the guides, then compare your finished map and Layers panel to Figure F-26.

    i. Save your work, then exit InDesign.

Independent Challenge 1

You were recently hired as a designer for a snowboarding magazine. Each month you update the magazine cover for the new issue. During your first week, you realize that the previous designer did not use layers when assembling the magazine cover template. You decide to add layers to it in order to keep the page elements organized.

    a. Start InDesign, open ID F-1.indd, then save it as **Snowboard Magazine**.

    b. Open the Layers panel.

    c. Create five layers named **Date**, **Title**, **Subtitle**, **Picture**, and **In this Issue**.

    d. Expand Layer 1, then drag each page item to its corresponding layer. (*Hint*: The orange background and the title are one item. "The Top 10 Mountains" is the subtitle.)

    e. Delete Layer 1 by clicking the Layers Panel options button, then click Delete Layer "Layer 1".

Independent Challenge 1 (continued)

f. Rearrange the order of the layers, as necessary, so that you see all five page elements.

g. Hide and show each layer to make sure that each item is placed correctly.

h. Press [W] to view your page without guides, then save your work.

i. Compare your screen and your Layers panel to Figure F-27, then exit InDesign.

Independent Challenge 2

You volunteer at a local farm stand each summer. Every Monday, Tuesday, and Wednesday, the farm offers a different item for $1.00 until it runs out of the item. You are in charge of creating ads for the sale item each morning. You have figured out how to make a different ad each day using the same InDesign document.

FIGURE F-27

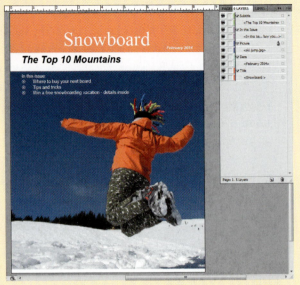

a. Start InDesign, open ID F-2.indd, then save it as **Quick Ad**.

b. Duplicate Layer 1, rename the new layer **Monday**, then change the selection color for the Monday layer to the color of your choice.

c. Hide Layer 1, select the Monday layer, then change the "Day of Week" text in the text box on the Monday layer to **Monday**.

d. Duplicate the Monday layer, rename the new layer **Tuesday**, then change the selection color for the Tuesday layer.

e. Hide the Monday layer, target the Tuesday layer, then change the "Monday" text in the text box to **Tuesday**.

f. Repeat Steps d-e to create new layers for Wednesday, Thursday, and Friday. (*Hint*: Remember to duplicate the layers instead of creating new layers.)

g. Check your work by showing each layer with all other layers hidden. (*Hint*: Press and hold [Alt] (Win) or [option] (Mac), then click the Toggles visibility button for a layer to show that layer and hide all others.)

h. Select the Friday layer, then hide all other layers on the Layers panel.

i. Place the file named seedless grapes.psd from the Fruit folder in the circle graphics frame, then fill the frame proportionally.

Advanced Challenge Exercise

- Show all of the layers on the Layers panel.
- Click the Layers Panel options button, then click Paste Remembers Layers to put a check mark next to it, if necessary.
- Click Edit on the Application bar, then click Select All.
- Click Edit on the Application bar, then click Copy.
- Create a new InDesign document with the default settings.
- Click Edit on the Application bar, then click Paste.
- Press and hold [Alt] (Win) or [option] (Mac), then click the Monday layer to show that layer and hide all others.

FIGURE F-28

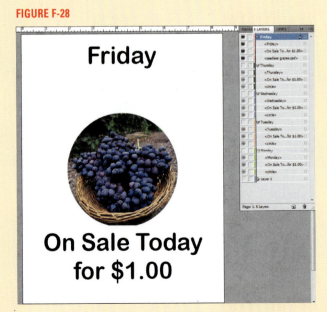

j. Deselect all, press [W], then compare your screen to Figure F-28.

k. Save your work, then exit InDesign.

Independent Challenge 3

You volunteer two hours a week doing community service work for school credit at your local library. Each week, you create some fun pages to be distributed at the weekly story hour. Since taking an InDesign class in school, you realize that you could improve the fun page document by organizing the page elements in layers.

a. Start InDesign, open ID F-3.indd, update links if necessary, then save it as **Fun Page Layers**.

b. Rename Layer 1 as **Text**.

c. Create four new layers named **Animals**, **Toys**, **Fruit**, and **Candy**.

d. Place each page item on the appropriate layer, then hide and show each layer to check your work.

e. Lock the Text layer.

f. Press and hold [Alt] (Win) or [option] (Mac), click Toys on the Layers panel to select all of the objects on it, change their stroke color to C=100 M=90 Y=10 K=0, then add the same color stroke to the dog image.

g. Deselect all objects, then save your work.

h. Press [W] to hide the guides, compare your screen and your Layers panel to Figure F-29, then exit InDesign.

FIGURE F-29

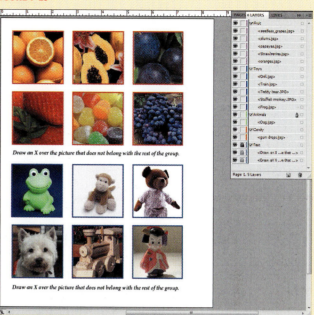

Real Life Independent Challenge

Determine two items that you no longer use but you think you could sell online. Before you post information about the items online, place a picture of each item in InDesign and add descriptions.

a. Start InDesign and create a new single-page 8.5" × 11" document without facing pages and with 1-inch margins.

b. Save the document as **Online Sale**.

c. Place at least two images of your own items in the document. (*Hint*: If you do not have your own photos, use any two photos from your Data Files folders for this book.)

d. Write a description for each item.

e. Place each item on a new layer and name the layer so that it describes the item on it.

f. Create a layer named **Text**, then place all of the text descriptions on the text layer.

g. Arrange the images and descriptions on the page as you like.

h. Drag the Text layer to the bottom of the Layers panel.

Advanced Challenge Exercise

- Select one layer, press and hold [Shift], then click the remaining layers.
- Click the Layers Panel options button, then click Merge Layers.
- Change the name of the merged layer to **Sale Items**.

i. Save your work, then exit InDesign.

Visual Workshop

Start InDesign and create a new 8.5" × 11" document with facing pages. Save the document as **Guide Layers**. Using Figure F-30 as a guide, open the A-Master and create all of the guides shown in the figure on the left and right pages of the A-Master. Place the horizontal guides on a layer named **Horizontal guides** and the vertical guides on a layer named **Vertical guides**. (*Hint*: Guides do not appear on the Layers panel.) Compare your screen to Figure F-30, save your work, then exit InDesign.

FIGURE F-30

Working with Color and Tables

Color can greatly enhance a document's appearance, and is a dynamic part of any InDesign document. InDesign offers an endless supply of colors to use for printed documents and for the Web. You can make your own process colors and save them in the Swatches panel or choose from several spot color libraries. You can also use two or more colors to create a fill in which colors blend from one to another, called a **gradient fill**. Using tables in InDesign helps you organize and display text in rows and columns, similar to a spreadsheet. There are many ways to format tables to create a professional presentation of your information, such as by applying colors and styles to table cells and text. The Happy Apple is raising money for a local animal shelter. At the checkout line, customers will be able to purchase a paper apple for $1.00 that they will hang in the store window. Ted asks you to create two apple cutouts, each with a different color, for customers to choose from. He also asks you to create a table showing the progress of the six Happy Apple stores that are participating in the fundraiser.

OBJECTIVES

Create a process color

Select a spot color

Create a gradient

Use the Gradient Swatch tool

Create a table

Format table cells

Insert, merge, and split table cells

Set tabs in a table

Creating a Process Color

A **process color** is a color that is made from using the four process inks: cyan, magenta, yellow, and black, also known as **CMYK**. Process inks are inks that are used for color printing; they are made by combining different percentages of one or more of these four colors, similar to combining the ingredients in a recipe. For example, the color red is made from 50% yellow and 50% magenta. Process colors are designated for documents that will be printed on paper. These colors are affected by the type of paper they are printed on and other elements such as light and air, and therefore are not guaranteed to look the same every time when printed. You open an InDesign document containing two apple graphics, create a new process color, and then apply it to one of the apple graphics.

STEPS

1. **Start InDesign, open ID G-1.indd, then save it as Apple Cutouts**

   The open document contains two apple vector graphics that were copied and pasted from Adobe Illustrator to InDesign. The images are modifiable because they were pasted rather than placed as preview files into the document.

2. **Click Window on the Application bar, point to Workspace, then click Reset Essentials**

3. **Click the Direct Selection tool ▶ on the Tools panel, then click the apple on the left**

   The apple is grouped to the stem and leaves. The Direct Selection tool selects just the apple.

4. **Click the Swatches panel button ▦ on the right side of the workspace to open the Swatches panel, then drag the lower-right corner of the Swatches panel down so that you can see all of the colors in it, as shown in Figure G-1**

   The top nine colors, starting with Paper, are the default colors on the Swatches panel. The three bottom colors are the three colors applied to the apple and stem in each of the graphics. Notice that all of the colors are named using C, M, Y, and K, followed by a percentage. The gray square icon to the right of each color indicates that each color is a process color. The color c15m100y100k0 is selected on the Swatches panel because it is the color that is applied to the selected object.

5. **Verify that the apple is still selected and that the Fill button ⬚ is active on the Tools panel, click the Swatches Panel options button ▤, then click New Color Swatch**

   The New Color Swatch dialog box opens, displaying the last swatch that was selected on the Swatches panel.

6. **Click the Name with Color Value check box to remove the check mark, then type Golden Delicious in the Swatch Name text box**

   By deselecting the Name with Color Value check box, you can add your own descriptive name, rather than using the default CMYK naming convention.

7. **Double-click the Cyan text box, type 10, press [Tab], type 12, press [Tab], type 90, press [Tab], type 0, then compare your New Color Swatch dialog box to Figure G-2**

   The color created from this combination of CMYK appears in the preview box.

8. **Click OK to close the New Color Swatch dialog box**

   The new color, Golden Delicious, is applied to the selected apple and appears at the bottom of the Swatches panel, as shown in Figure G-3. If you wanted to continue to create additional new colors, you could click Add instead of OK in the dialog box. When you click Add, the new color is added to the Swatches panel and the New Color Swatch dialog box remains open.

9. **Click the Color panel icon ◉ to open the Color panel, click the Color Panel options button ▤, then click CMYK**

   The Color panel shows the CMYK combination for the Golden Delicious color swatch.

FIGURE G-1: Identifying colors on the Swatches panel

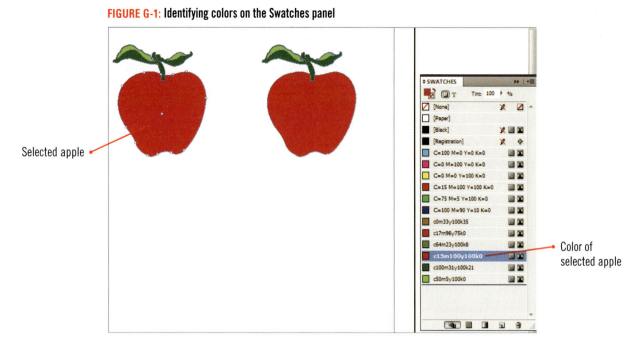

Selected apple

Color of selected apple

FIGURE G-2: New Color Swatch dialog box

Preview of new color

Swatch Name text box

Type color amounts here

FIGURE G-3: New process color applied to artwork

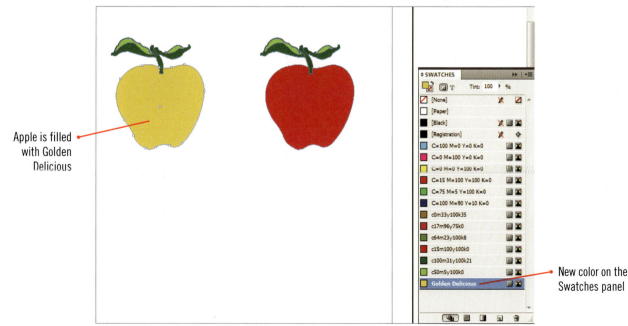

Apple is filled with Golden Delicious

New color on the Swatches panel

Selecting a Spot Color

Spot colors are another type of color used for documents printed on paper. Unlike process colors that you can create yourself, **spot colors** are manufactured by paint companies. Spot colors are helpful to use when you are unsuccessful at creating a color you need with CMYK. They are more reliable than process colors because they print exactly the same each time they are used. Spot colors can be used for documents printed on your home computer, but they are often used for high-end commercial documents such as magazines and catalogs that will be printed on large printing presses. Spot colors are listed on the Swatches panel. You choose a spot color for the second apple and then apply it to the apple shape.

STEPS

1. **Deselect the Golden Delicious apple, open the Swatches panel, click the Swatches Panel options button ▾≣, then click New Color Swatch**

   The New Color Swatch dialog box opens.

2. **Click the Color Type list arrow, then click Spot**

3. **Click the Color Mode list arrow, then click PANTONE solid matte**

   Pantone is the company name of a large color manufacturer. Solid matte is a category of paint that Pantone makes.

> **QUICK TIP**
> If you are not sure of the number of the color that you want, you can scroll through the list to view them all.

4. **Click the PANTONE text box, then type 390**

   The color PANTONE 390 M, a light green, is selected in the list, as shown in Figure G-4. You want to apply this to the next apple to make it the color of a Granny Smith apple.

> **QUICK TIP**
> When you use a commercial printer to publish a document, you must purchase the spot colors you use in your print piece.

5. **Click OK to close the New Color Swatch dialog box**

   PANTONE 390 M appears at the bottom of the Swatches panel, as shown in Figure G-5. To the right of the color, the square icon with the circle at its center indicates that the color is a spot color. If you position the mouse pointer over the CMYK mode icon to the right of the spot color icon, a tool tip shows the combination of CMYK you would use to create a process color that is the closest possible match to the spot color. This is known as a **process match**. Creating a process match is useful when the color you need does not have to be a perfect match and you don't want to purchase the spot color ink for use in your publication.

6. **Click the Fill button ◩ on the Tools panel, if necessary**

> **QUICK TIP**
> You can load swatches from another InDesign document into the open document by clicking the Swatches Panel options button, clicking Load Swatches, then opening the desired file.

7. **Click the Direct Selection tool ▶, click the apple on the right, then click PANTONE 390 M on the Swatches panel**

   The apple is filled with a light green color, PANTONE 390 M.

8. **Deselect all, compare your screen to Figure G-6, then save your work**

Creating a new tint swatch

If you need a lighter version of a color, you can make a new tint swatch from it. To create a tint swatch from an existing color, select the color in the Swatches panel, click the Swatches panel options button, then click New Tint Swatch. Drag the Tint slider to the left in the New Tint Swatch dialog box until the desired percentage appears in the text box to the right, then click OK. The new tint swatch appears in the Swatches panel with the same name and tint percentage next to the name.

FIGURE G-4: Spot color in New Color Swatch dialog box

PANTONE text box

Selected color

Click to select Color Mode

FIGURE G-5: Viewing **PANTONE 390 M** on the Swatches panel

CMYK mode icon

Spot color icon

FIGURE G-6: Spot color applied to apple

Pantone 390 M spot color

Creating a Gradient

A **gradient** is a type of fill for an object that contains at least two colors that gradually blend from one to the other, such as from black to white. **Linear** gradients blend from one point to another horizontally, vertically, or diagonally, depending on the angle of the gradient. **Radial** gradients blend from the center outward to the border(s) of the object. Gradient fills can add texture to an object and also give the illusion of lightness and darkness in an object. You create a gradient fill for the apple leaves to give them a more three-dimensional look.

STEPS

1. **Click the Swatches Panel options button** 📑 **, then click New Gradient Swatch**

   The New Gradient Swatch dialog box opens with the default Linear type and the default gradient colors (white to black) showing in the Gradient Ramp, as shown in Figure G-7. The two icons below the Gradient Ramp are called **color stops**. The first color stop, located at 0% on the Gradient Ramp, represents the starting color of the gradient. The second color stop, located at 100% on the Gradient Ramp, represents the ending color of the gradient. A diamond icon appears above the Gradient Ramp. By default its location is at 50%, which indicates the point in the gradient where there is 50% of each color. You can drag the diamond slider to change its location.

2. **Click the right color stop, click the Stop Color list arrow, then click Swatches**

   The colors on the Swatches panel are available in the dialog box.

3. **Scroll down in the list of swatches, then click c100m31y100k21 (dark green)**

   Green is applied to the 100% color stop and becomes the last color in the new gradient. The gradient blends from white to green, as shown in Figure G-8.

   > **QUICK TIP**
   > To remove a color from a gradient, drag a color stop off of the Gradient Ramp.

4. **Click just below the Gradient Ramp anywhere between the color stops to add a new color stop, then drag the new color stop until you see approximately 50% in the Location text box**

   The new color will begin halfway between the starting color stop and the ending color stop. Diamond icons now appear halfway between the 0% and 50% color stops, and halfway between the 50% and 100% color stops.

5. **Using Figure G-9 as a guide, drag the sliders for the middle color stop to C=36 M=0 Y=70 K=0**

   The gradient blends from white to a lighter green and then to a darker green.

   > **QUICK TIP**
   > To rename a gradient swatch, double-click it to open the Gradient Options dialog box, then change its name in the Swatch Name text box.

6. **Click OK to close the dialog box**

   The gradient swatch is added to the bottom of the Swatches panel and is named New Gradient Swatch by default.

7. **Click the Zoom tool** 🔍 **on the Tools panel, then drag the Zoom tool pointer** ⊕ **around the left apple to zoom in on it**

8. **Click the Direct Selection tool** ▸ **, click the dark green part of the left leaf, click New Gradient Swatch on the Swatches panel, then apply the New Gradient Swatch to the dark green part of the right leaf**

   The New Gradient Swatch is applied to the left and right leaves, as shown in Figure G-10.

9. **Apply the New Gradient Swatch to the dark green areas of the left and right leaves on the Granny Smith apple, then save your work**

Filling text with a gradient fill

By default, you cannot fill text with a gradient fill. However, you can convert text to outlines and then fill the outlines with a gradient. To do so, select the text, click Type on the Application bar, then click Create Outlines. Each character in the text object is converted to a vector graphic made up of anchor points and line segments. It is no longer text, but rather an object that can be filled with a gradient.

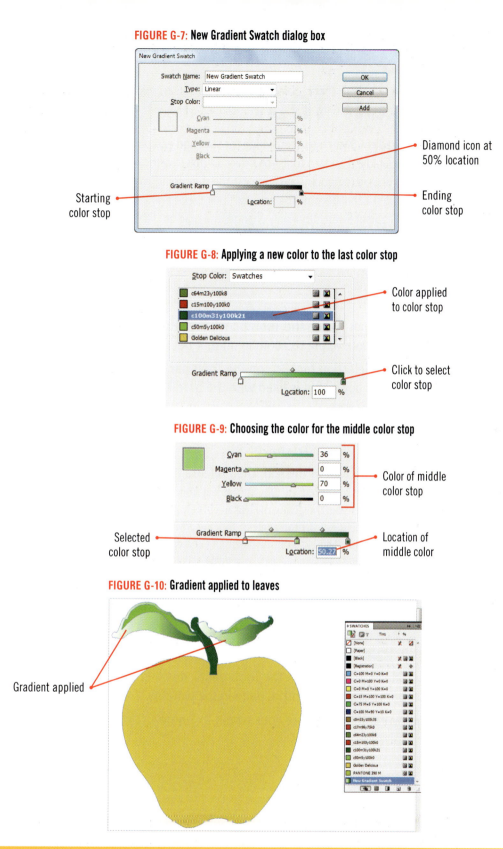

FIGURE G-7: New Gradient Swatch dialog box

Diamond icon at 50% location

Starting color stop

Ending color stop

FIGURE G-8: Applying a new color to the last color stop

Color applied to color stop

Click to select color stop

FIGURE G-9: Choosing the color for the middle color stop

Color of middle color stop

Selected color stop

Location of middle color

FIGURE G-10: Gradient applied to leaves

Gradient applied

Changing the view of the Swatches panel

The default view in the Swatches panel is the Name view in which all swatches are listed by name. To change the view of swatches in the Swatches panel, click the Swatches Panel options button, and then click Small Name, Small Swatch, or Large Swatch. You can also choose which swatches you want to view in the panel using the buttons at the bottom of the panel. The Show All Swatches button is selected by default, and all color swatches and gradient swatches are displayed in the panel. Click the Show Color Swatches button to show only color swatches in the panel. Click the Show Gradient Swatches button to display only the gradient swatches in the panel.

Using the Gradient Swatch Tool

You can use the Gradient Swatch tool to change the start and end points, direction, and/or angle of a gradient fill. To use the Gradient Swatch tool, you select an object with the gradient fill, then drag the tool over the object. As you drag, a temporary line appears. The start point, end point, direction, and angle of the line created by dragging the tool become the new start point, end point, direction, and angle of the gradient fill, respectively. The Gradient Swatch tool only changes the gradient fill of the selected object or objects; it does not affect the gradient swatch on the Swatches panel. You use the Gradient Swatch tool to change the start and end points and the direction of the gradient fill on each set of leaves so that the two apples are not identical.

STEPS

1. Click the Zoom tool 🔍 on the Tools panel, then drag the Zoom tool pointer ⊕ around the Golden Delicious apple to zoom in on it, if necessary

2. Click the Direct Selection tool ▸ on the Tools panel, then click the left leaf of the Golden Delicious apple that is filled with the gradient

3. Click the Gradient Swatch tool ▣ on the Tools panel

   The mouse pointer becomes a crosshair icon.

4. Using Figure G-11 as a guide, click slightly above the left leaf, drag in a downward direction to the bottom of the leaf, then release the mouse button

   As shown in Figure G-12, the gradient fills the left leaf from just above the top of it to just below the bottom of it, instead of from left to right, giving the leaf an entirely new look, since the bottom is darker than the top. The angle of the gradient follows the angle of the line created when you dragged. The parts of the leaf not included within the line are filled with the beginning and ending colors used in the gradient.

5. Press and hold the [Spacebar] to switch to the Hand tool 🖑, then drag the page to the left until you see the Granny Smith apple

6. Click ▸, then click the section of the right leaf filled with the gradient

7. Click ▣, drag the Gradient Swatch tool pointer -¦- from the bottom of the leaf to the top, then release the mouse button

8. Click the Selection tool ▸ on the Tools panel, deselect the leaf, then double-click 🖑 on the Tools panel to view the entire page in the window

9. Save your work, then compare your screen to Figure G-13

Using the Gradient panel

The Gradient panel includes the same options as the New Gradient Swatch dialog box for creating a new gradient. When you use the Gradient panel to create a new gradient, you will need the Swatches panel and/or the Color panel open at the same time so that you can choose colors for each color stop. When you select a color stop and are ready to choose a swatch on the Swatches panel to apply to that color stop, be sure to press and hold [Alt] (Win) or [option] (Mac) before clicking the swatch. Otherwise, the selected object will be filled with the color swatch chosen on the Swatches panel. Pressing [Alt] (Win) or [option] (Mac) ensures that the color chosen on the Swatches panel is only applied to the color stop of the gradient fill.

Start dragging
here

Stop dragging
here

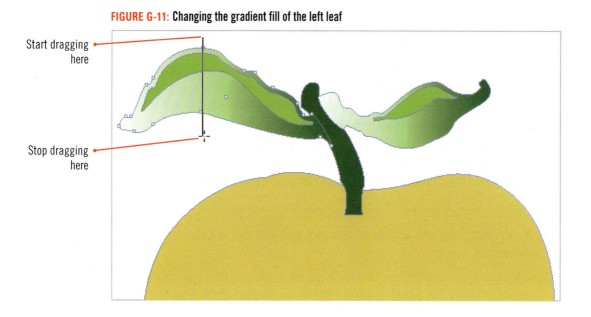

FIGURE G-12: Viewing the result of the Gradient tool

Gradient is
reversed

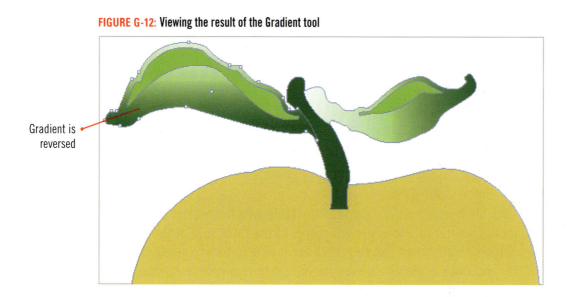

FIGURE G-13: Viewing the gradient fills

Creating a Table

There are some types of information, such as weekly schedules, that are best presented in documents as tables. In InDesign, a **table** is a rectangular object that is made up of many smaller rectangles called **cells**. Cells are laid out horizontally in **rows** and vertically in **columns**. Tables are used primarily for text, but it is possible to insert graphics into cells too. To create a table, you must first create a text box to put the table into. To make changes to a table, you can select individual cells, rows, or columns, or you can select the entire table. You are ready to create a table that shows how much money has been raised so far. The Happy Apple will match the donation for each dollar donated.

STEPS

1. Verify that the rulers are displayed and that you can see the entire page in the document window

2. Click the Type tool T on the Tools panel, position the Type tool pointer at approximately the 5-inch mark on the vertical ruler, then drag to create a text box that snaps to the left, bottom, and right margin guides, as shown in Figure G-14

   The text box in the figure is selected so that you can see its four borders.

3. Click T if necessary, click inside the text box, click Table on the Application bar, then click Insert Table

   The Insert Table dialog box opens.

4. Type 7 in the Body Rows text box, press [Tab], type 3 if necessary in the Columns text box, then click OK

   A table with seven rows and three columns appears in the text box.

> **QUICK TIP**
> To select a row, position the mouse pointer on the left edge of the row, then click the mouse button.

5. Position the mouse pointer on the top edge of the first column of the table until the pointer becomes a black arrow ↓, as shown in Figure G-15, then click the mouse button

   The first column of cells is selected. When an element of the table is selected, settings for modifying the table appear on the Control panel.

> **QUICK TIP**
> You can also use the Select command on the Table menu to select a cell, row, column, or table.

6. Click the mouse button outside of the table area to deselect the column, position the mouse pointer on the upper-left corner of the table so that the mouse pointer becomes a diagonal black arrow ↘, then click the mouse button to select the entire table

   The entire table is selected. Selecting the entire table is useful to make changes to every cell in the table at once.

7. Click in the top cell of the first table column, type Store Locations, press [Tab], type Number of Apples Sold, press [Tab], type Total Amount Donated, then press [Tab]

   The insertion point appears in the second cell of the first table column. Pressing [Tab] when in a table cell moves the insertion point to the next cell in the table.

8. Type the text shown in Figure G-16 in the remaining table cells

9. Save your work

Using the Table panel

The Table panel includes some of the same options for modifying a table that are on the Control panel when a table or table element is selected. Both panels include buttons that allow you to rotate the text inside a cell, change the number of columns and rows, choose an exact width or height for table cells, and change the cell inset value. The **inset** value is the amount of space between the top, bottom, right, and/or left sides of text and its cell borders. The Table panel menu includes the same menu items found on the Table menu on the Application bar, such as Merge Cells, Table Options, and Cell Options. Choosing whether to use the Table panel, Control panel, or Table menu is merely a matter of preference. To open the Table panel, click Window on the Application bar, point to Type & Tables, then click Table.

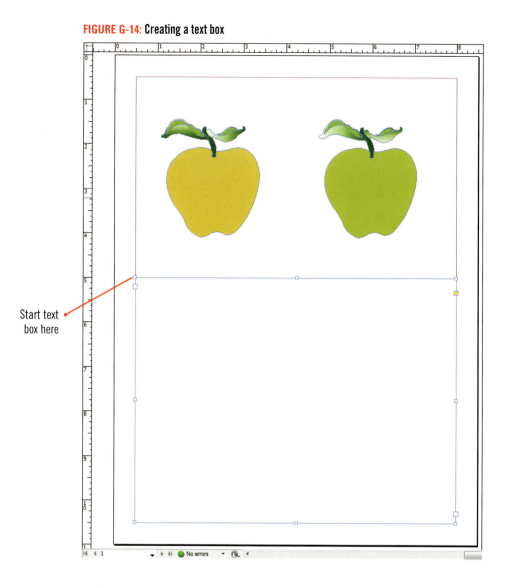

Start text
box here

FIGURE G-15: Preparing to select a column

FIGURE G-16: Text entered into table

Store Locations	Number of Apples Sold	Total Amount Donated
Presque Isle, Maine	550	$1,100.00
Bangor, Maine	360	$720.00
Burlington, Vermont	471	$942.00
Concord, New Hampshire	292	$584.00
Hartford, Connecticut	379	$758.00
Cambridge, Massachusetts	650	$1,300.00

Formatting Table Cells

There are many formatting options for table cells. You can format the text inside cells the same way that you format text inside a text box. You can apply borders and shading to table cells, and also change the width and height of table cells in order to fit more information inside them. After entering all of the data in the table, you are ready to format the table cells. You increase the height of each table cell, vertically align the text inside the cells, and then change the weight and color of the cell borders.

STEPS

1. **Click the Type tool T. on the Tools panel, if necessary, select the entire table, click Table on the Application bar, point to Cell Options, then click Rows and Columns**
   The Cell Options dialog box opens with the Rows and Columns tab displayed.

2. **Click the Row Height list arrow, then click Exactly**
   The Exactly setting is used when you want the row height to be an exact number. The At Least setting is used when the height of a row should be at least a specific value that you choose.

3. **Double-click the value in the Row Height text box, type .35, press [Tab], then click the Preview check box to add a check mark**
   The height of each table row changes to 0.35 inches tall in the document. Compare your screen and Cell Options dialog box to Figure G-17.

4. **Click the Text tab in the Cell Options dialog box, click the Align list arrow, then click Align Center**
   The text is vertically centered inside each of the cells.

5. **Click the Strokes and Fills tab**
   Notice that there is already a default 1-pt black stroke applied to table cells.

6. **Click the Weight list arrow, click 2 pt, click the Color list arrow, click C=75 M=5 Y=100 K=0 (green), then click OK**

7. **Click the Selection tool on the Tools panel, deselect the table, then press [W]**
   A 2-pt green border is added to the table cells, as shown in Figure G-18.

8. **Save your work**

Row Height text box

Preview of rows as 0.35 inches tall

Preview check box

FIGURE G-18: New formatting applied to table cells

Store Locations	Number of Apples Sold	Total Amount Donated
Presque Isle, Maine	550	$1,100.00
Bangor, Maine	360	$720.00
Burlington, Vermont	471	$942.00
Concord, New Hampshire	292	$584.00
Hartford, Connecticut	379	$758.00
Cambridge, Massachusetts	650	$1,300.00

Converting text to tables and tables to text

You can easily convert existing text to a table using the Convert Text to Table command on the Table menu. Select the text that you wish to convert to a table, click Table on the Application bar, then click Convert Text to Table. The Convert Text to Table dialog box opens. In this dialog box, you need to indicate how you initially separated the text horizontally and vertically. Typically, you would use a tab, a space, or a comma to separate pieces of text horizontally, and a paragraph return to separate pieces of text vertically. Whatever you used will determine how the text will be separated into columns and rows. Click the Column Separator list arrow, then click the item (Tab, Comma, or Paragraph) that you used to separate the pieces of text horizontally. Click the Row Separator list arrow, then click the item (Tab, Comma, or Paragraph) that you used to separate the pieces of text vertically. You can also convert tables into text by selecting a table and then clicking the Convert Table to Text command on the Table menu. In the Convert Table to Text dialog box, you indicate what type of separator you would like to use to separate each piece of text.

Inserting, Merging, and Splitting Table Cells

When working with tables, you may need to add table rows and/or columns because you don't have enough or delete them because you have too many. You can easily add rows and columns in a table using the Insert Row or Insert Column dialog box. You can choose how many rows or columns you want to insert, and if they should be added above or below the selected row or column. To delete a row or column, select the row or column, click Table on the Application bar, point to Delete, then click Row or Column. You can also combine, or **merge**, table cells into one cell and break up, or **split**, a table cell into smaller cells. You realize you need a heading row and a totals row for the table, so you insert two new rows, merge the cells in the new top row for the heading, and split the last table cell in the new bottom row to add the company goal next to the total dollar amount.

STEPS

1. **Press [W] to view guides, click the Type tool T on the Tools panel, position the mouse pointer on the left edge of the top row of the table until the pointer becomes a black arrow ➔, then click the mouse button**
   The top row is selected.

2. **Click Table on the Application bar, point to Insert, then click Row**
   The Insert Row(s) dialog box opens.

3. **Click the Above option button if necessary, then click OK**
   A new row is inserted above the selected row.

4. **Select the new row, then click the Merge cells button ⊠ on the Control panel**
   The three cells in the top row are merged into one cell.

5. **Click the merged cell, type The Happy Apple Fundraiser, change the font size of the text in the merged cell to 18 pt, click the Align center button ☰ on the Control panel, click the Selection tool ▸, deselect all, then compare your table to Figure G-19**

6. **Click T, select the bottom table row, click Table on the Application bar, point to Insert, click Row, click the Below option button in the Insert Row(s) dialog box, then click OK**

7. **Click the first cell of the bottom row, type Total, press [Tab], type 2,702, then press [Tab]**

8. **Click Table on the Application bar, point to Select, then click Cell**
   The current cell is selected.

9. **Click Table on the Application bar, click Split Cell Vertically, then deselect the cell**
   As shown in Figure G-20, the cell is split evenly into two cells.

10. **Click the left side of the split cell, type $5,404.00, press [Tab], type Goal: $3,000.00, then save your work**

Creating a table style

To add visual interest to your table, you may want to fill table cells with color. For example, you can apply alternating fill colors to rows in order to place emphasis on specific rows and make the table easier to read, or just to make the table more attractive. Once you have finished formatting a table, you can save all of the formatting as a table style in the Table Styles panel and then apply the style to new tables in the future. To create a new table style, click the Table Style Panel options button, then click New Table Style. The New Table Style dialog box opens with the General category displayed. The Style Settings section lists a summary of the style currently applied to the table. You can further modify the table style using the categories provided on the left of the dialog box. When you close the dialog box, the new style is added to the Table Styles panel.

The Happy Apple Fundraiser		
Store Locations	Number of Apples Sold	Total Amount Donated
Presque Isle, Maine	550	$1,100.00
Bangor, Maine	360	$720.00
Burlington, Vermont	471	$942.00
Concord, New Hampshire	292	$584.00
Hartford, Connecticut	379	$758.00
Cambridge, Massachusetts	650	$1,300.00

Merged cell

The Happy Apple Fundraiser			
Store Locations	Number of Apples Sold	Total Amount Donated	
Presque Isle, Maine	550	$1,100.00	
Bangor, Maine	360	$720.00	
Burlington, Vermont	471	$942.00	
Concord, New Hampshire	292	$584.00	
Hartford, Connecticut	379	$758.00	
Cambridge, Massachusetts	650	$1,300.00	
Total	2,702		

InDesign CS5

Setting Tabs in a Table

Tab stops are ruler settings that work together with the [Tab] key to allow you to position, or **justify**, text at specific horizontal locations within a text box or table cell. Using tab alignments, you can left-, right-, or center-justify text. You can also align numbers by their decimal point using the Align to Decimal button. You use the Align to Decimal button to align the dollar amounts in the third column of the table.

STEPS

1. Click the Type tool [T] on the Tools panel, if necessary, then drag from the second cell of the third column ($1,100.00) through the remaining six cells in the column

   The text in the second cell and in all cells beneath it in the column is selected.

2. Click Type on the Application bar, then click Tabs

   The Tabs panel appears directly above the selected text, as shown in Figure G-21. The Tabs panel includes a ruler and four alignment buttons in its upper-left corner.

3. Click the Align to Decimal button [↓] on the Tabs panel, then click directly above the 1-inch mark on the ruler on the Tabs panel

   As shown in Figure G-22, the Align to Decimal tab stop appears in the ruler. The numbers in the column shift to the right and are aligned by their decimal points at the location of the Align to Decimal tab stop. The text "1 in" in the X text box on the Tabs panel indicates the location of the selected tab stop.

4. Drag the Align to Decimal tab stop on the ruler to the right to approximately the 1.25-inch mark in order to move the aligned numbers to a new position

   The numbers in the selected cells move $1/4$" to the right. The information in the right half of the split cell also moves $1/4$" to the right.

5. Select just the cell that contains Goal: $3,000.00, drag the Align to Decimal tab stop down and off of the tab ruler to remove the tab setting for this cell, close the Tabs panel, then deselect all

   Dragging a tab stop out of the ruler removes the tab stop for the selected text only.

6. Select all of the numbers in the second column, click Type on the Application bar, click Tabs, then set an Align to Decimal tab stop at the 1-inch mark

7. Close the Tabs panel, select the second row, click the Font Style list arrow, then click Bold Italic to format the column headings

8. Deselect all, press [W] to hide guides, then compare your finished table to Figure G-23

9. Save your work, then exit InDesign

   You can also type a number in the X text box to place the selected tab stop type at that spot on the ruler.

FIGURE G-21: Tabs panel above selected text

Tab buttons

Ruler

FIGURE G-22: Align to Decimal tab set

X text box

Align to Decimal button

Align to Decimal tab stop

1-inch mark on ruler

Numbers are aligned by decimal point

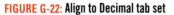

FIGURE G-23: Finished table

The Happy Apple Fundraiser			
Store Locations	**Number of Apples Sold**	**Total Amount Donated**	
Presque Isle, Maine	550	$1,100.00	
Bangor, Maine	360	$720.00	
Burlington, Vermont	471	$942.00	
Concord, New Hampshire	292	$584.00	
Hartford, Connecticut	379	$758.00	
Cambridge, Massachusetts	650	$1,300.00	
Total	2,702	$5,404.00	Goal: $3,000.00

InDesign CS5

Practice

Concepts Review

For current SAM information, including versions and content details, visit SAM Central (http://www.cengage.com/samcentral). If you have a SAM user profile, you may have access to hands-on instruction, practice, and assessment of the skills covered in this unit. Since various versions of SAM are supported throughout the life of this text, check with your instructor for the correct instructions and URL/Web site for accessing assignments.

Label the elements of the InDesign screen shown in Figure G-24.

FIGURE G-24

1. _____   4. _____
2. _____   5. _____
3. _____

Match each term with the statement that best describes it.

6. **Merge**   a. A type of gradient fill
7. **Linear**   b. Made from cyan, magenta, yellow, and/or black
8. **Color stop**   c. Found on the Gradient Ramp
9. **Spot color**   d. A color made by an ink manufacturer
10. **Process color** e. Combining two or more table cells

Select the best answer from the list of choices.

11. **Which of the following are associated with table columns and rows?**
    a. Alternating fills
    b. Exact width or height measurements
    c. Borders
    d. All of the above

12. **What is the Gradient tool used for?**
    a. Create a gradient
    b. Change a gradient
    c. Apply a gradient
    d. None of the above

13. **What are process inks used for?**
    a. Web graphics
    b. Color printing
    c. Multimedia
    d. Creating spot colors

14. **What is Pantone an example of?**
    a. Process color
    b. Process match
    c. Manufacturer of spot colors
    d. CMYK color

15. **Which of the following steps do you perform to add a new color stop to the Gradient Ramp?**
    a. Click just below the Gradient Ramp
    b. Double-click the far-left color stop
    c. Double-click the first color stop
    d. Click the Gradient panel list arrow, then click New Color Stop

Skills Review

1. **Create a process color.**
   a. Start InDesign, open ID G-2.indd, then save it as **Fall Schedule**.
   b. Click Window on the Application bar, point to Workspace, then click Essentials or, if Essentials is already selected, click Reset Essentials.
   c. Click the Swatches panel button to open the Swatches panel, then drag the lower-right corner of the Swatches panel down so that you can see all of the colors in it.
   d. Click the Swatches Panel options button, then click New Color Swatch.
   e. Type **0** in the Cyan text box if necessary, press [Tab], type **45**, press [Tab], type **100**, press [Tab], then type **0** if necessary.
   f. Click the Name with Color Value check box to remove the check mark, then type **Pumpkin Orange** in the Swatch Name text box.
   g. Click OK to close the New Color Swatch dialog box, click the far-left leaf, click the Fill tool on the Tools panel if necessary, click Pumpkin Orange in the Swatches panel, then deselect the leaf.
   h. Click Color on the right side of the workspace to open the Color panel, then notice the CMYK combination for the Pumpkin Orange color swatch.
   i. Open the Swatches panel again, then create a new process color using **0%** Cyan, **25%** Magenta, **100%** Yellow, and **0%** Black. Name the color **Gold**, click OK, then apply the Gold fill color to the middle leaf.
   j. Deselect the middle leaf.

Skills Review (continued)

    k. Create a third new process color using **25%** Cyan, **100%** Magenta, **100%** Yellow, and **0%** Black. Name the color **Rust**, click OK, then apply the Rust fill color to the far-right leaf.

    l. Deselect the far-right leaf, then save your work.

2. Select a spot color.

    a. Click the Swatches Panel options button, then click New Color Swatch.

    b. Click the Color Type list arrow, then click Spot.

    c. Click the Color Mode list arrow, then click PANTONE solid matte.

    d. Click the PANTONE text box, then type **1605**.

    e. Click OK to close the New Color Swatch dialog box.

    f. Open the Color panel and notice the spot color along with its process match.

    g. Click the stem on the far-left leaf, press and hold [Shift], click the other two leaf stems in the document, then release [Shift].

    h. In the Swatches panel, click PANTONE 1605 M.

    i. Deselect all, then save your work.

3. Create a gradient.

    a. Click the Swatches Panel options button, then click New Gradient Swatch.

    b. Click the first color stop on the Gradient Ramp in the New Gradient Swatch dialog box, click the Stop Color list arrow, then click Swatches if necessary.

    c. Click Gold in the list of swatches.

    d. Click just below the Gradient Ramp anywhere between the first color stop and the second color stop to add a new color stop, then drag the new color stop until you see approximately 50% in the Location text box.

    e. Click the new color stop, click the Stop Color list arrow, then click Swatches.

    f. Click Pumpkin Orange in the list of swatches, click the third color stop, then click Rust in the list of swatches.

    g. Click OK to close the dialog box.

    h. Click the Selection tool if necessary, click the middle leaf, then click New Gradient Swatch in the Swatches panel.

    i. Click Window on the Application bar, point to Color, then click Gradient to see the selected gradient on the Gradient panel.

    j. Close the Gradient panel, then save your work.

4. Use the Gradient Swatch tool.

    a. Verify that the middle leaf is still selected.

    b. Click the Gradient Swatch tool on the Tools panel.

    c. Position the Gradient Swatch tool just above where the middle leaf's stem meets the leaf, drag straight up to the approximate middle of the leaf, then release the mouse button. (*Hint*: The top points of the leaf are rust-colored.)

    d. Click the Selection tool, then deselect all.

    e. Save your work.

5. Create a table.

    a. Click the Type tool, then create a text box below the three leaves that is 6 inches wide and 3.5 inches tall and whose bottom edge snaps to the bottom margin guide.

    b. Show the Align panel, align the text box to the horizontal center of the page, then close the Align panel. (*Hint*: Select Align to Page in the Align panel.)

    c. Click the Type tool if necessary, click inside the text box, click Table on the Application bar, then click Insert Table.

    d. Type **6** in the Body Rows text box, press [Tab], type **3** if necessary, then click OK.

    e. Position the mouse pointer on the top edge of the first column of the table so that the pointer becomes a black arrow, then click to select the column.

    f. Position the mouse pointer on the upper-left corner of the table so that the mouse pointer becomes a diagonal black arrow, then click to select the table.

  g. Click in the top cell of the first table column, type **Weekday**, press [Tab], type **Name of Class**, press [Tab], type **Drop-In Cost**, then press [Tab].

  h. Enter the following text in the remaining table cells:

Monday	**Pilates**	**$18.00**
Tuesday	**Hatha Yoga**	**$16.00**
Wednesday	**Ballet Stretch**	**$12.00**
Thursday	**Vinyasa Yoga**	**$16.00**
Friday	**Zumba**	**$20.00**

  i. Save your work.

6. Format table cells.

  a. Select the entire table, click Table on the Application bar, point to Cell Options, then click Rows and Columns.

  b. Click the Row Height list arrow, then click Exactly.

  c. Double-click the value in the Row Height text box, type **.375**, press [Tab], then select the Preview check box, if necessary.

  d. Click the Text tab in the Cell Options dialog box, click the Align list arrow, then click Align Center.

  e. Click the Strokes and Fills tab, click the Weight list arrow, click 1 pt if necessary, click the Color list arrow, click Pumpkin Orange, then click OK.

  f. Deselect the table, then press [W].

  g. Save your work.

7. Insert, merge, and split table cells.

  a. Press [W] to show guides again, click the Type tool if necessary, select the top table row, click Table on the Application bar, point to Insert, then click Row.

  b. Click the Above option button if necessary, then click OK.

  c. Select the new row, then click the Merge cells button on the Control panel.

  d. Click the merged cell, then type **Fall Class Schedule**.

  e. Change the font size of the text in the merged cell to 24 pt, click the Align center button on the Control panel, then deselect all.

  f. Select the bottom table row, click Table on the Application bar, point to Insert, click Row, click the Below option button in the Insert Row(s) dialog box, then click OK.

  g. Click the first cell of the bottom row, type **Saturday**, press [Tab], type **Nia**, then press [Tab].

  h. Click Table on the Application bar, point to Select, then click Cell.

  i. Click Table on the Application bar, click Split Cell Vertically, then deselect the cell.

  j. Click the left side of the split cell, type **$14.00**, press [Tab], type **Two classes**, then save your work.

8. Set tabs in a table.

  a. Click the Type tool if necessary, then drag from the second cell of the third column ($18.00) through the remaining six cells in the column.

  b. Click Type on the Application bar, then click Tabs.

  c. Click the Align to Decimal button on the Tabs panel if necessary, then click directly above the 0.5-inch mark on the ruler on the Tabs panel.

  d. Select only the cell that contains "Two classes," then drag the Align to Decimal tab stop down and off of the ruler to remove the tab stop for this cell only.

  e. Close the Tabs panel, then deselect all.

  f. Select the first row of the table, click the Font Style list arrow, then click Bold Italic to format the title.

  g. Deselect all, press [W], then compare your finished table to Figure G-25.

  h. Save your work, close Fall Schedule.indd, then exit InDesign.

FIGURE G-25

Fall Class Schedule			
Weekday	Name of Class	Drop-In Cost	
Monday	Pilates	$18.00	
Tuesday	Hatha Yoga	$16.00	
Wednesday	Ballet Stretch	$12.00	
Thursday	Vinyasa Yoga	$16.00	
Friday	Zumba	$20.00	
Saturday	Nia	$14.00	Two classes

Independent Challenge 1

You are a textbook cover designer, and you have been asked to design the cover for a tenth grade math book. You first want to create a palette of three vibrant colors that work well together and that you will use when you design the cover.

    a. Start InDesign, create a new default document, then save it as **Textbook colors**.

    b. Create three rectangles on the page that are 3 inches wide and 2 inches tall.

    c. Create three new colors and name them in the Swatches panel. Create colors that you think would appeal to the audience. For example, the sample shown in the figure uses lime green, purple, and yellow.

    d. Apply each new color as a fill color to one of the rectangles.

    e. Overlap the rectangles in any arrangement to demonstrate how the colors look together.

    f. Save your work, press [W], then compare your screen to Figure G-26.

Advanced Challenge Exercise

FIGURE G-26

    ■ Select all three rectangles, then press and hold [Alt] (Win) or [option] (Mac) while you drag them below to create a copy.

    ■ Create a tint swatch for each of the three new colors, using 75% for each tint swatch.

    ■ Apply the three tint swatches to the copied rectangles.

    ■ Save your work.

    g. Close Textbook colors.indd, then exit InDesign.

Independent Challenge 2

You work in the sales office of a local car dealer. Your boss has asked you to help him improve the appearance of an advertisement he is running in the local newspaper for an upcoming sale. You decide to create some colors and a gradient fill to apply to the balloon graphics in the document.

a. Start InDesign, open ID G-3.indd, then save it as **Car Ad**.

b. Create two new process colors and name them in the Swatches panel.

c. Select two PANTONE solid coated spot colors and save them in the Swatches panel.

d. Apply the four new colors to four of the balloons.

e. Using the four new colors, create a new four-color, radial gradient swatch and name it **Balloon Gradient**.

f. Apply the Balloon Gradient as the fill color to the last unfilled balloon in the document.

g. Use the Gradient Swatch tool to change the highlight point by clicking on the balloon somewhere other than the center of it.

h. Save your work, press [W], then compare your screen to Figure G-27. (*Hint*: The appearance of the balloons in your document will differ.)

Advanced Challenge Exercise

- Select the text box at the top of the document.
- Click Type on the Application bar, then click Create Outlines.
- Click the Balloon Gradient on the Swatches panel.
- Deselect all, then save your work.

i. Close Car Ad.indd, then exit InDesign.

FIGURE G-27

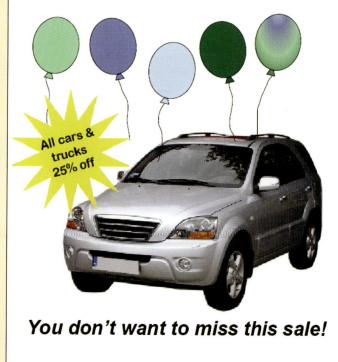

Independent Challenge 3

The local high school lacrosse team needs new equipment and uniforms. As the volunteer manager of the team, you plan to present a document outlining the needs of the team to the school budget committee. You plan to incorporate the team colors, royal blue and gray, into the document. You use a table in InDesign to present the information.

a. Start InDesign, create a new 8.5" × 11" document with 1-inch margins, without facing pages, and with Portrait orientation, then save the document with the name **Lacrosse**.

b. Create a text box that snaps to all four margin guides.

c. Insert a table in the text box with seven rows and three columns.

d. Enter the following text in the first seven rows. (*Hint*: Include the header row.)

Quantity	Equipment	Price (each)
12	Lacrosse sticks	$87.00
12	Lacrosse helmets	$109.00
12	Team jerseys	$26.00
12	Arm pads	$35.00
12	Lacrosse shorts	$24.99

e. Merge the first two cells in the bottom row, type **Total** in the merged cell, press [Tab], then type **$3,383.88**.

f. Select the table, then change the cell height to exactly 1 inch.

g. Change the text alignment to Center.

h. Change the font size of all text in the table to 18 pt, then center-align the cells in the Quantity and Equipment columns.

i. Insert a new row above the top row, merge the new row, then type **Fairbanks High School Lacrosse Team**.

j. Center the new heading, then change the font size to 24 pt.

k. Create two new process colors named **Aqua** and **Light Gray**. (*Hint*: Use your own CMYK percentages to create the colors.)

l. Click Table on the Application bar, point to Table Options, then click Alternating Fills.

m. Apply alternating fills using 10% Aqua and 100% Light Gray for all rows.

n. Apply the Aqua color to the heading text.

o. Add Aqua, 2-pt borders around each cell in the table.

p. Use an Align to Decimal tab stop to align all of the amounts in the third column and then center-align the "Price (each)" text above the amounts.

q. Save your work, press [W], compare your screen to Figure G-28, close Lacrosse.indd, then exit InDesign.

FIGURE G-28

Fairbanks High School Lacrosse Team		
Quantity	Equipment	Price (each)
12	Lacrosse sticks	$87.00
12	Lacrosse helmets	$109.00
12	Team jerseys	$26.00
12	Arm pads	$35.00
12	Lacrosse shorts	$24.99
Total		$3,383.88

Working with Color and Tables

Real Life Independent Challenge

Tables are a great tool to help you organize information. Use InDesign to create a table of your weekly schedule. You can include school, work, and/or all extracurricular activities, such as exercise classes, meetings, and tasks. Adding color to a table can help emphasize specific cells.

a. Start InDesign, create a new document with 1-inch margins, without facing pages, and with Landscape orientation, then name it **Weekly Schedule**.

b. Create an 9" × 5" text box that snaps to the left and right margin guides.

c. Insert a table in the text box that has five rows and five columns.

d. Type the days of the week from Monday through Friday in the five cells in the first row, then fill the cells below the column headings with your activities for each day, such as **School 7-2**. (*Hint*: You do not have to add times to each item or use all of the rows. If you run out of rows, you can add more by clicking in the last cell of the last column, then pressing [Tab].)

e. Insert a new row above row 1, merge the cells in row 1, then type **My Schedule** in the merged cell.

f. Delete any extra rows, if necessary.

g. Format the text as you like.

h. Format the cells using the Cell Options dialog box.

i. Save your work, then exit InDesign.

Visual Workshop

Start InDesign and create a new 8.5" × 11" document without facing pages. Save the document as **Rainbow Gradient**. Using Figure G-29 as a guide, create a rectangle and place it just above the approximate center of the page. Create a color swatch named **Orange** from 0% Cyan, 50% Magenta, 100% Yellow, and 0% Black. Create a linear gradient named **Rainbow** using the Orange swatch and the default red, yellow, green, and blue colors in the Swatches panel. (*Hint*: Orange should appear in the gradient between red and yellow.) Space each color stop 25% to the right of the previous color stop on the Gradient Ramp. Select the blue color stop on the Gradient Ramp, compare your screen to Figure G-29, save your work, then exit InDesign.

FIGURE G-29

Adding Interactivity and Exporting Documents

Files You Will Need:

Logo RGB.ai
ID H-1.indd
Logo CMYK.ai
Donations.pdf
Leaf RGB.ai
ID H-2.indd
Leaf CMYK.ai
New class.pdf
ID H-3.indd
ID H-4.indd
ID H-5.indd
Fruit folder

Interactive documents include buttons and links that you click to visit specific sections in a document or a Web site. Imagine viewing a college catalog online; you could click a link for only those schools that are in a specific part of the country or only those schools that offer a culinary program. In InDesign, you can build interactivity into a document by adding buttons, hyperlinks, and animation. When you export the document as a PDF or a Flash Player file, the interactive elements become active. You can open PDF files in Adobe Reader and view Flash Player files in a Web browser. The Happy Apple wishes to share its fundraising efforts with its customers. Ted asks you to apply a hyperlink to an apple graphic that jumps to a pet shelter Web site where donations will be sent. Ted also asks you to create an interactive apple button that when clicked shows how much money the Happy Apple has raised. This graphic will be exported as an interactive Adobe PDF and used in the company's e-mail marketing service.

OBJECTIVES

Create a document for the Web

Create a hyperlink

Create an animation

Export a document as a Flash Player file

Create a button

Create a rollover

Export a document as an interactive Adobe PDF file

Understand export options for the Web

Creating a Document for the Web

In InDesign, you can create documents for print and for the Web. Although you can convert an existing document to a Web document, it is ideal to create a Web document from scratch in the New Document dialog box. The New Document dialog box allows you to choose Print or Web as the intended output for the document. When you choose Web, some settings in the dialog box change to reflect the Web environment. The current unit of measure changes to pixels because all graphics displayed on monitors are viewed as pixels. The color mode changes from CMYK to **RGB** (red, green, blue), the color system for graphics displayed on a monitor. You create a new Web document, then place an apple graphic on the page. The apple will be the source for the hyperlink.

STEPS

1. Start InDesign, click File on the Application bar, point to New, then click Document

2. In the New Document dialog box, click the Intent list arrow, then click Web

   As shown in Figure H-1, the unit of measure is displayed in pixels. The page orientation changes from Portrait to Landscape, and the Facing Pages check box is deselected. The page size, 800×600, is equivalent to an InDesign page that is approximately 11 inches wide by 8.5 inches tall. Notice the margin guides are 36 pixels. There are 72 pixels in 1 inch; therefore, the margins are ½ inch.

3. Click OK to close the New Document dialog box, then notice that the rulers display pixels

   QUICK TIP
   If your rulers are not visible, click View on the Application bar, then click Show Rulers.

4. Click the workspace switcher on the Application bar, then click Interactive

   The Interactive workspace offers panels appropriate for building Web documents, such as the Buttons and Hyperlinks panels.

5. Save the document as Web hyperlink

6. Click File on the Application bar, click Place, navigate to the drive and folder where you store your Data Files, click Logo RGB.ai, click Open, then click the approximate center of the artboard

   You will use the Happy Apple as a source for the hyperlink. Click **View** on the Application bar, point to **Display Performance**, then click **High Quality Display**.

7. Click the Swatches panel icon ▦ to open the Swatches panel

   As shown in Figure H-2, the Swatches panel displays the default set of RGB colors used for Web documents. Web colors were applied to the apple graphic when it was originally created in Adobe Illustrator.

8. Close the Swatches panel, then save your work

FIGURE H-1: New Document dialog box

Intent list arrow

Page size and margins are measured in pixels

FIGURE H-2: Viewing the Interactive workspace

Rulers displayed in pixels

Swatches panel

Web swatches

Interactive panels

InDesign CS5

Creating a Hyperlink

Like buttons, hyperlinks offer another way to incorporate interactivity into an InDesign document. You use the Hyperlinks panel to create a **hyperlink** that opens an e-mail message window, jumps to another location in the current document or another document, or opens a Web site. Hyperlinks can appear as a rectangle or they can be invisible. Each hyperlink requires a source and a destination. The **source**—the actual link that a user will click—can be a text selection, a text frame, or a graphics frame. The **destination** is the place the source jumps to. Hyperlinks are only active in InDesign documents that have been exported as Adobe PDF or SWF files, although you can test them on the Hyperlinks panel. You are ready to add a hyperlink to the apple. The apple will serve as the source for an invisible hyperlink. When clicked, the hyperlink will take viewers to the Web site of the pet shelter receiving the donations.

STEPS

1. **Click the Hyperlinks panel icon** 🔲 **to open the Hyperlinks panel, click the Selection tool** ▸ **on the Tools panel, then click the apple**

   The Hyperlinks panel opens in the workspace.

2. **Click the Hyperlinks Panel options button** 🔲, **then click New Hyperlink**

   The New Hyperlink dialog box opens, as shown in Figure H-3. It allows you to choose the type of link, such as a URL, the name of the destination, and the appearance of the hyperlink. Notice that the Appearance section describes the physical characteristics that will be used for the hyperlink. You can choose whether you want the hyperlink to be visible or not. By default, hyperlinks are invisible.

   > **QUICK TIP**
   > To link to another InDesign document, click Page in the Link To list, click the Document list arrow, then click Browse to choose the file.

3. **Click the Link To list arrow, then click URL, if necessary**

   A **Uniform Resource Locator (URL)** is the address of a Web site on the Internet.

   > **QUICK TIP**
   > URL information remains stored in the Hyperlinks panel. You can click the URL list arrow on the panel to choose a stored URL.

4. **Click after the** // **in the Destination text box, then type www.buddydoghs.com**

   The URL, www.buddydoghs.com, is the Buddy Dog Humane Society Web site, which is the destination for the hyperlink. The hyperlink will appear on top of the selected apple as an invisible rectangle.

5. **Click OK to close the New Hyperlink dialog box**

   The New Hyperlink dialog box closes. The hyperlink has been added to the document on top of the apple, but it is invisible because its appearance is set to Invisible Rectangle.

6. **Click Hyperlink on the Hyperlinks panel, if necessary**

   The URL for Hyperlink appears in the URL text box in the panel, as shown in Figure H-4. You can test the hyperlink without exporting the document.

7. **Click the Go to destination of the selected hyperlink or cross-reference button** 🔲 **on the Hyperlinks panel**

   The Buddy Dog Humane Society Web site opens in the browser, as shown in Figure H-5.

8. **Close the browser window, close the Hyperlinks panel, then save your work**

Using the Web swatch library

If you use InDesign to create pages or graphics for the Web, you should apply color from the Web swatch library to the objects in your documents in order for them to display correctly on the Web. Colors in the Web swatch library are displayed the same on both Windows and Macintosh computers, and are all made from a combination of RGB instead of CMYK. To access the Web swatch library, click the Swatches Panel options button, click New Color Swatch, click the Color Type list arrow, click Spot, click the Color Mode list arrow, then click Web.

FIGURE H-3: New Hyperlink dialog box

Options for changing the
hyperlink's appearance

FIGURE H-4: Viewing the hyperlink

URL for
Hyperlink

FIGURE H-5: Buddy Dog Humane Society Web site

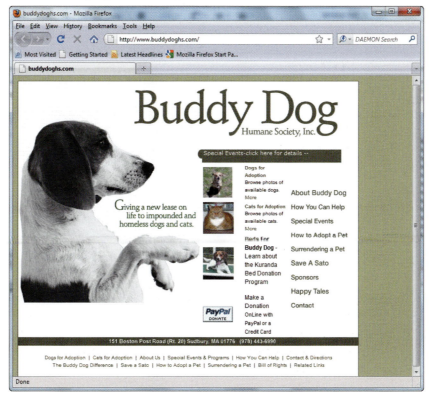

Adding Interactivity and Exporting Documents

Creating an Animation

Animation is an effect that you can apply to an InDesign object to cause it to move in a specific way, such as zoom in from the side or spin. Animating objects can add a lot of fun and visual interest to your InDesign document. Using the Animation panel is easy; you select the object that you wish to animate, then choose a type of animation from the Preset menu on the panel. You can choose how many seconds the animation should last, how many times it should occur, and the event that will cause it to occur. A preview of the animation appears as a pink butterfly graphic in the Animation panel. However, you can preview how the InDesign objects will look when animated using the Preview panel. You animate the apple to spin one time when the Web page loads in the browser. You then preview the animation on the Preview panel.

STEPS

1. **Select the apple on the artboard**

2. **Click the Animation panel icon** to open the Animation panel

   The Animation panel opens in the workspace.

3. **Notice that Logo RGB.ai appears in the Name text box**

4. **Click the Preset list arrow, then click Spin**

   The butterfly shows a preview of how the apple will look when animated.

> **QUICK TIP**
> You can also **loop** an animation, which means to have it continually play without stopping, by clicking the Loop check box.

5. **Click the Event(s) list arrow, then click On Page Load, if necessary**

   The apple will rotate once when the Web page is loaded. An animation icon appears next to the button icon on the apple graphic. You preview the animation in the Preview panel. You can choose how many times an animation will occur by changing the value in the Play text box. Compare your screen to Figure H-6.

6. **Click the Preview Spread button** on the Animation panel to open the Preview panel

   You can also play the animation in the Preview panel.

7. **Click the Play preview button** on the Preview panel to preview the animation, as shown in Figure H-7

   The apple spins one time when the page is loaded in the panel. Now you are ready to export your InDesign document as an SWF file and preview it in a browser.

8. **Save your work**

Preview

Name
text box

Preset list
arrow

Event

Animation icon

Preview of
animation preset

Play preview
button

InDesign CS5

Exporting a Document as a Flash Player File

Shockwave Flash (or SWF) is a very popular format for online animations and games. SWF files are scalable and compact, which makes them perfect for the Web. SWF files can be viewed by anyone with Flash Player installed on his or her computer. To export an InDesign document as an SWF file, choose Flash Player (SWF) in the Save as type list (Win) or Format list (Mac) in the Export dialog box. If you wish to quickly preview your SWF file in a browser window after exporting, be sure to click the Generate HTML File check box and the View SWF After Exporting check box in the Export SWF dialog box that opens before the file export is complete. All hyperlinks and buttons are active in the exported SWF file. You export the Web hyperlink document so that you can test the hyperlink in a browser window.

STEPS

1. **Click File on the Application bar, then click Export**

    The Export dialog box opens.

2. **Navigate, if necessary, to the drive and folder where you store your Data Files, click the Save as type list arrow (Win) or the Format list arrow (Mac) at the bottom of the Export dialog box, then click Flash Player (SWF), if necessary**

    The .swf filename extension is added to Web hyperlink in the File name (Win) or Save As text box (Mac).

    > **QUICK TIP**
    > You can apply page transitions to multipage documents in the Pages panel.

3. **Click Save**

    The Export SWF dialog box opens, as shown in Figure H-8, showing the default General settings for exporting a document as an SWF file. You can change the settings depending on your needs. The Export section allows you to choose a selection, a range of pages, or all pages to export. You can also choose to view the SWF file after the export is complete. The Size section lets you control the output size of the exported file. You can choose a transparent background or the paper color of the document. Finally, you can choose to include the interactivity and media applied, or not, and any page transitions that may have been applied.

4. **In the Export SWF dialog box, verify that the Paper Color option button is selected as the Background, then click OK to accept the default settings in the Export SWF dialog box**

    The SWF file opens in your default browser.

5. **Position the mouse pointer over the apple, then notice that the pointer changes to an interactivity pointer 🖑, as shown in Figure H-9**

6. **Click the red apple to open the Buddy Dog Humane Society Web site**

    The Buddy Dog Humane Society Web site opens.

7. **Close the Web browser, then close Web hyperlink.indd**

Understanding Global Security

If you receive a warning in the browser, click Settings in the dialog box. In the Global security settings for content creators box, click Edit locations, click Add location, click Browse for files, navigate to where you store the file, then click Confirm. Close the browser window, then go back to InDesign and re-export the file.

Paper Color
option button

InDesign CS5

Creating a Button

In InDesign, a **button** refers to an interactive, clickable item that becomes active when the document is exported as an interactive Portable Document Format (PDF) or SWF file. You can create a button using just about any object in InDesign. You can use a shape, a placed image, or even a text box as a button. To create a new button, select the object that you would like to use as a button, then click the Convert to Button command on the Object menu. The Buttons panel opens, prompting you to choose an action and an event for the new button. The **event** refers to the required treatment of the button, such as a rollover or a click, and the **action** refers to what will happen as a result of the action, such as opening a Web page. You convert an apple graphic to a button that will open a document showing how much money the Happy Apple has raised so far for the shelter.

STEPS

1. **Open the file ID H-1.indd from the drive and folder where you store your Data Files, then save the file as Apple button**

   The document is a custom size document that is 4.25" × 5.5".

2. **Click the workspace switcher, click Reset Interactive, then change the display to High Quality Display**

3. **Click the Selection tool ▶ on the Tools panel, then click the apple**

   > **QUICK TIP**
   > You can also convert an object to a button by clicking the Convert Object to a Button button 🔲 on the Buttons panel. You can convert a button back into an object by clicking the Convert Button to an Object button 🔲 on the Buttons panel.

4. **Click Object on the Application bar, point to Interactive, then click Convert to Button**

   The Buttons panel opens, displaying the button with its Normal appearance; the way it will look on the Web site or in a PDF document before it is clicked. The Buttons panel allows you to create a button name, and choose an action and an event for the button. As shown in Figure H-10, a semi-transparent button icon appears in the lower-right corner of the graphic, indicating that the graphic is now a button.

5. **Highlight the text in the Name text box, then type Donations button**

6. **Click the Event list arrow, then click On Click**

   The On Click event is assigned to the button, indicating that users must click the button to trigger an action. You assign an event that will open a file.

   > **QUICK TIP**
   > You can remove an action by clicking the Delete selected action button 🔲 on the Actions panel.

7. **Click the Add new action for selected event button 🔲 on the Buttons panel, then click Open File**

   The action appears in the panel. When a user clicks the button, a PDF file will open, showing a chart that tracks the amount of donations.

8. **Click the Select File button 🔲 on the Buttons panel, navigate to the drive and folder where you store your Data Files, click Donations.pdf, then click Open**

   The link to the Donations document appears in the Select File text box, as shown in Figure H-11. To test the button, you must export the document as an Adobe PDF (Interactive) or SWF file. In a later lesson, you will export the file as an Adobe PDF (Interactive) file to test the button.

9. **Save your work**

Adding sample buttons

In a multipage document that users will view in Adobe Reader or Adobe Acrobat or on the Web, you may need to create buttons for the viewer to use to navigate through the document or to view additional information. InDesign comes with preset buttons stored in the Sample Buttons panel that can help you easily add this interactivity. Each button is programmed with a prewritten script, called an action, that runs when the user clicks the button or moves the mouse pointer over it.

Semi-transparent
button icon

FIGURE H-11: Defining the action for the event

Select File button

Path of the file that will open
when the button is clicked

Creating a Rollover

When you create a button, you can choose to change its appearance, or **state**, when an event takes place. For example, it's common to change the button's appearance when a user rolls the mouse over the button or when the user clicks the button. To define the new appearance, you first select the button, then click either [Rollover] or [Click] on the Buttons panel. Make the changes you would like to make to the button and you're done. The button's new appearance appears on the Buttons panel. You create a rollover effect for the apple graphic so that when a user rolls the mouse over the button, a drop shadow appears behind it.

1. **Verify that the apple button is still selected**

2. **On the Buttons panel, click [Rollover] in the Appearance section, as shown in Figure H-12**
   The [Rollover] appearance becomes active on the Buttons panel. You want to modify the button's appearance in its rollover state.

QUICK TIP
You can also press [Ctrl][Alt][M] (Win) or ⌘[option][M] (Mac) to open the Effects dialog box.

3. **Click Object on the Application bar, point to Effects, then click Drop Shadow**
   The Effects dialog box opens with the Drop Shadow effect selected, as shown in Figure H-13. A **drop shadow** is an effect that adds the illusion of depth to an object by placing a shadow behind it. The Drop Shadow effect has many settings that you can adjust in the Effects dialog box, but the default settings are acceptable for the rollover.

4. **Click OK to accept the default settings in the Effects dialog box**
   A drop shadow appears behind the apple graphic and the preview of the apple in the [Rollover] section of the Buttons panel updates to show the drop shadow, as shown in Figure H-14.

5. **Save your work**

Working with effects

You can apply 10 effects to InDesign objects from the Object Effects menu. The Effects dialog box opens with the effect that you chose both highlighted and checked on the left side of the dialog box. The main panel of the dialog box displays all of the possible settings for that effect. The settings that you first see are the default settings. For example, the Drop Shadow settings use a 75% opaque black color for the shadow. Each effect has dials, check boxes, menus, and text boxes for you to use to enter new setting values. You can preview the changes by clicking the Preview check box in the lower-left corner of the dialog box. If you want to apply an effect just to an object's stroke, fill, or text, click the Settings for list arrow above the list of effects on the left side of the dialog box, then click Fill, Stroke, or Text.

You can apply more than one effect to an object at a time. Click the effect check box or highlight the effect name to choose that effect. If you click the effect check box, the main panel continues to display the settings for the highlighted effect, even if it's not the one whose check box you just selected. In this case, the new effect is added to the object using InDesign's default settings. However, if you click the name of the effect, the effect is highlighted and its corresponding check box is automatically checked. The main panel displays the settings for the highlighted effect, allowing you to modify the new effect's settings while adding it to the object. To remove an effect, remove the check mark next to the effect name. The Transparency effect does not have a check box. Simply click Transparency to apply it, and deselect it to remove it. Effects are listed on the Effects panel after they are applied to an object.

[Rollover]
appearance
is selected

FIGURE H-13: Effects dialog box

Drop Shadow effect

Settings for the Drop
Shadow effect

FIGURE H-14: Viewing the drop shadow effect

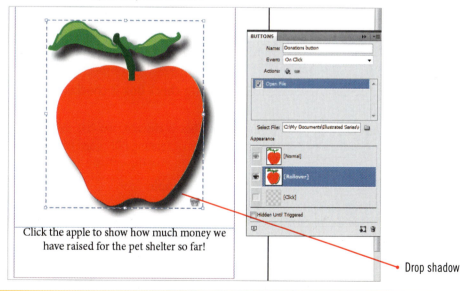

Click the apple to show how much money we
have raised for the pet shelter so far!

Drop shadow

Using the Preflight panel

When you complete a document, it is very important to find and correct any errors in the document to ensure that it prints correctly. The Preflight feature is an InDesign utility that you can use to check an open document for errors such as missing fonts, missing or modified links, and overset text. Any errors that are found are listed in the Preflight panel; you can use this list to fix any problems by substituting fonts, fixing overset text issues, and/or updating missing and modified files. A green circle on the left side of the status bar indicates that there are no preflight errors in a document; when the circle is red, there are errors. You can create customized preflight profiles in which you indicate what you would like the Preflight panel to flag as errors to be fixed. For example, you may want InDesign to flag font sizes smaller than 12 points as an error because your document cannot contain any font sizes smaller than 12 points.

InDesign CS5

Exporting a Document as an Interactive Adobe PDF File

Portable Document Format, or **PDF**, is the file format used in Adobe Reader and Adobe Acrobat software programs that allows you to view documents created by other programs and saved in the PDF file format. For example, an InDesign document exported as a PDF file can be opened and viewed by someone who does not have InDesign. PDF files make it much easier for a large audience to view your work whether or not they have the software used to create it. You can export an InDesign document as an Adobe PDF (Print) format or as an Adobe PDF (Interactive) format. When your document includes any type of interactivity, choose Adobe PDF (Interactive) format from the Export dialog box. All hyperlinks, bookmarks, animation, transitions, and buttons added in InDesign have full functionality in an exported Adobe PDF (Interactive) file. You export the Apple button document as an interactive Adobe PDF and then test the button.

STEPS

1. **Click File on the Application bar, then click Export**
2. **Navigate to the drive and folder where you store your Data Files, click the Save as type list arrow (Win) or the Format list arrow (Mac) at the bottom of the Export dialog box, then click Adobe PDF (Interactive)**

   The .pdf filename extension is added to Apple button in the File name (Win) or Save as text box (Mac).

3. **Click Save**

   The Export to Interactive PDF dialog box opens, as shown in Figure H-15, showing the default General settings for exporting a document as an interactive PDF file. You can change the settings depending on your needs. The Pages section allows you to choose an individual page, a range of pages, or all pages to export. You can choose how many pages to view at a time in the Layout menu as well as the zoom level at which to view the PDF in the View menu. For a multipage interactive document, you can choose page transitions and show the presentation in full screen mode. Be sure to choose the Include All option button in the Buttons and Media section. This will activate the interactivity built into the document. Finally, in the Image Handling section of the dialog box, you can choose compression and quality settings.

QUICK TIP
Click the Security button in the Export to Interactive PDF dialog box to apply password protection to the PDF file.

4. **Verify that the View After Exporting check box is checked, then click OK to accept the default settings in the dialog box**

   When the View After Exporting check box is checked, the PDF file will open in Adobe Reader or Adobe Acrobat when the export is complete. The Generating PDF progress bar appears and then the PDF file opens in Adobe Reader or Adobe Acrobat. Your version of the software may differ from Figure H-16.

5. **Position the mouse pointer over the apple**

   As shown in Figure H-16, the pointer changes to an interactivity pointer 🖑, and the drop shadow appears behind the apple.

6. **Click the apple to open the Donations.pdf file**

7. **Close the Donations.pdf file, then close Adobe Reader or Adobe Acrobat**

8. **Close the Apple button document**

Creating an Export preset

You can save your Export Adobe PDF dialog box settings as a named preset so that you do not have to choose the same settings each time you export to PDF. Once you've chosen the settings you need, click the Save Preset button in the lower-left corner of the Export Adobe PDF dialog box. Name the preset in the Save Preset dialog box, then click OK. The new preset is added to the list of presets in the Adobe PDF Preset list at the top of the dialog box. Click the Adobe PDF Preset list arrow, click the preset you need, then click Export.

FIGURE H-15: Export to Interactive PDF dialog box

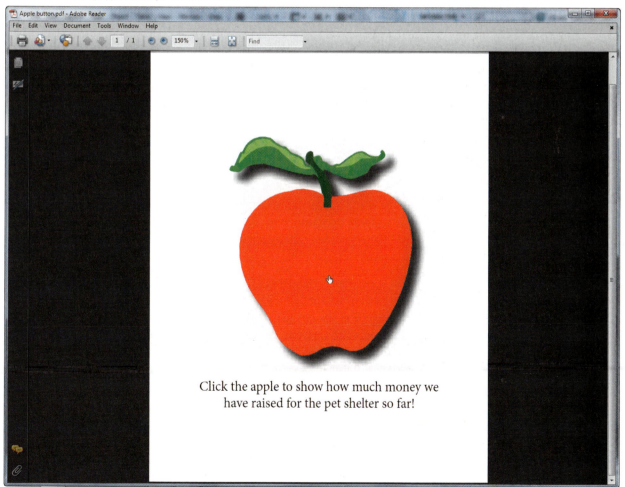

FIGURE H-16: Viewing Apple button.pdf in Adobe Reader

Click the apple to show how much money we have raised for the pet shelter so far!

InDesign CS5

Understanding Export Options for the Web

Many of today's designers face the dual task of creating printed materials and then translating those same materials for use on the Web. InDesign makes it easy to prepare Web-ready graphics and pages that can be exported for use in Adobe Flash, Adobe Dreamweaver, or another HTML editor. Hyperlinks and buttons created in an InDesign document become active in these exported Web formats. Ted explains to you that your job will start to involve preparing marketing materials for the Web, and that you'll be working with the Web department to get the materials put online. He asks you to research methods for exporting InDesign for use on the Web.

DETAILS

InDesign documents can be exported for use on the Web as the following file types:

- **JPEG (Joint Photographic Experts Group)**

  A JPEG is a compressed graphic file format that has a smaller file size than other graphic formats and is ideal for use on the Web. You can export objects on an InDesign document page as JPEG files. You can also export one page, a range of pages, or an entire InDesign document as a JPEG. Having the ability to export InDesign objects or document pages as JPEG files is useful when you want to post a selection, a page, or pages as an image on the Web. To export a selected object, page, or document as a JPEG file, choose JPEG in the Save as type list (Win) or Format list (Mac) in the Export dialog box.

QUICK TIP
You can use Dreamweaver to create complex Web sites or individual Web pages.

- **Dreamweaver**

  Adobe Dreamweaver CS5 is a Web development program that lets you create Web pages containing text, images, hyperlinks, animation, sounds, and video. To export an InDesign document as a Dreamweaver file, click File on the Application bar, point to Export for, then click Dreamweaver. In the XHTML Export Options dialog box that opens, you can choose options for exporting a selection or the entire document, image quality options, color palette options, and options for dealing with cascading style sheets (CSS) and JavaScript. When you export an InDesign document for Dreamweaver, you create an HTML file of the document and a folder containing all of the optimized images.

- **SWF (Shockwave Flash)**

  SWF is a very popular format for online animations and games. SWF files are scalable and compact, which makes them perfect for the Web. SWF files can be viewed by anyone with Flash Player installed on his or her computer. To export an InDesign document as an SWF file, choose SWF in the Save as type list (Win) or Format list (Mac) in the Export dialog box. All hyperlinks and buttons are active in the exported SWF file.

- **FLA**

  You can edit FLA files in Adobe Flash Professional CS5, a development program you can use to create Web sites, animations that are used on Web sites, and applications. An FLA file is an editable version of the file you originally created in InDesign. You you can add sample buttons to an InDesign document and then attach complex actions to them in Flash. To export an InDesign document as an FLA file, choose Flash Professional CS5 (FLA) in the Save as type list (Win) or Format list (Mac) in the Export dialog box, then click OK in the Export dialog box. Figure H-17 shows an exported InDesign file opened in Adobe Flash Professional CS5.

- **XML**

  You can export InDesign files as **eXtensible Markup Language (XML)** files. XML files store and transport data in a format accessible by other programs. The XML format allows others to build, modify, and collaborate on projects using shared files by adding **tags** that describe the data. You can edit individual elements of a project in InDesign, then export the file as an XML file. Other users can access the same or different elements, allowing multiple users to build on your project. Advanced users can modify an element directly in the XML file.

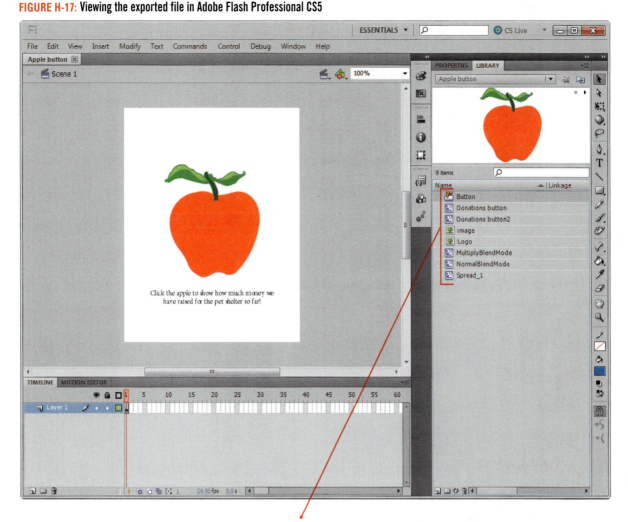

The Library contains the
symbols and elements you
created in the InDesign file

Packaging a document

There are times when you may need to send an InDesign document to someone else. For example, you may need to send it to your internal production department to have it printed, or you may need to send it to a client so that he or she can archive it. When you send an InDesign document to someone else, you need to send the file, any linked graphics, and any fonts used in the document that the recipient may not have. To make sure you have gathered all necessary elements for your recipient, you can use InDesign's Package feature. Just like its name implies, the Package feature "packs up" everything needed to print the document by creating a folder and copying the InDesign file, all fonts and graphics used in the document, and a report into the folder.

Practice

For current SAM information, including versions and content details, visit SAM Central (http://www.cengage.com/samcentral). If you have a SAM user profile, you may have access to hands-on instruction, practice, and assessment of the skills covered in this unit. Since various versions of SAM are supported throughout the life of this text, check with your instructor for the correct instructions and URL/Web site for accessing assignments.

Concepts Review

Label the elements of the InDesign screen shown in Figure H-18.

FIGURE H-18

1. _____   4. _____
2. _____   5. _____
3. _____

Match each term with the statement that best describes it.

6. **Button**   a. Where the source jumps to
7. **Preset**   b. Can be visible or invisible
8. **Destination**   c. Allows you to jump to another location
9. **Action**   d. Applied to a button
10. **Hyperlink**   e. An animation style

Select the best answer from the list of choices.

11. InDesign documents can be exported for use in which program?
- **a.** Photoshop
- **b.** Dreamweaver
- **c.** Excel
- **d.** Premiere Pro

12. Which of the following refers to a prewritten script?
- **a.** Template
- **b.** Event
- **c.** Destination
- **d.** Action

13. A hyperlink has both a destination and a _____.
- **a.** package
- **b.** source
- **c.** template
- **d.** folder

Skills Review

1. Create a document for the Web.
- **a.** Start InDesign, click File on the Application bar, point to New, then click Document.
- **b.** In the New Document dialog box, click the Intent list arrow, then click Web.
- **c.** Click OK to close the New Document dialog box, then notice that the rulers display pixels.
- **d.** Click the workspace switcher on the Application bar, then click Interactive.
- **e.** Save the document as **Class hyperlink**.
- **f.** Click File on the Application bar, click Place, navigate to the drive and folder where you store your Data Files, click Leaf RGB.ai, then click Open.
- **g.** Click the approximate center of the artboard to place the leaf.
- **h.** Click View on the Application bar, point to Display Performance, then click High Quality Display.
- **i.** Save your work.

2. Create a hyperlink.
- **a.** Click the Hyperlinks panel button to display the Hyperlinks panel, then click the Selection tool on the Tools panel.
- **b.** Click the leaf, click the Hyperlinks Panel options button, then click New Hyperlink.
- **c.** Click the Link To list arrow, then click URL if necessary.
- **d.** Click after the // in the Destination text box, then type **www.clayroom.com**.
- **e.** Click OK to close the New Hyperlink dialog box.
- **f.** Click Hyperlink on the Hyperlinks panel.
- **g.** Click the Go to destination of the selected hyperlink or cross-reference button on the Hyperlinks panel.
- **h.** Close the browser window, close the Hyperlinks panel, then save your work.

3. Create an animation.
- **a.** Verify that the leaf is selected.
- **b.** Click the Animation panel button to open the Animation panel.
- **c.** Notice that Leaf RGB.ai appears in the Name text box.
- **d.** Click the Preset list arrow, then click Dance.
- **e.** Click the Event(s) list arrow, then click On Page Load, if necessary.
- **f.** Click the Preview Spread button on the Animation panel to open the Preview panel.
- **g.** Click the Play preview button on the Preview panel to preview the animation.
- **h.** Save your work.

4. Export a document as a Flash Player file.
- **a.** Click File on the Application bar, then click Export.
- **b.** Navigate if necessary to the drive and folder where you store your Data Files, click the Save as type list arrow (Win) or the Format list arrow (Mac) at the bottom of the Export dialog box, then click Flash Player (SWF).
- **c.** Click Save.
- **d.** Click OK to accept the default settings in the Export SWF dialog box.
- **e.** Position the mouse pointer over the leaf graphic and notice that the pointer becomes a hand pointer.

    f. Click the hyperlink to open the Clayroom Web site.

    g. Close the browser window, save your work, then close Class hyperlink.indd.

5. Create a button.

    a. Open ID H-2.indd from the drive and folder where you store your Data Files, then save the file as **Leaf button**.

    b. Click the workspace switcher, click Reset Interactive, then change the display to High Quality Display.

    c. Click the Selection tool on the Tools panel, then click the leaf.

    d. Click Object on the Application bar, point to Interactive, then click Convert to Button.

    e. Highlight the text in the Name text box, then type **New Class button**.

    f. Click the Event list arrow, then click On Click.

    g. Click the Add new action for selected event button on the Buttons panel, then click Open File.

    h. Click the Select File button on the Buttons panel.

    i. Navigate to the drive and folder where you store your Data Files, click New class.pdf, then click Open.

    j. Save your work.

6. Create a rollover.

    a. Verify that the leaf button is still selected.

    b. On the Buttons panel, click [Rollover].

    c. Click Object on the Application bar, point to Effects, then click Drop Shadow.

    d. Click OK to accept the default settings in the Effects dialog box.

    e. Save your work.

7. Export a document as an Interactive Adobe PDF file.

    a. Click File on the Application bar, then click Export.

    b. Navigate to the drive and folder where you store your Data Files, click the Save as type list arrow (Win) or the Format list arrow (Mac) at the bottom of the Export dialog box, then click Adobe PDF (Interactive).

    c. Click Save.

    d. Verify that the View after Exporting check box is checked, then click OK to accept the default settings in the dialog box.

    e. Position the mouse pointer over the leaf, as shown in Figure H-19.

    f. Click the leaf to open the New class.pdf file.

    g. Close the New class.pdf file, then close Adobe Reader or Adobe Acrobat.

    h. Close the Leaf button document.

FIGURE H-19

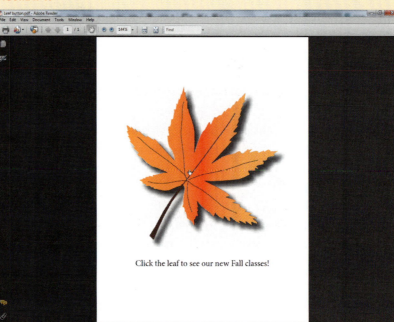

Independent Challenge 1

You've created a logo for a client, and now she would like you to make another version of it that can be used on her Web site as a button. She also would like you to use two new colors. You apply Web swatches to the logo and then convert it to a button.

a. Open H-3.indd from the drive and folder where you store your Data Files, then save it as **Button**.

b. Click the Selection tool, then click one of the green objects to select the group of green objects.

c. Open the Swatches panel, click the Swatches Panel options button, then click New Color Swatch.

d. Click the Color Type list arrow, click Spot, click the Color Mode list arrow, then click Web.

e. Choose a color in the list of Web swatches, then click OK to close the New Color Swatch dialog box.

f. Repeat Steps b-e to change the color of the yellow group to a Web color.

g. Select both color groups, then group them together.

h. Convert the logo to a button.

i. Change the event to On Click and the action to Go To URL.

j. Click after the // in the URL text box, then type **www.course.com**.

Advanced Challenge Exercise

- Select the button.
- Click Object on the Application bar, point to Effects, then click Bevel and Emboss.
- Click the Style list arrow, then click Pillow Emboss.
- Close the Effects dialog box.

k. Save your work, compare your button to the sample shown in Figure H-20, then close the document.

FIGURE H-20

Independent Challenge 2

You've created a set of alphabet flash cards, and now you would like to promote them to an educational Web site. Before you send your prototype, you add interactivity to the set of cards and test out your idea in a browser.

a. Open H-4.indd from the drive and folder where you store your Data Files, then save it as **Web cards**.

b. Open the Pages panel, then double-click the A-Master to open it in the document window.

c. Create two buttons on the master page that viewers can click that will move to the next page and the previous page. You can use anything as the buttons: text, small photos, or simple shapes.

d. Name the buttons **Previous Page** and **Next Page** on the Buttons panel.

e. For the Previous Page button, add an On Click event that will take viewers to the previous page.

f. For the Next Page button, add an On Click event that will take viewers to the next page.

g. Remove the Next Page button on page 26 (Z) and the Previous Page button on page 1 (A). (*Hint*: Open each page in the document window, override all master items, then delete the respective buttons.)

h. Save your work, then export the document as a Flash Player (SWF) file.

Advanced Challenge Exercise

- Select all of the pages in the Pages panel.
- Click the Page Panel options button, point to Page Transitions, then click Choose.
- Click the Uncover option button in the Page Transitions dialog box, then click OK.
- Save your work, then export the document as a Flash Player (SWF) file.
- Test your buttons and view the page transitions in the browser window.

i. Test your buttons in the Web browser, compare your screen to Figure H-21, then close the browser window.

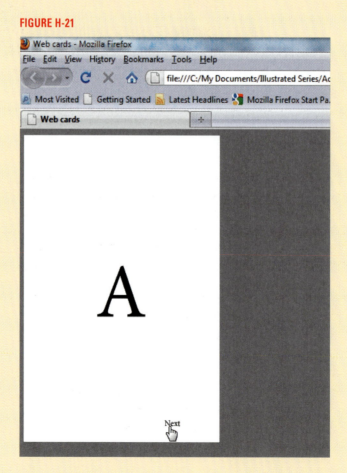

Independent Challenge 3

You volunteer each week at the local library, and each week you put together fun pages for the children's weekly story hour. The library is looking for new ideas to keep you busy, so you suggest putting the fun pages online so kids can play with them on the library Web site. You get to work by adding animation to the correct answers to the fun page questions.

    a. Start InDesign, open ID H-5.indd, then save it as **Animation**.

    b. Select the gumdrops image, then display the Animation panel.

    c. Click the Preset list arrow, then click Disappear.

    d. On the Animation panel, click the Event(s) list arrow, remove the check mark next to On Page Load, then choose On Roll Over (Self).

    e. Click the Reverse on Roll Off check box.

    f. Verify that the gumdrops image is still selected, then convert the image into a button.

    g. Name the button **Gum Drops button**.

    h. On the Buttons panel, add the On Roll Over event and then choose Animation as the action.

    i. On the Buttons panel, verify that the Options setting is set to Play, then click the Reverse on Roll Off check box.

    j. Export the file as a Flash Player (SWF) file, then test the button.

    k. Compare your screen to Figure H-22, then close the browser window.

    l. Save your work, then close Animation.indd.

FIGURE H-22

Point to the picture that does not belong with the rest of the group.

Real Life Independent Challenge

When you are planning a vacation, it is helpful to organize some of the trip's agenda so that your time is used wisely. Think of a place where you would like to go on your next vacation, and a friend or family member whom you would like to take with you. Identify four places or points of interest, or an event you'd like to attend while there. For example, if you were going to New York, you might want to attend a Broadway show, see the Empire State Building and the Statue of Liberty, or visit the Central Park Zoo. Use InDesign to create an interactive document with hyperlinks attached to the name of each point of interest. You'll then export the file as a PDF file so that you can send it to your traveling companion.

    a. Start InDesign, create a new document using Letter – Half as the page size, then save it as **Trip Planner**.

    b. Create a text box at the top of the page that includes the name of your destination.

    c. Create four more text boxes below it that include the names of four points of interest.

    d. Format the text to your liking.

    e. Add an invisible hyperlink to each of the four text boxes that link to URLs for Web sites containing more information about the planned activity in the text box. (*Hint*: If you are not able to research the exact URLs for your points of interest, create made-up URLs to use in the hyperlinks.)

    f. Test the hyperlinks using the Hyperlinks panel, if possible, then close any open browser windows and save your work.

    g. Close Trip Planner.indd, then exit InDesign.

Visual Workshop

Start InDesign, then create a new 800 px × 600 px Web document. Save the document as **Navigation**. Using Figure H-23 as a guide, create a 50 px × 50 px circle, then fill it with RGB Blue. Add a rollover appearance (RGB Red) and a click appearance (RGB Green). Convert the circle to a button that will play a sound when it is clicked. Compare your screen to Figure H-23, save your work, then exit InDesign.

FIGURE H-23

Adding Interactivity and Exporting Documents

Glossary

Action A prewritten script attached to a button.

Align (objects) To position one or more selected objects in relation to each other, in relation to the margins of a document, or in relation to the boundaries of the page or spread.

Alignment (paragraph) The way a paragraph is horizontally spread out between the left and right sides of a text box.

Anchor points The small dots that connect straight or curved line segments of a path.

Application bar Bar that sits at the top of the InDesign workspace and includes several menu options.

Baseline grid Type of grid that is useful for working with columns of text.

Bitmap graphic A graphic that is made up of pixels.

Bleed An item that extends one or more of the page borders. Bleed elements require an additional .25" size added to them to prevent white space appearing when the document is trimmed.

Bounding box A rectangle whose size matches the width and height of the selected object; includes eight selection handles that can be used to resize the object.

Bullets Small symbols, such as circles or squares, that appear before the beginning of a paragraph; typically used for lists of items.

Cells Small rectangles laid out horizontally in rows and vertically in columns that make up a table.

Character style Formatting that can be applied consistently to text characters; enables you to control font, font size, and color.

CMYK (cyan, magenta, yellow, and black) Process inks; combinations of CMYK create process colors.

Color stop Icon below the Gradient Ramp that represents a color used in the gradient.

Content Indicator The content indicator, a donut-shaped icon, appears over a placed graphic when you move the Selection tool over the graphic. The content indicator allows you to move a graphic in a frame without moving the frame.

Column Vertical arrangement of cells in a table.

Control panel Workspace area that can be used to view or modify information about a selected object, such as the object's size or location on the page.

Crop To hide part of an image without permanently removing it.

Destination The place the source jumps to from a hyperlink.

Detach To convert a master item on a document page into a regular object so that the item is no longer associated with changes made to the corresponding master item on the master page.

Distribute To place equal space between three or more objects.

Document grid Type of grid that is useful for aligning objects.

Document tab Appears just above the horizontal ruler; includes the document name, the current magnification level of the document, and a Close button.

Document window In a workspace, the white space surrounded by a black border and drop shadow that represents the open InDesign document.

Dreamweaver Adobe Web development program that lets you create Web pages containing text, images, hyperlinks, animation, sounds, and video.

Effect Special feature that you add to an object to improve its appearance or to create a particular impression about the object.

Embed To make a file a permanent part of the InDesign file so that the embedded file cannot be affected by changes made to the original file outside of InDesign.

Event The activity that needs to take place for an action to occur, such as when the user clicks a button or moves the mouse pointer over a button.

Facing pages Left and right pages in a multiple-page document.

Fill The color that fills an object.

Font A set of characters based on a typeface using a specific size and style.

Gradient fill A type of fill in which two or more colors blend from one to another.

Grid Preset group of vertical and horizontal lines equidistant from each other in the document window, much like traditional grid paper.

Group To select two or more objects and make them into one selectable object.

Guide Horizontal or vertical line that is used to create and position objects in the document window.

Gutter The space between two columns.

Hanging indent A type of text indent in which the first line in each paragraph is positioned to the left of the remaining lines in the paragraph.

Hidden character A non-printing character, such as a space between words or a paragraph return.

Hyperlink Object that, when clicked, jumps to another location in the same document, to another document, or to a Web site.

Indent A blank space between text and its margin or frame border.

Inset The amount of space between the top, bottom, right, and/or left sides of text and its table cell borders.

Island spread A spread whose pages remain together when pages are moved within a document.

JPEG (Joint Photographic Experts Group) Compressed graphic file format that is ideal for use on the Web.

Justify To position text at specific horizontal locations within a text box or table cell.

Layers The designated levels within a document on which objects appear.

Leading The amount of space between the baselines of two lines of type.

Library A type of InDesign file used for storing often-used text, graphics, and InDesign pages.

Linear gradient A type of gradient fill that blends from one point to another, horizontally, vertically, or diagonally, depending on the angle of the gradient.

Link The connection between a placed graphic in a frame and the original graphic file on the hard drive.

Margin guide Colored horizontal or vertical line within a document that indicates a margin.

Master item Object placed on a master page; appears on every document page to which the master page is applied.

Master page Page design that can be applied consistently to multiple document pages.

Merge (cells) To combine table cells into one cell.

Merge (layers) To consolidate multiple layers into one single layer.

Normal mode The default view in InDesign; it displays all of the non-printing elements, such as frame borders, guides, grids, margin guides, and column guides.

Object Anything that can be selected, such as a text box, logo, picture, simple shape, line, or guide.

Override To "unlock" a master item on a document page in order to work with it.

Page guide Guide that appears on a single page and doesn't extend to other pages in a document.

Page item The name given to an item placed on a layer.

Page layout software Software that includes tools that allow you to easily position text and graphics on document pages.

Panel Small floating window that contains options for working with selected objects.

Paragraph style Formatting that can be applied consistently to paragraphs of text; enables you to control character formatting, indents, spacing before and after paragraphs, and alignment.

Paragraphs Lines of text that are separated by the space created when you press [Enter] (Win) or [return] (Mac).

Pasteboard Gray or white area surrounding the document window.

PDF The file format used in Adobe Reader, a free software program that allows you to view documents created from other software programs without needing those programs installed on your computer.

Pixels Tiny color squares arranged in a grid that are used to display graphics shown on a monitor or television screen.

Point of origin The point on an object from which the object is transformed.

Portable Document Format *See* PDF.

Preset A collection of document settings that is saved and stored with a descriptive name and is available for use in the New Document dialog box.

Preview A graphical representation of an original image file and not the file itself.

Preview mode InDesign view that hides all of the non-printing elements.

Process color A color that is made from using the four process inks (CMYK).

Process ink Ink used for color printing; different percentages of one or more process inks (CMYK) combine to create process colors.

Process match A combination of process inks (CMYK) that is the closest possible match to a spot color.

Proportion The original relationship between an object's width and height.

Radial gradient A type of gradient fill that blends from the center outward to the border(s) of the object.

RGB Stands for Red, Green, Blue. RGB is the color system for graphics displayed on a monitor.

Resolution The number of pixels per inch (ppi) used to display computer graphics on a monitor.

Row Horizontal arrangement of cells in a table.

Screen resolution *See* Resolution.

Selection color The color of the bounding box that appears around selected objects on a specific layer in a document.

Shuffle To change the order and location of pages by moving one or more pages within a document.

Smart Guides Smart guides are guides that appear automatically as you position objects on a page. Smart guides are visual clues that let you know when the object you are positioning is touching a side or the center of another object, a margin guide, or the center of the page.

Snap To exactly align with something, such as a guide.

Source A hyperlink that, when clicked, goes to a destination location, document, or Web site.

Split To break a table cell into smaller cells.

Spot color Color that is manufactured by a company and must be purchased when used in a publication that will be professionally printed.

Spread A set of left and right pages in a multiple-page document.

Spread guide Guide that extends to the pasteboard and appears on all of the pages in a spread.

Story All of the text in one text box or all of the text in linked text boxes.

Status bar A bar along the bottom of the document window. It shows the status of the document, such as the active page.

Stroke The color that outlines an object; similar to a border or an edge.

Swatch Color sample available on the Swatches panel.

SWF (Shockwave Flash) Scalable and compact file format that is popular for online animation and games; can be viewed by anyone with Flash Player installed on his or her computer.

Tab stop Ruler setting that works together with the [Tab] key to enable you to position, or justify, text at specific horizontal locations within a text box or table cell.

Table A rectangular object that is made of up rows and columns of smaller rectangles called cells.

Text box Object that is a container for text; also called a text frame.

Text frame *See* Text box.

Thread To flow text into linked text boxes.

Tools panel Panel that contains all available InDesign tools, such as those for creating objects, transforming objects, changing the page view, and navigating the workspace.

Typeface A design created for a set of characters including the alphabet, numbers, and some symbols.

Uniform scale A type of scale in which an object is scaled both horizontally and vertically by the same percentage.

Vector graphic A graphic that is made up of straight or curved line segments connected by anchor points.

Weight The thickness of a stroke; measured in points.

XML XML stands for **eXtensible Markup Language** and is a file format that InDesign documents can be saved as. XML files store and transport data in a format accessible by other programs. The XML format allows others to build, modify, and collaborate on projects using shared files by adding tags that describe the data.

Index

Note: Page numbers in boldface indicate key terms.

A

actions, InDesign 178
Add Bullets dialog box, InDesign 40–41
adding
 graphics to libraries, InDesign 90–91
 master items, InDesign 106
 pages to documents, InDesign 100
 sample buttons, InDesign 178
Adobe Community Help window,
 InDesign 16–17
Adobe Creative Suite 5 (CS5), InDesign 1
Adobe Dreamweaver CS5, InDesign 184
Adobe Flash Professional CS5, InDesign 184
Adobe Illustrator, creating vector graphics using,
 InDesign 78
Adobe InDesign CS5
 See also InDesign
 described, InDesign 1
 Help, InDesign 16–17
 starting, InDesign 4–5
Adobe PDF, InDesign 182–183
align described, InDesign 66
Align panel, using, InDesign 66–67
aligning
 guides on rulers, InDesign 14
 objects, InDesign 66–67
 snapping using guides, InDesign 14
 text, numbers in tables, InDesign 158
alignment
 described, InDesign 32
 paragraph options (table), InDesign 33
A-Master, InDesign 102–103, InDesign 108,
 InDesign 110
anchor points, InDesign 78
 manipulating graphics using, InDesign 78,
 InDesign 83
 moving, InDesign 79
Animation panel, using, InDesign 174–175
animations, creating, InDesign 174–175
Application bar, workspace, InDesign 6
Apply Master to Pages command,
 InDesign 110–111
Arrange commands, InDesign 126
arranging and locking objects, InDesign 60–61
Autoflow, InDesign 29

B

baseline grid, InDesign 15
Beveled corners, InDesign 68
bitmap graphics
 described, InDesign 78
 and resolution, InDesign 79

bleeding, InDesign 6
borders, applying to table cells, InDesign 154
bounding boxes, InDesign 56
Bring Forward command, InDesign 60,
 InDesign 126
Bring to Front command, InDesign 60,
 InDesign 61, InDesign 126
browser, security settings, InDesign 176
bullets, applying to text, InDesign 40–41
buttons
 creating, InDesign 178–179
 using, InDesign 2
Buttons panel, InDesign 178–179

C

cells, table, InDesign 152
 formatting, InDesign 154–155
 inserting, merging, splitting, InDesign 156–157
centering images, InDesign 84–85
changing
 See also modifying
 character styles, InDesign 38
 fonts, InDesign 30–31
 layer order, InDesign 134–135
 master items, InDesign 104–105
 strokes, InDesign 68–69
 Swatches panel view, InDesign 149
 text, InDesign 42–43
 vertical order of objects, InDesign 60
 workspaces, InDesign 7
character styles, creating and applying,
 InDesign 38–39
CMYK colors, InDesign 144
collapsing panels to icons, InDesign 12
color stops, InDesign 148
colors
 applying color labels to pages, InDesign 112–113
 applying fill, to objects, InDesign 56–57
 changing tint, InDesign 56
 CMYK, InDesign 144
 process, InDesign 144–145
 RGB, InDesign 170–171
 selection color, InDesign 124
 spot, InDesign 146–147
 swatches. See swatches
 working with, InDesign 143
column guides, InDesign 8
columns, table
 described, InDesign 152
 formatting, InDesign 154
commands
 See also specific command
 fitting (table), InDesign 84
 on Pages Panel options menu, InDesign 112–113
content indicator, InDesign 82–83

Control panel
 adding effects to frames, images, InDesign 84
 viewing, InDesign 85
Control panel, workspace, InDesign 6
converting
 graphics to buttons, InDesign 178–179
 shapes to different shapes, InDesign 56
 text to outlines, InDesign 148
 text to tables, InDesign 155
copying
 layers, InDesign 128–129, InDesign 134
 objects with Step and Repeat, InDesign 62–63
corners
 editing, InDesign 59
 modifying, InDesign 68–69
creating
 animations, InDesign 174–175
 character styles, InDesign 38–39
 documents, InDesign 8–9, InDesign 100–101
 documents for the Web, InDesign 170–171
 export preset, InDesign 182
 frames, InDesign 80, InDesign 102
 gradients, InDesign 148–149
 guides, InDesign 14
 hyperlinks, InDesign 172–173
 layers, InDesign 126–127
 master items, InDesign 102–103
 master pages, InDesign 108–109
 multipage documents, InDesign 100–101
 paragraph styles, InDesign 34–35
 process colors, InDesign 144–145
 rollovers, InDesign 180–181
 tables, InDesign 152–153
 text boxes, InDesign 26–27, InDesign 152–153
 tint swatches, InDesign 146
cropping described, InDesign 82
custom workspaces, InDesign 7
customizing
 InDesign presets, InDesign 11
 Pages panel, InDesign 110
 workspaces, InDesign 7

D

destination (hyperlink), InDesign 172
detaching master items, InDesign 111
dictionary, changing, InDesign 11
Direct Selection tool, InDesign 78, InDesign 83
Display Performance, InDesign 122,
 InDesign 170
displaying rulers, InDesign 170–171
distributing objects, InDesign 64–65
docking panels, InDesign 13
document grid, InDesign 15
document tab, workspace, InDesign 6
document window, InDesign 6

documents
See also paragraphs, text
changing page order in, InDesign 107
creating for the Web, InDesign 170–171
creating multipage, InDesign 100–101
creating new, InDesign 8–9
embedding files, InDesign 88–89
exporting, InDesign 2
exporting as Flash player files, InDesign 176–177
exporting as PDF files, InDesign 182–183
interactive elements, InDesign 169
layers. *See* layers
loading master pages, InDesign 112–113
master items, InDesign 102–105
naming and saving, InDesign 10–11
packaging, InDesign 185
page numbering, InDesign 103
pasting layers into, InDesign 134–135
shuffling, preventing, InDesign 113
Dreamweaver CS5, **InDesign 184**
Drop Shadow effects, InDesign 180–181
duplicating
See also copying
layers, InDesign 128–129

E

Edit Original command, InDesign 89
editing
corners, InDesign 59
links, InDesign 89
with Story Editor, InDesign 30
effects
See also specific effect
working with, InDesign 180
Effects dialog box, InDesign 180–181
Ellipse tool, InDesign 56
em spaces, **InDesign 31**
embedding files, InDesign 88–89
Essentials workspace, InDesign 6–7
events, InDesign 178
Export SWF dialog box, InDesign 176–177
exporting
documents, InDesign 2
documents as Flash player files,
InDesign 176–177
documents as PDF files, InDesign 182–184
for the Web, options, InDesign 184–185
eXtensible Markup Language (XML),
InDesign 184

F

facing pages, **InDesign 8**, InDesign 100
Fast Display, InDesign 122
files
embedding, InDesign 88–89
link status, InDesign 88
locations, and links, InDesign 4
Fill button, Tools panel, InDesign 126
fills
applying color, to objects, InDesign 56–57
gradient, **InDesign 143**
Find/Change dialog box, InDesign 42–43
finding and changing text, InDesign 42–43
Fit content proportionately button,
InDesign 122

FLA files, InDesign 184
Flash, exporting documents as Flash player files,
InDesign 176–177
flash cards, InDesign 100
flowing text, InDesign 28–29
fonts
described, **InDesign 30**
Macintosh substitutes, InDesign 4
formatting
controls on Control panel, InDesign 32
paragraphs, InDesign 32–33
table cells, InDesign 154–155
text, InDesign 30–31
frames
creating, InDesign 80, InDesign 102
master text, **InDesign 108**
placing graphics in, InDesign 80–81

G

Global security settings, InDesign 176
gradient fills, InDesign 143
filling text with, InDesign 148
and Gradient Swatch tool, InDesign 150
Gradient panel, using, InDesign 150
Gradient Swatch tool, using, InDesign 150–151
gradients, creating, **InDesign 148–149**
graphics
adding to libraries, InDesign 90–91
converting to buttons, InDesign 178–179
links. *See* links
placing in frames, InDesign 80–81
types of, InDesign 78–79
working with, InDesign 77
grid, InDesign 15
grouping objects, InDesign 62
guides
described, **InDesign 14**
lock, InDesign 130
margin, **InDesign 8**
page, **InDesign 6**
smart, InDesign 54–55
working with, InDesign 14–15
gutter, InDesign 26
viewing value, InDesign 26

H

Hand tool, InDesign 28, InDesign 124
Help, InDesign 16–17
hidden characters, **InDesign 32**
hidden objects, finding and selecting, InDesign 61
hiding
layers, InDesign 130–131
Links panel, InDesign 86
High Quality Display, InDesign 122,
InDesign 170
hyperlinks
creating, **InDesign 172–173**
using, InDesign 2

I

icons, collapsing panels to, InDesign 12
Illustrator vector graphics, copying and pasting
into InDesign, InDesign 78

images
cropping, InDesign 82–83
placing multiple, InDesign 80
relinking, InDesign 88–89
.indd files, InDesign 10
indents, InDesign 34
InDesign
features and capabilities of, InDesign 2–3
guides, grids, InDesign 14–15
preferences, InDesign 11
starting, InDesign 4–5
workspace elements, InDesign 6–7
inserting
pages, InDesign 100
table cells, InDesign 156–157
text boxes, InDesign 26–27
inset values, InDesign 152
Interactive workspace, InDesign 7,
InDesign 170–171
interactivity
creating animations, InDesign 174–175
creating buttons, InDesign 178–179
creating documents for the Web,
InDesign 170–171
creating hyperlinks, InDesign 172–173
creating rollovers, InDesign 180–181
designing into documents, InDesign 169
exporting documents as Flash player files,
InDesign 176–177
exporting documents as PDF files,
InDesign 182–183
Inverse Rounded corners, InDesign 68–69
island spreads, InDesign 113

J

JPEG (Joint Photographic Experts Group),
InDesign 184
justify (text), InDesign 158

K

kerning, InDesign 31

L

landscape page orientation, InDesign 170
layers, InDesign 121
changing options, InDesign 124–125
changing order of, InDesign 134–135
creating new, InDesign 126–127
locking and hiding, InDesign 130–131
merging, InDesign 132–133
moving objects to another, InDesign 132–133
pasting into documents, InDesign 134–135
placing objects on, InDesign 122–123
selecting items on, InDesign 126
selection color, **InDesign 124**
targeting, **InDesign 124**
Layers Option dialog box, InDesign 131
Layers panel, InDesign 122–124, InDesign 128
leading, InDesign 32
legend, map, InDesign 122
libraries
adding graphics to, InDesign 90–91
described, **InDesign 2**

linear gradients, InDesign 148
lines, grids, InDesign 15
links, InDesign 77
  editing, InDesign 89
  and file locations, InDesign 4
Links panel
  changing options, InDesign 89
  using, InDesign 86–87
lock guides, InDesign 130
locking
  layers, InDesign 130–131
  objects, InDesign 60–61
looping (animations), InDesign 174

M

Macintosh users
  InDesign workspace, InDesign 6
  opening InDesign, InDesign 4
  substitute fonts, InDesign 4
magnifying. See zooming
manipulating graphics, InDesign 78–79
map legend, InDesign 122
margin guides, InDesign 8
marquees, InDesign 78
master items
  creating, InDesign 102–103
  described, InDesign 102
  detaching, InDesign 111
  overriding, InDesign 104–105
master pages
  applying, InDesign 110–111
  creating new, InDesign 108–109
  loading, InDesign 112
  modifying, InDesign 106–107
  using, InDesign 99
  working with, InDesign 112–113
master text frames, InDesign 108
merge described, InDesign 132
merging layers, InDesign 132–133
merging table cells, InDesign 156–157
modifying
  See also changing
  master pages, InDesign 106–107
  paragraph styles, InDesign 36–37
Move command, InDesign 63
moving
  objects, InDesign 63
  objects between layers, InDesign 132–133
  pages, InDesign 107

N

naming documents, InDesign 10–11
New Color Swatch dialog box,
  InDesign 144–145
New Dialog dialog box, InDesign 170–171
New Document dialog box, InDesign 8–9
New Gradient Swatch dialog box,
  InDesign 148–149
New Hyperlink dialog box, InDesign 172–173
New Master dialog box, InDesign 108–109
New Tint Swatch dialog box, InDesign 146–147
newsletter, example of, InDesign 3
Normal mode, InDesign 12
numbers
  aligning in tables, InDesign 158

applying to paragraphs, InDesign 40–41
options for page, InDesign 103

O

objects
  See also specific object
  aligning, InDesign 66–67
  animating, InDesign 174–175
  arranging, InDesign 60–61
  converting to buttons, InDesign 178–179
  creating, InDesign 56–57
  editing corners, InDesign 59
  grouping, InDesign 62
  hidden, InDesign 61
  locking, InDesign 60–61
  modifying corners, strokes, InDesign 68–69
  moving, InDesign 63
  moving to another layer, InDesign 132–133
  placing on layers, InDesign 122–123
  point of origin, InDesign 58
  positioning, InDesign 66–67
  resizing, InDesign 64
  rotating, InDesign 64
  stepping and repeating, InDesign 62–63
  transforming, InDesign 58–59
  using Live Distribute feature, InDesign 64–65
  working with, InDesign 53
On Click events, InDesign 178
opening InDesign, InDesign 4–5
outlines, converting text to, InDesign 148
overriding master items, InDesign 104–107

P

packaging documents, InDesign 185
page guides, InDesign 6, InDesign 14
page items, InDesign 122
  placing on layers, InDesign 122–123
  selecting, InDesign 124
page layout software, InDesign 2
pages
  changing order in documents, InDesign 107
  facing, InDesign 8, InDesign 100
  inserting, InDesign 100
  master. See master pages
  numbering options, InDesign 103
Pages panel, InDesign 100–101
Pages Panel menu, InDesign 110
Pages Panel options menu, InDesign 112–113
Panel Options dialog box, InDesign 110
panels, InDesign 6
  See also specific panel
  docking, InDesign 13
  working with, InDesign 12–13
Pantone colors, InDesign 146–147
Paragraph panel, InDesign 32, InDesign 34
paragraph styles, InDesign 34
paragraphs, InDesign 32
  alignment options (table), InDesign 33
  applying bullets, numbers to, InDesign 40–41
  formatting, InDesign 32–33
parent/child relationships with styles,
  InDesign 35
Paste Remembers Layers command, Panel
  options menu, InDesign 134
pasteboard, InDesign 6

patterns, creating, InDesign 64–65
PDF files, exporting documents as,
  InDesign 182–183
Pen tool, InDesign 2, InDesign 78
pixels, InDesign 78
  and resolution, InDesign 79
  ruler measurements, InDesign 170–171
Place dialog box, InDesign 80–81
placed graphics. See links
placeholder text, InDesign 36
placing and flowing text, InDesign 28–29
planning InDesign documents, InDesign 8
plus sign (+) and paragraph styles, InDesign 34
point of origin, InDesign 58
Polygon tool, InDesign 56
Portable Document Format (PDF),
  InDesign 182–183
portrait page orientation, InDesign 170
positioning
  objects, InDesign 66–67
  shapes, InDesign 58–59
  text and graphics, InDesign 2
  text boxes, InDesign 107
pound sign (#), hidden character, InDesign 32
preferences, InDesign, InDesign 11
presets described, InDesign 8
Preview mode, InDesign 12
Preview panel, InDesign 174–175
previews, InDesign 86
printing InDesign documents with linked files,
  InDesign 86
process colors, creating, InDesign 144–145

R

radial gradients, InDesign 148
Rectangle Frame tool, InDesign 80, InDesign 102,
  InDesign 122
Rectangle tool, InDesign 56
removing
  actions, InDesign 178
  local overrides, InDesign 105
renaming layers, InDesign 128
resizing objects, InDesign 64
resolution, InDesign 79
RGB color system, InDesign 170
rotating objects, InDesign 58, InDesign 64
Rounded corners, InDesign 68
rows, table
  described, InDesign 152
  formatting, InDesign 154
rulers, InDesign 6
  aligning guides on, InDesign 14
  displaying, InDesign 170–171

S

Save As dialog box, InDesign 10–11
saving documents, InDesign 10–11
Scale X Percentage, InDesign 84–85
Scale Y Percentage, InDesign 85
scaling
  images, InDesign 84–85
  objects, InDesign 58
searching help topics, InDesign 16–17
security, global, InDesign 176

selecting
 items on layers, InDesign 126
 objects, InDesign 61
 page items, InDesign 124
selection color, InDesign 124
Selection tool, InDesign 26, InDesign 80
 and content indicator, InDesign 82–83
 editing corners, InDesign 59
Send Backward command, InDesign 60,
 InDesign 126
Send to Back command, InDesign 126
shape tools, InDesign 56
shapes
 creating, InDesign 56–57
 positioning, InDesign 58–59
Shockwave Flash (SWF) format, InDesign 176
showing
 See also viewing
 and hiding layers, InDesign 130–131
 Links panel, InDesign 86
 text threads, InDesign 28
sizing fonts, InDesign 30
smart guides, InDesign 54–55
snap described, InDesign 14
source (hyperlink), InDesign 172
spacing
 kerning and tracking, InDesign 31
 leading, InDesign 32
splitting table cells, InDesign 156–157
spot colors
 described, InDesign 146
 selecting, InDesign 146–147
spread guides, InDesign 14
spreads, InDesign 8
spreads, island, InDesign 113
squares, creating, InDesign 62–63
starting InDesign, InDesign 4–5
states described, InDesign 180
status bar, InDesign 6
Step and Repeat feature, InDesign 62–63
stepping, repeating objects, InDesign 62–63
Story Editor, using, InDesign 30
Stroke button, Tools panel, InDesign 126
strokes, modifying, InDesign 68–69
styles
 character, InDesign 38–39
 paragraph, InDesign 34–37
 parent/child relationships, InDesign 35
swatches, InDesign 2
 creating new color, InDesign 144–145
 Web swatch library, InDesign 172

Swatches panel, InDesign 12–13, InDesign 56,
 InDesign 128, InDesign 144–145, InDesign 149
SWF (Shockwave Flash) format, InDesign 176,
 InDesign 184

T

tab stops, setting in tables, InDesign 158–159
Table panel, using, InDesign 152
tables, InDesign 152
 converting text to, InDesign 155
 formatting cells, InDesign 154–155
 inserting, merging, splitting cells,
 InDesign 156–157
 setting tabs in, InDesign 158–159
tags, InDesign 184
targeting layers, InDesign 124
text
 applying bullets to, InDesign 40–41
 character styles, InDesign 38–39
 converting to tables, InDesign 155
 entering in tables, InDesign 152–153
 filling with gradient fills, InDesign 148
 finding and changing, InDesign 42–43
 formatting, InDesign 30–31
 inset values, InDesign 152
 justifying, InDesign 158
 kerning and tracking, InDesign 31
 methods of flowing (table), InDesign 29
 paragraph styles, InDesign 34–37
 placeholder, InDesign 36
 working with, InDesign 25
text boxes, InDesign 26
 creating, InDesign 26–27, InDesign 152–153
 filling with 'fake' text, InDesign 36
 flowing text into, InDesign 28
 placing, flowing, InDesign 28–29
text threads, viewing, InDesign 28
threading text, InDesign 28
tint swatches, creating, InDesign 146
Toggles visibility icon, Layers panel, InDesign 130
Tools panel, workspace, InDesign 6
tracking, InDesign 31
Transform Again command, InDesign 58
transforming
 frame contents, InDesign 84–85
 objects, InDesign 58–59
transparency, InDesign 110
Type tool, InDesign 26, InDesign 28, InDesign 102,
 InDesign 106
typefaces, InDesign 30

U

Uniform Resource Locator (URL) as hyperlink
 destination, InDesign 172–173
updating
 linked files, InDesign 86
 paragraph styles, InDesign 36–37

V

vector graphics
 described, InDesign 78
 and resolution, InDesign 79
vectors described, InDesign 78
View, Application bar, InDesign 170
viewing
 gutter value, InDesign 26
 hyperlinks, InDesign 173
 library items, InDesign 90
 master pages, InDesign 108
 objects in order, InDesign 122
 smart guides, InDesign 55
 text threads, InDesign 28

W

Web
 creating documents for the, InDesign 170–171
 creating hyperlinks, InDesign 172–173
 export options for the, InDesign 184–185
Web swatch library, InDesign 172
Welcome Screen, InDesign 4
workspaces
 overview of, InDesign 6–7
 using custom, InDesign 7

X

XML files, InDesign 184

Z

Zoom tool, InDesign 126
zooming on bitmap graphics, InDesign 78